Fluent Selves

Fluent Selves

Autobiography, Person, and History in Lowland South America

Edited by SUZANNE OAKDALE
and MAGNUS COURSE

University of Nebraska Press
Lincoln & London

Library of Congress Cataloging-in-Publication Data
Fluent selves: autobiography, person, and history in
lowland South America / edited by Suzanne Oakdale,
Magnus Course.
pages   cm
Includes bibliographical references and index.
ISBN 978-0-8032-4990-5 (hardback: alk. paper)
ISBN 978-0-8032-6515-8 (epub)
ISBN 978-0-8032-6516-5 (mobi)
ISBN 978-0-8032-6514-1 (pdf)
1. Indians of South America—Ethnic identity. 2. Indians
of South America—Biography. 3. Autobiography—Social
aspects—South America. 4. Discourse analysis, Narrative—
South America. 5. Group identity—South America. 6.
Ethnology—South America. I. Oakdale, Suzanne, editor of
compilation. II. Course, Magnus, editor of compilation.
F2230.1.E84F58 2014
305.80098—dc23
2014019559

Set in ITC New Baskerville by L. Auten.

In memory of Steve Rubenstein, our dear friend

Contents

Illustrations

Images

Maps

Tables

Acknowledgments

This volume grew out of a Wenner-Gren, British Academy, and University of Edinburgh (School of Social and Political Science) funded workshop, titled "Autobiographical and Biographical Narratives in Lowland South America: Unexpected Relations between Persons, Language, and History," held at the University of Edinburgh, September 16–17, 2010. We wish to thank each of these institutions for their support. Magnus Course, who had the idea of having such an event, was an untiring and gracious host in Edinburgh along with Maya Mayblin. Our intent was to bring scholars together from Europe and North and South America who work on this cluster of topics in one way or another in their lowland research. We succeeded in attracting anthropologists and linguists trained in many different traditions, and the discussion was much richer for this diversity. The essays in this volume do not, therefore, have a uniformity with respect to their theoretical orientations. We were also joined by three other colleagues in this workshop, whose work does not appear here: Ana Mariella Bacigalupo (State University of New York, Buffalo), Pierre Déléage (Laboratoire d'anthropologie sociale), and the late Steve Rubenstein (formerly of the University of Liverpool). All our chapters profited from Mariella's, Pierre's, and Steve's comments, and the workshop from their sociability and goodwill.

The title of this work—*Fluent Selves*—is drawn from Kenneth Rexroth's famous poem "Lute Music," a work that focuses on the transience and fluidity of selves as they move into, through, and out of language. It is precisely this movement of selves and persons through the medium of language that is our focus in this volume.

The volume benefited greatly from the careful reviews given by the readers enlisted by the University of Nebraska Press. We also thank the School of Social and Political Science at the University of Edinburgh for the funding it provided for the volume's indexing. Finally, we are very grateful to Bill Mayblin for creating the map in the volume's introduction.

Fluent Selves

Introduction

Suzanne Oakdale and Magnus Course

Much of the recent research in lowland South America fore-
grounds history—a significant departure in a literature long
marked by a commitment to a structural functional emphasis
on integrated systems (Fausto and Heckenberger 2007; Hill
1988; Whitehead 2003). Yet despite the attention to historical
consciousness and "historicity" in this literature, remarkably few
studies have explicitly focused on autobiographical or biographical narrative.[1] In this volume we set out to address this lacuna
through the exploration of narrative practices in a wide variety
of lowland communities. We explore how they illuminate the
social and cultural processes that make the past meaningful for
indigenous peoples in lowland South America and what these
narrative practices show us about the contemporary enactment
of persons in these locales.[2] In brief this volume concerns the
relationships between personhood and the ways people relate
to the past as these come together in narrative practices.

The authors represented in *Fluent Selves* focus on a variety of
autobiographical and biographical narrative forms and employ
a range of different theoretical approaches. Chapters explore
both oral and written genres, in rural and urban settings in
such countries as Ecuador, Brazil, Peru, and Chile, active in
a range of contexts from highly ritualized performances to
ethnographic interviews and moments of self-presentation in
large public events. This volume unites scholars from Europe,

North America, and Latin America, trained in several different intellectual traditions of social, cultural, and linguistic anthropology as well as linguistics. Some authors are more interested in culturally distinct models of personhood and historical consciousness, others in how actors draw simultaneously on multiple models or invoke social personae from a wide range of social fields. Authors also focus on different aspects of these narratives, from thematic content, to form, to the role they play in social life. Despite these differences, all the contributors consider these narrative practices primarily in terms of how the construction of history and personhood are in some way interlinked.

We have divided this volume into four sections. The first section, "Neither Myth nor History," is concerned with how modes of engagement with temporality—frequently dichotomized into "myth" and "history"—are often transformed and reconciled in lowland autobiographical and biographical narrative forms. The second section, "Persons within Persons," unites chapters that together offer a refinement of the "perspectivist" model of personhood. The third, "Creating Sociality across Divides," encompasses chapters that speak to the social life of these kinds of narratives in lowland societies. Here we focus on the sorts of effects they have, how their performance can, for example, be a means of structuring engagement between very different types of people who are working to create allies, forging interethnic networks, or enlarging a moral community. The fourth section, "Hybridity, Dissonance, and Reflection," concentrates on the accounts of several lowland leaders who tell about becoming intermediaries, working between multiple social spheres, simultaneously inhabiting conflicting roles and identities. Here the psychological stress and the creative potential of this sort of hybridity are apparent. Before we introduce the four sections of this book in more detail, let us review the insights of the small but growing body of research on lowland autobiographical and biographical narrative practices.

OAKDALE AND COURSE

Map 1. Map of South America indicating locations of groups mentioned in this book. (Courtesy of Bill Mayblin)

Autobiographical and Biographical Narratives
in Lowland Ethnography

While there have always been a few exceptions, autobiographical and biographical narrative practices have been overlooked
in most lowland research, especially in contrast with their
prominence in the anthropology of other regions such as that
of Native North America (e.g., Radin 1999[1926]; DeMallie
1984, among many others; see Sáez 2006). Lowland societies
were often typecast as the inverse of so-called modern societies, celebrated primarily as "still enchanted," integrated systems, societies in which communal cohesion was intact (Sáez
2006). Collective institutions therefore seemed a much more
fitting focus for ethnography than material about distinctive, individualized, or personal experiences, individuation
being considered a mark of disenchantment. Oscar Calavia
Sáez (2006), in the context of discussing the absence of this
material in Brazilian ethnographic literature, suggestively contrasts the creation of a coherent native "I" through published
nineteenth-century Native North American autobiographies
and photo portraits with the equally constructed "collective
indigenous subject" produced in mid-twentieth-century Brazilian ethnography and ethnographic photography.

Lowland peoples are also usually characterized as living
in societies in which there is an absence of the idea of "the
individual," with its classic "Western" connotations, including
autonomy, will, uniqueness, interiority, and indivisible unity—a
term that has an illusory air of coherence (see Lukes 1973;
also La Fontaine 1985 and Strathern 1988). While we would
agree with the need to question the applicability of this "Western individual" for lowland peoples, we wonder if the fear of
ethnocentric projection may also have led to an unnecessary
avoidance of first-person narrative forms. In shifting our attention to these forms, we would also like to return to thinking
about how kinds of individuality may in fact be emphasized

in some lowland societies, albeit an individuality distinct from that associated with the "Western individual." We do not wish, however, to automatically yoke autobiographical narrative practices to the expression of individuality or processes of self-actualization, much less the whole conceptual package of the "Western individual," unless, of course, narrators themselves are in social domains where this idea is at play.

Research by Greg Urban (1989) and Ellen Basso (1995) has been some of the first to creatively disengage lowland first-person narration from introspection and the expression of unique individuality. They show that the social power and transformative potential of some of these narrative practices in lowland societies can rest on their use of quoted speech. These narrative forms work to subjectively connect persons in the present to persons from the past or from alternate modes of existence such as mythical time or the position of enmity. These insights have led others to examine these processes elsewhere in the lowlands, especially in the more highly ritualized practices of the Wanano, Mapuche, Sharanawa, Xavante, and Kawaiwete (Kayabi) (Bacigalupo 2007; Chernela 2011; Course 2007, 2009; Déléage 2007; Graham 1995; Oakdale 2002, 2005, 2009).

In the body of research focusing squarely on history in the lowlands, biographical and autobiographical narratives have been valuable for understanding structural shifts and continuities in the contexts of colonization, missionization, guerrilla struggle, and urbanization (Bacigalupo 2001; Brown and Fernández 1993; Crocker 2007; Fausto 2012; Fernández 1986; Langdon 2007; Muratorio 1991; Rubenstein 2002; Veber 2009; Vilaça 2010; Watson 1968, 1970; Wright 2005). *La chute du ciel* (2010) stands out for the evocative way it presents the experiences of Davi Kopenawa, a Yanomami shaman and leader living with and fighting against the environmental destruction his people have faced over the course of his life. It also presents his experiences with missions and working within government institutions.

Those who have understood autobiographical and biographical forms in terms of their distinctive cultural saliency have found that in many societies these narratives are in fact central to the construction of historical consciousness. Ellen Basso, for example, has observed that for the Kalapalo of central Brazil, "history is first and foremost biographical" and "emerges from particular intelligences and insights, decisions and choices, that together constitute enactments of specific persons" (Basso 1995:295; Basso 2003:89). Likewise, Anne-Christine Taylor writes that for the Ecuadorian Shuar autobiographical forms play an important part in building up a "regime of history" (2007:147). Both observations show that the growing interest in these forms is not simply a symptom of "the new 'subjectology'" in anthropology (Sahlins 2004:140; Fausto and Heckenberger 2007:4) but is, in part at least, also driven by the importance of these narrative forms in lowland traditions themselves.

Those interested in historical narrative have also pointed out the importance of the absence of these forms in certain domains. Nádia Farage (2003) observes that Wapishana avoid speaking about certain past events because of their association with the dead. Only when the dead have reached a certain remoteness, when, in Wapishana terms, their individualized faces have been forgotten and they can less easily affect the living, can they be featured in narratives by those who knew them (see also Taylor 1993, 2007).

In addition to these veins of research, there are other seemingly incongruous areas where attention to autobiographical and biographical narrative practices in one form or another have consistently appeared: research on lowland dreams and visions, shamanism, and leadership. While much of the research on dreams has centered on beliefs about the nature and efficacy of dreaming, Waud Kracke (1979), drawing on psycho-

6   OAKDALE AND COURSE

logical anthropology, has explored Kagwahiv dream accounts as they relate to the social-psychological dynamics between headmen and their followers. Ellen Basso (1992) has examined how Kalapalo dreams are interpreted as being about "self becoming." Likewise, Steve Rubenstein (2012) has focused on the centrality of the vision quest in the narrative formation of the Shuar subject. In the northwest Amazon, Robin Wright (2013) has written extensively on shamanic apprenticeship by focusing on the autobiographical account of Mandu da Silva, a Baniwa jaguar shaman. Davi Kopenawa's (2010) account of his life centers on his shamanic training and how he has drawn upon this body of knowledge to critique the destruction and greed of industrial society.

Much like Davi Kopenawa's account, some of the most extensive presentations of autobiographical narratives are book-length accounts of leaders, such as those of the Ecuadorian Shuar warrior Tukip' (Hendricks 1993) and shaman Alejandro Tsakimp (Rubenstein 2002). Research on millenarian leaders in the northwest Amazon has also long featured biographical material (Hill and Wright 1988; Wright and Hill 1986; Wright 1998). Additionally, Alcida Ramos (1988) has focused on the autobiographical aspects of political speeches made by indigenous leaders involved in the pan-Indian movement in Brazil; Linda Rabben (2004) on the lives of Payakan and Davi Yanomami as international activists; Joanne Rappaport (2005) on the lives of Colombian indigenous intellectuals; and Hanne Veber (2007) on the narratives of a Peruvian Ashéninka activist, Mihuel Camaiteri, as well as several other Asháninka and Ashéninka leaders (Veber 2009). While not focused on leadership per se, Janis Nuckolls (2010) discusses the autobiographical narratives of a Runa "strongwoman," or woman of strength and vitality, an unofficial status that rests in part on engagement with a range of nonhuman as well as human beings. In these seemingly disconnected areas of research on dreams/visions and on lowland leaders, autobiographical narratives appear to be linked to the display of fluency between different domains, both social and ontological.[3]

Finally, autobiographical accounts written by or coauthored by lowland individuals are also currently appearing in the context of indigenous activism, especially in those places where indigenous leaders have emerged in the last few decades as high-profile political actors. As Bruce Albert has observed, "self-representation formulae" have become "highly effective political instruments on the postmodern scene of globalization and multi-ethnicity" (1997:59). The modes in which this is done, he continues, borrow from the rhetoric of official state "indigenism," from the rhetorics of nongovernmental and church organizations, and from local discourses (1997:59; see also Rappaport 2005). Autobiographical narratives in a range of genres are effective parts of these projects. Published testimonials and autobiographies by lowland indigenous activists are beginning to appear, such as that centering on the life of Mapuche leader Rosa Isolde Reuque Paillalef (2002), Kayapo leader Raoni (Raoni and Dutilleux 2010), in addition to that of Davi Kopenawa (Kopenawa and Albert 2010).

Indigenous autobiographies are also increasingly salient in the context of global networks. Websites of institutions such as Survival International as well as those dedicated specifically to the preservation of the Amazon feature short biographies (in translation for international audiences) of leaders such as Davi Kopenawa and Kayapo leader Raoni (Survival International 2012; Raoni.com 2012). Resonating with national and international audiences, these narrative forms are becoming an important part of the way large numbers of people around the world are drawn into complex global networks of support. Davi Kopenawa's accounts of his experiences, for example, are effective pleas for readers to become involved in movements centered on both indigenous rights and environmentalism. These works show that such texts not only describe cosmopolitan lives (Albert 2010) but also work to engage readers situated across various sorts of boundaries.

Neither Myth nor History

The autobiographical and biographical narratives discussed here are, at least in part, embedded in and constitutive of indigenous conceptions of time, most obviously the past but also the present and the future. The precise nature of the way in which indigenous peoples in lowland South America engage with temporality has been the topic of much heated debate in recent years, a debate for which the parameters were set by Claude Lévi-Strauss's elaboration of the simple observation that different societies engage differently with the past (1966). Whereas some societies seek to obliterate the appearance of cumulative change, through "myth," other societies seek to make it the very core of the way they understand themselves, through "history." Lévi-Strauss utilized the ideal types of "cold" mythical modes and "hot" historical modes to refer to each of these tendencies respectively. Yet later critiques have suggested that through the characterization of lowland societies as predominantly "cold" in their engagement with temporality, Lévi-Strauss was denying them "history" and thus contributing to the perceived isolation of indigenous peoples from global historical and political trends. In response to these critiques, others have argued that, on the contrary, Lévi-Strauss is simply allowing for indigenous conceptions of temporality that are autonomous from Western expectations of what "history"—with its emphasis on cumulative change and flows of capital—should look like (Gow 2001; Fausto and Heckenberger 2007). Careful ethnographic studies of indigenous engagements with the past, have revealed the coexistence of multiple and heterogenous forms of understanding temporality, something that, at least if we understand "cold" and "hot" as ideal types, is precisely what Lévi-Strauss would have predicted as well as something that would logically follow from these peoples' involvement in the larger political econo-mies of nations and transnational communities (Hugh-Jones 1988, 1989; Turner 1988).[4]

This book is situated somewhat tangentially to the debate described here since the contributors to the volume come from a variety of different disciplinary and national traditions and each has his or her own view of the relative merits of the var-ious positions in this debate. Our purpose in this introduc-tion is not to take sides on this issue but rather to point out that the autobiographical and biographical narratives that are the subject matter of this book go beyond any simple cat-egorization as either "myth" or "history." They are rather the very medium in which a variety of modes of engagement with temporality meet, are reconciled, and reemerge.

To advance this argument, we need to be somewhat clearer about exactly what we take the idealized modes of "myth" and "history" to mean. Perhaps the key point is that the dis-tance between myth and history is not simply chronologi-cal but ontological. Myth refers to a mode of being in which all entities remain incompletely differentiated, and thus ani-mals, spirits, and humans are not entirely distinct. It is the continued copresence of this ontological domain of unspeci-fied becoming that forms the basis of perspectivism, the posi-tion that there exists a widely held understanding across the indigenous Americas that all entities see themselves as human (Viveiros de Castro 1998). It is precisely within this mythic domain that shamans enter into relations with other beings and seek to manipulate the mythical correlates of the non-mythic world. Indeed, through shamanism, dreaming, and visions, the domain of myth remains accessible in a way that history, even recent history, does not. What is strange about this domain of myth, and the mythic narratives of it, is that it evades the epistemological "rules" of the everyday. For this reason Lévi-Strauss has described myths as emerging from "nowhere" (1970:18; cf. Gow, this volume). Thus ultimately the distinction between mythic and historical modes finds at least one of its sources in the nature of the linguistically encoded relationship between narrator and narrated. Perhaps as much as an opposition of myth and history, what we are actually observing is an unresolved tension or oscillation between lives as singular, unique, and irreducible, and lives as instantiations of a shared, collective, and enduring experience that transcends any one life. While this statement might be more or less true for people in general, it is given a particular inflection through both epistemologies that set firsthand experience apart from knowledge gained in other ways and ontologies in which what is shared extends far beyond the realms of the human as usually understood.

The implications of this point are addressed in detail in Peter Gow's chapter on exemplary personal experience narratives among the Piro. In this case, the figure-ground relationship of the generic and the particular is framed as a relationship between multiplicity and individuality. As Gow notes, "the Piro person is a precipitate out of an a priori multiplicity." The autobiographical narratives mark a transition outward from multiplicity to individual experience, from myth to history, from the generic to the singular, or "a special case of self-singularization," to use Gow's phrase. Yet just as autobiography marks a transition out of the generic into the particular, out of myth and into history, it can equally mark the reverse, for as Gow points out, myths themselves are neither more nor less than the biographies of ancestral beings shorn of the evidential and epistemic markers that would otherwise make them "historical." It is their strange quality as originating from "nowhere" that allows them to reside alongside lived experience and thus provide a generic form that can subsequently be "inhabited" in personal experience. This is more than just saying that myths serve as a "template" for biographies, for we could equally say that biographies serve as a template for myths.

The essays collected here, but especially those in the first section, lead us to argue strongly for the absolute centrality of personal experience in indigenous lowland engagements with temporality. From the "biographies" of ancestral beings that constitute the realm of myth to the biographies and autobiographies of contemporary people that constitute the realm of "history," the world and its transformations are accessible through individual experience rather than generic collective templates (see also Basso 1995; Urban 1989). Yet as Casey High's chapter suggests, the transformation of such an understanding into the kind of collective histories required by contemporary claims to indigeneity has necessarily involved the adoption of new narrative forms, new sites of narration, and new kinds of audiences (Course 2010; Turner 1988; Veber, this volume). For what High's chapter demonstrates is that invention of new and heterogeneous narrative forms is always rooted in and emergent from very particular social positions. This leads to a striking contrast between senior peoples' autobiographical accounts of spear fighting in which they celebrate Waorani past openness to SIL missionaries and their nature as "real persons," and young activists' nonverbal, staged performances of "wildness" in urban centers that enact a firm boundary between Waorani and non-Waorani. High shows not only that these two genres of self-presentation work very differently with respect to how they model sociality but also that they correspond to different generational experiences of both past and future.

Hanne Veber's chapter describes the challenges and difficulties of a similar process in the movement towards the development of Asháninka "historical consciousness." It is precisely the rootedness of experience in autobiographical narratives, with their fundamentally "self-singularizing" qualities, that stand in the way of narratives about "the Asháninka." A common task that both historians and historically minded anthropologists take upon themselves is the production of a collective history out of the cumulation of autobiographical narratives, yet this act is as much an act of destruction as it is of creation. For the transformation of autobiographical narratives into "history" is primarily achieved through the process of "contextualization," a process that we often assume adds something to a narrative but, as Gow points out in his chapter in this volume, can equally be seen as stripping something away. Or as Silverstein and Urban (1996) have phrased the point, any act of "contextualization" is premised upon a prior "decontextualization." It is precisely the immediacy and singularity of personal experience that is lost as indigenous autobiographies become placed in their "historical context." Ironically, in creating "history" historians end up with "myth" as narratives become stripped of their anaphoric correlate. What is clear is that the understandings of time, both implicit and explicit in these autobiographical and biographical narratives, cannot be disassociated from understandings of what it means to be a person. Much as Raymond Williams (1977) has argued that theories of language are ultimately always theories of the nature of persons, we argue that theories of personhood are equally and necessarily at the foundation of theories of temporality, and it is to this topic that we now turn.

Persons within Persons

Recent decades have seen a genuine paradigm shift in anthropological approaches to the conceptualization of personhood. While several important studies have followed Marcel Mauss's famous demonstration of the cultural, historical, and religious particularities of the "Western individual" (Mauss 1985[1938]; Dumont 1985), others have turned toward alternative conceptualizations of personhood in non-Western societies (Dumont 1970[1966]; Strathern 1988, 1992; Wagner 1991). These two approaches are of course interlinked, and several writers have demonstrated that deep-rooted culturally specific assumptions about personhood have led anthropologists to systematically overlook and misinterpret alternative understandings of personhood elsewhere (for example, Strathern 1992).

This rethinking of what personhood might mean at the conceptual level has perhaps been nowhere more revolutionary than in the anthropology of indigenous lowland South America. Seminal writings by Anthony Seeger and his colleagues (Seeger, Da Matta, and Viveiros de Castro 1979), Joanna Overing Kaplan (1977), and Eduardo Viveiros de Castro (1998) have turned upside down previous anthropological models of both "individuals" being recruited into "society" and of the place of humanity within a "multicultural" framework. Through detailed ethnographic investigation of the contingent nature of what constitutes the "human," a new "perspectival" and "multinaturalist" understanding of the person was established and has become the dominant paradigm for many analyses of lowland South American personhood.

Put simply, perspectivism is the observation that in many indigenous American ontologies different kinds of beings see different worlds in the same way. For example, in an Amazonian context, it is common to hear that peccaries see one another as human and that they see humans as jaguars. Jaguars, on the other hand, see one another as human but see humans as peccaries. Viveiros de Castro has described this phenomenon of Amerindian perspectivism in terms of deixis (1998). In a conventional use of the term, deixis refers to the referential meaning of an utterance being dependent on the spatial, temporal, or personal position from which it is emitted. Yet in the deixis characteristic of perspectivism, it is the world itself that is dependent on the position from which its perception emanates, hence Viveiros de Castro's label of "cosmological deixis." A key point is that in perspectival ontologies not only do all beings appear human to themselves, but they act toward one another as humans would—in other words they all possess human "culture." For example, peccaries see themselves as living in villages, having shamans, and frequently holding manioc beer parties (although what constitutes manioc beer for peccaries appears to humans as mud, while what constitutes manioc beer for jaguars appears to humans as human blood). The crucial point is that "Amerindian ontological perspectivism proceeds along the lines that the *point of view creates the subject*; whatever is activated or 'agented' by the point of view will be a subject" (Viveiros de Castro 1998:476, emphasis in original). And it is the occupation of this subject position, rather than any "natural" essence, that defines one as "culturally" human.

While such a model offers a penetrating analytical framework for a wide variety of indigenous social practices—and indeed its influence is evident in many of the chapters in this volume—it nevertheless leaves certain questions unanswered. First, although derived from close ethnographic observation, the theory is formulated at an abstract and generic level. In fact the level of abstraction is so great that "the Amerindian person" frequently seems only tangentially connected to actual indigenous people. A second, related problem is that the creation of a "model of the Amerindian person" tends to homogenize the multiplicity of actually quite different ideas about sociality and personhood across lowland societies. Key questions such as why some societies, such as the Mapuche, the Asháninka, or the Achuar, insist on "living apart" while others, such as the Piro, the Piaroa, or numerous Gê-speaking groups, insist on "living together" remain unanswered or outside the paradigm.[5] Finally, although contemporary anthropological approaches influenced by this perspectival approach recognize indigenous conceptualizations of personhood, not as a fixed, enduring, and bounded essential states, but rather as a contingent processes of becoming through engagement with others, relatively little attention has been paid to the role of discursive interaction in this process. Thus despite the centrality of biographical and autobiographical narratives to the description of perspectival ontologies by anthropologists, surprisingly little attention has been given to such narratives in their own right. For example, Viveiros de Castro (1992) makes extensive use of the encompassment of enemy others through specific forms of autobiographical songs in his account of the Araweté, while Anne-Christine Taylor (1993) also relies on biographical *anent* songs to describe the transformative personhood among the Achuar in Ecuador.

While many anthropologists of lowland South America based in Europe and Brazil have greatly advanced understandings of indigenous conceptualizations of personhood from both within and without this perspectival paradigm, a parallel tradition of U.S.-based linguistic and cultural anthropology advanced greatly our understandings of socially situated discourse as it relates to the enactment of personhood. Participants in the workshop from which this volume has emerged were drawn from both (or in some cases neither) of these approaches, but all agree to some extent on taking these sorts of narrative practices more fully into account in the exploration of personhood. The chapters in this second section speak to some of the issues surrounding the conceptualization of personhood according to this perspectival paradigm. For some authors who have contributed to this volume, a focus on autobiographical narratives is important because they are precisely the medium in which the connection between the abstract "Amerindian person" and actual people becomes visible. Yet these same authors insist that a focus on autobiographical narratives offers more than just an exemplification or instantiation of broader structural features of "Amerindian thought"; it also provides a refining perspective on the model itself. Other authors (especially in parts 3 and 4) represented here maintain that without attention to the discursive practices within which personhood is enacted, it is hard to understand how individual persons draw on several different models of personhood simultaneously or how they invoke a range of "voices" or linguistically constructing social personae through drawing on the different ways of speaking associated with "different character types, professions, genders, social statuses, kinship roles, moral stances, ideological systems, age groups, ethnicities" (Keane 2001:269).[6]

For those more interested in a lowland "model of personhood," the ethnographic accounts of autobiographical and biographical narratives presented in the volume's second section suggest that this model needs to be complicated by attention to two distinct sets of processes. Borrowing a pair of spatial metaphors from Mikhail Bakhtin, we call the first set "centrifugal" and the second "centripetal." Centrifugal processes involve an engagement with and incorporation of aspects of others, while centripetal processes involve a condensation of those aspects into a singular person. The incorporation of aspects of others has long been recognized as a defining feature of personhood in lowland societies. From symbolic appropriations, such as the emphasis on utilizing the clothing or body ornaments of other groups, to the literal incorporation of others through cannibalism, the idea that the self is premised on the incorporation of others is recognized throughout the region. In the most highly ritualized events, the wide-ranging invocation of ways of speaking associated with exotic or "otherworldly" social personae is also often directly linked to the production of subjective transformations (Chernela 2003; Graham 1995; Londoño-Sulkin 2012; Oakdale 2005; Urban 1989). Such a process is seen in the autobiography of the Marubo shaman Robson Venãpa described by Pedro de Niemeyer Cesarino in this volume. Venãpa's journey as a shaman involves an incorporation of spirit beings into the "longhouse" of his body and the continual engagement of his "double" with these same spirit beings. It is precisely through these relations that both spiritual power is acquired and the self transformed and reconstituted to the extent that Venãpa asserts, "I am another person."

What we call centripetal processes, in contrast, refers to the way in which singular, encapsulated identities emerge at points in time, from the continual flow of perspectives and invoked social positions how, to use Marilyn Strathern's phrase, the network is cut, and a recognizable entity, a named person, emerges. While this aspect of personal narratives has received perhaps less attention than the centrifugal engagement with others, it nevertheless seems to be present in many of the ethnographic case studies included in this volume. This centripetal process of singularization appears to be at stake in the emphasis, described by Magnus Course, that rural Mapuche place on each individual's unique and singular destiny, an emphasis at first glance at odds with a copresent model of personhood predicated on an outward expansion toward others through exchange. Yet these two aspects are, of course, two sides of the same coin. The centripetally created named persons are premised on the conjunction of a multiplicity of relationships, while this processual plane of relationships only becomes tangible through these fixed "voices." Strathern has made a similar point with regard to kinship, that processes of extending networks of relationships necessarily go hand in hand with processes of limiting them; "one kind of reckoning never operates alone" (1996:530). Likewise, the invocation of "voices" allows for the expansion of the person across a multiplicity of others while simultaneously cutting that network through the anchoring of specific words to a specific person and thereby producing singular persons. Chapters in this second section argue that the copresence of models of the person as multiple, relational, and "dividual" and models of the person as singular, unique, and "individual" are not, contrary to what we might expect, necessarily contradictory or opposed but rather can also be mutually constitutive.

Creating Sociality across Divides

The third section of this volume diverges from the previous two in that authors focus on the "social life" or the effects of autobiographical and biographical narratives. The two contributions in this section suggest that not only do these narrative practices have the potential to bridge ontological domains and bring disparate "voices" into conjunction, but that their performances can also be a powerful means of structuring interpersonal relationships across large social divides. By focusing on the social life of narratives, the chapters in this section offer insight on some of the ways that interethnic relationships are created through these types of narrative performances. A number of recent archeological, ethnographic, and linguistic works have been concerned with the extent to which lowland peoples are and have been involved in wide-ranging networks beyond regional, ethnic, or language groups. This research has been insightful in illuminating the way a shared lingua franca, the trade in objects, pottery styles, or joint participation in music, ritual, or indigenous movements has linked peoples together across vast expanses (see especially Hill 1996; Hill and Santos-Granero 2002; Hornborg and Hill 2011). In archeology, Alf Hornborg has called for moving away from the "billiard-ball model" of migration according to which reified "peoples" "push each other across the Amazon basin" and toward looking at "communicative processes within a system of exchange relations in the lowlands" (2005:602). Through this sort of archeological work, the lowlands are coming into view as a place marked for centuries by wide-ranging relationships, as a place of partnerships and networks rather than a terrain marked by small villages, separated from one another by vast expanses of jungle, that have only just recently been "contacted" by outsiders. In linguistic anthropology, Christopher Ball, intentionally moving away from depicting the Wauja of the Upper Xingu in Brazil as a bounded whole, focuses instead on the "cultural structures that guide Wauja ideas about relation making" and how they are "picked up and circulated, applied and transformed in ever widening spaces" (2007:5, 8). Ellen Basso's earlier work on Kalapalo warrior biographies

(1995) is seminal for showing that at least in the case of the Kalapalo of the Upper Xingu these sorts of narratives function as exactly one of these structures. They move people in the Upper Xingu to consider the expansion of their moral community and to accept outsiders as consociates.

The chapters by Ellen Basso and Oscar Calavia Sáez each show how biographical and autobiographical narrative practices are, in fact, communicative processes that are employed, sometimes successfully, sometimes not, to structure interethnic relationships (see also High's chapter). Basso's chapter examines Kalapalo biographies as "repositories of speech heard in extraordinary contexts" that are useful for other situations in which strangers are engaged. Focusing on the contrast between verbal and nonverbal channels, she considers how the aesthetics of the performances of these accounts enable the further development of multilingual networks. Yet such attempts to cross ethnic divides do not always meet with success. Thus Sáez's chapter, about an urban Tukanoan leader's attempt to publish his sexually explicit autobiography, is in some sense an account of a thwarted attempt to communicate across boundaries. According to Sáez, Gabriel Gentil drew on both the idea of an anonymous reading public and images of a kind of "public" sexuality found in Tukanoan origin stories to creatively stake his claim to a type of shamanic empowerment while living in Manaus. His autobiography was, however, repeatedly rejected by publishers, effectively thwarting his attempt to communicate it to a larger reading public.

One way that autobiographical and biographical narrative practices work to structure social relations is by translating the experiences of distinct kinds of people for each other, between both people in the present and people from distant times and places. In some of these cases, such as those described by Basso (and also High in this volume), language barriers are clearly a problem to be overcome. In other cases, such as Basso's previous work (1995), these narrative forms operate on only a portion of those involved, in this case, Kalapalo speakers, encouraging in them a receptivity to the enlargement of their community. Chapters in this section keep open the possibility as well that while these narrative practices have the potential to bring new connections, they also carry the possibility of structuring new kinds of boundaries or of simply falling upon deaf ears, as Sáez describes.

The very act of recording experiences of any kind for a researcher, such as an anthropologist or linguist, as well as performing or publishing them for a national or international audience is also, of course, to be involved in structuring some sort of interethnic relationship in and of itself. All the contributions to this volume are, therefore, in some sense fundamentally part of these processes. Bruna Franchetto's chapter is particularly interesting with respect to considering how narrative performances structure relations between narrators and social science researchers, highlighting the power dynamics inherent in these relationships as well as how interchangeable these roles are at present. These sorts of relations between researchers and "research subjects" are not trivial, for the lowlands are a terrain in which the practice of research, particularly social science research, is a significant framework for structuring indigenous peoples' place in national societies. As Antonio Carlos de Souza Lima has noted about Brazil, anthropology has been bound to processes of nation-building from its outset (2005:199).

Hybridity, Dissonance, and Reflection

In the final section, we move from a focus on how these forms of discourse might work to structure social relations, to consider what these narrative forms express about the experience of entering into interethnic networks, a situation that can mean simultaneously participating in social spheres that require conflicting allegiances or that promote opposed values and models of personhood. These accounts give a sense for how larger political economic structures such as those connected to the extraction of resources, missionization, regimes of media, or academic production are partially entered into by narrators and how they become meaningfully integrated with (or work in opposition to) other, more local ideas and relationships.

Much as in the previous chapters, narrators here are also remarkable for the way they articulate images, discourses, and ideas from these "outside" institutions, in many cases circulating at a global level, with those that are more locally specific. Also notable are their skill and bravery with respect to these mixtures. The most successful blend resources in a way that is mutually intelligible, even if in different ways, for audience members who are situated across significant social divides.

These last chapters all concern the narratives of men who are or were, at one point, political leaders, individuals who played a significant role in spearheading the first sustained relationship or reshaping existing relations with "the whites" sent out from institutions such as the state or church. These narrators (as well as some authors) describe the dissonant, often jarring manner in which hybrid identities have taken shape over their lifetimes. In some sense, these texts allow a glimpse of the "processes of hybridization" taking place at a subjective level (Canclini 2005:43; see also Santos-Granero 2009 on the "hybrid bodyscape" in Amazonia).[7] These particular leaders appear as skillful interethnic negotiators and transculturites in these chapters, in contrast to the stereotypical media image of isolated, "uncontacted" warriors raising their bows at "the modern world."

The fact that similar hybrid identities are described in many of the narratives throughout this volume suggests that these multiple affiliations are integral to local cultural participation for many and have likely been so for a long time, certainly over the course of the last century and probably well before. This is of course what one would expect from lowland institutions promoting a "centrifugal model" of personhood and nations working to integrate "remote" or culturally distinct peoples through a variety of social and economic means. The narratives presented here give some account of what it feels like to engage with radically different social personae such as that of "pacification" expedition leader, urban media star, or "Owner of the Whites" as well as what it might feel like to step back and "cut the network" at certain points.

While the pleasure of successful engagement with new people, values, discourses, and ideas is not absent, narrators in this section focus more on the stress and cognitive dissonance caused by the simultaneous involvement in multiple worlds. In each of these three chapters the personal strain caused by entering simultaneously into disparate social institutions or positions in which social fields collide is apparent. In Suzanne Oakdale's chapter, a Kawaiwete leader, Sabino, describes being rushed into a hybrid leadership role, working as an organizer of rubber tappers and a "pacification" team leader, before he had an established family of his own, feeling as though he was forced to grow up too soon without gaining the culturally appropriate knowledge or maturity for such authority. Laura Graham focuses on the account of Xavante leader and activist Hiparidi Top'tiro, who grew up partially in a Xavante village and partially in urban Brazil, a leader torn between his fame as an urban media sensation and the effacement of ego required from Xavante leaders. Bruna Franchetto's chapter is a biographical sketch of a twentieth-century Kuikuro intercultural mediator, an "Owner of the Whites," Nahu. This portrait, woven together from his autobiographical narratives, accounts of other anthropologists, her own field notes, and an account from his grandson, is remarkable for the way it shows her own conflicting emotions with respect to her friendship with Nahu over a thirty-year period, one in which she and he struggled to define the terms of their relationship.

For each of the narrators in this section, the stress and dissonance of participating in conflicting social worlds also brings a self-reflexivity about (and at times, a critique of) aspects of "culture," social life, or "tradition"—both their own and that of other peoples. Participation in multiple social worlds allows these leaders to hold several ideas and ways of life at arm's length and critically examine them all. The stress of the dissonance in each is linked ultimately to innovations and creativity as well as sometimes a romantic return to an imagined past, but always to visions of better ways to live. In these chapters, this critical examination seems to come with the passage of time. In Franchetto's contribution this is most poignantly depicted in her own autobiographical narrative portions. The guilt and interest, repulsion and attraction she felt toward Nahu in the earlier years of her research in the Xingu are resolved in the present by Mutua, who is both a student in Franchetto's anthropology department and Nahu's grandson, someone who feels himself to be an embodiment of his grandfather.

Conclusion

To conclude, contributors to this volume argue for the centrality of autobiographical and biographical narrative genres in lowland constructions of history and personhood. They are forms that allow for an appreciation of indigenous understandings of myth and history (and their relationship to each other) and provide both a grounding and a reevaluation of the "perspectivist" model of the person. Furthermore, understanding how the performance of these narratives is tied to social life also provides a purchase on one of the mechanisms that subjects employ to form relationships across social divides, offering a more experiential perspective on such networks. Finally, they suggest that participation in multiple social worlds has been taking place for quite some time in the lowlands and that the resulting hybrid identities do not signal the end of these societies but rather demonstrate the very openness at the core of their existence.

Notes

1. Neil Whitehead defines historicity as "cultural schema and subjective attitudes that make the past meaningful" (Whitehead 2003:xi).

2. We take "lowland" to stem from neither a simply geographical nor a cultural area, but rather from an arbitrary academic division of labor that has traditionally segregated "highlands" from "lowlands" and "Andes" from "Amazonia." The Mapuche have usually been treated by scholars as neither "highland" or "lowland," but given the striking social and cultural continuities with many "lowland" peoples, they have been incorporated here.

3. Michael Brown (1987), in fact, has observed that lowland leaders are often required to demonstrate through an account of their dreams that they are able to cross ontological boundaries. The vast literature on lowland shamanism also offers insights on the degree to which these sorts of leaders engage with a wide variety of others across ontological divides.

4. This is no more than a cursory description of a complex debate. See Fausto and Heckenberger 2007 for a comprehensive overview.

5. See Viveiros de Castro 2001 for an attempt to account for diversity within a perspectival paradigm.

6. "Voice" here refers to types of "role inhabitance in discursive practices" (Silverstein and Urban 1996:8; see also Dinwoodie 1998) or the "linguistic construction of social personae" by virtue of the fact that ways of speaking are associated with these different statuses, roles, stances, groups, and so on (Keane 2001:269). See also Hastings and Manning 2004 on alterity in language as well.

7. Fernando Santos-Granero (2009) looks at the correlation between identity shifts and shifts in dress over the lifetimes of several Yanesha people, including new ways of being Yanesha and the hybridity of dress that results.

Bibliography

Albert, Bruce
    1997 "Ethnographic Situation" and Ethnic Movements. Critique of Anthropology 17(1):53–65.
    2010 Avant-Propos. In La chute du ciel: Paroles d'un chaman Yanomami. Davi Kopenawa and Bruce Albert, authors. Pp. 1–10. Paris: Terre Humaine, Plon.
Bacigalupo, Ana Mariella
    2001 La voz del kultrun en la modernidad: Tradición y cambio en la terapéutica de siete Machi Mapuche. Santiago: Editorial Universidad Católica de Chile.
    2007 Shamans of the Foye Tree: Gender, Power, and Healing among Chilean Mapuche. Austin: University of Texas Press.

Ball, Christopher

2007 "Out of the Park": Trajectories of Wauja (Xingu Arawak) Language and Culture. PhD dissertation, Department of Linguistics and the Department of Anthropology, University of Chicago.

Basso, Ellen B.

1992 The Implications of a Progressive Theory of Dreaming. *In* Dreaming: Anthropological and Psychological Interpretations. Barbara Tedlock, ed. Pp. 86–104. Santa Fe: School of American Research.

1995 The Last Cannibals: A South American Oral History. Austin: University of Texas Press.

2003 Translating "Self-Cultivation." *In* Translation and Ethnography: The Anthropological Challenge of Intercultural Understanding. Tullio Maranhão and Bernhard Streck, eds. Pp. 85–101. Tucson: University of Arizona Press.

Brown, Michael

1987 Ropes of Sand: Order and Imaginary in Aguaruna Dreams. *In* Dreaming: Anthropological and Psychological Interpretations. Barbara Tedlock, ed. Pp. 154–70. Santa Fe: School of American Research Press.

Brown, Michael, and Eduardo Fernández

1993 War of Shadows. Berkeley: University of California Press.

Canclini, Néstor García

2005 Hybrid Cultures: Strategies for Entering and Leaving Modernity. Minneapolis: University of Minnesota Press.

Chernela, Janet M.

2003 Language Ideology and Women's Speech: Talking Community in the Northwest Amazon. American Anthropologist 105(4):794–806.

2011 The Second World of Wanano Women: Truth, Lies, and Back-Talk in the Brazilian Northwest Amazon. Linguistic Anthropology 21(2):193–210.

Course, Magnus

2007 Death, Biography, and the Mapuche Person. Ethnos 72(1):77–101.

2009 Why Mapuche Sing. Journal of the Royal Anthropological Institute 15(2):295–313.

2010 Los generos sobre el pasado en la vida Mapuche rural. Revista Chilena de Antropologia 21:39–58.

Crocker, William H.

2007 The Canela Diaries: Their Nature, Uses and Future. Theme issue, "Life History," Tipití 5(1):33–58.

Déléage, Pierre

2007 A Yaminahua Autobiographical Song: Caqui Caqui. Theme issue, "Life History," Tipití 5(1):79–95.

DeMallie, Raymond, ed.

1984 The Sixth Grandfather: Black Elk's Teachings Given to John G. Neihardt. Lincoln: University of Nebraska Press.

Dinwoodie, David

1998 Authorizing Voices: Going Public in an Indigenous Language. Cultural Anthropology 13(2):193–223.

Dumont, Louis

1970[1966] Homo Hierarchicus: The Caste System and Its Implications. London: Weidenfeld and Nicolson.

1985 A Modified View of Our Origins. In The Category of the Person. Michael Carrithers, Steven Collins, and Steven Lukes, eds. Pp. 93–122. Cambridge: Cambridge University Press.

Farage, Nádia

2003 Rebellious Memories: The Wapishana in the Rupununi Uprising, Guyana, 1969. In Histories and Historicities in Amazonia. Neil L. Whitehead, ed. Pp. 107–22. Lincoln: University of Nebraska Press.

Fausto, Carlos

2012 Warfare and Shamanism in Amazonia. Cambridge: Cambridge University Press.

Fausto, Carlos, and Michael Heckenberger

2007 Introduction: Indigenous History and the History of the "Indians." In Time and Memory in Indigenous Amazonia: Anthropological Perspectives. Carlos Fausto and Michael Heckenberger, eds. Pp. 1–43. Gainesville: University Press of Florida.

Fernández, Eduardo

1986 Para que nuestra historia no se pierda. Lima: Centro de Investigación y Promoción Amazónica.

Gow, Peter

2001 An Amazonian Myth and Its History. Oxford: Oxford University Press.

Graham, Laura

1995 Performing Dreams: Discourses on Immortality among the Xavante of Central Brazil. Austin: University of Texas Press.

Hastings, Adi, and Paul Manning

2004 Introduction: Acts of Alterity. Language & Communication 24(4):291–311.

Hendricks, Janet

1993 To Drink of Death: The Narrative of a Shuar Warrior. Tucson: University of Arizona Press.

Hill, Jonathan

1988 Introduction: Myth and History. *In* Rethinking History and Myth: Indigenous South American Perspectives on the Past. Jonathan Hill, ed. Pp. 1–17. Champaign: University of Illinois Press.

Hill, Jonathan, and Fernando Santos-Granero

2002 Comparative Arawakan Histories. Urbana: University of Illinois Press.

Hill, Jonathan, and Robin Wright

1988 Time, Narrative, and Ritual: Historical Interpretations from an Amazonian Society. *In* Rethinking History and Myth: Indigenous South American Perspectives on the Past. Jonathan Hill, ed. Pp. 78–105. Champaign: University of Illinois Press.

1996 History, Power, and Identity: Ethnogenesis in the Americas, 1492–1992. Iowa City: University of Iowa Press.

Hornborg, Alf

2005 Ethnogenesis, Regional Integration and Ecology in Prehistoric Amazonia. Current Anthropology 46(4):595–620.

Hornborg, Alf, and Jonathan D. Hill, eds.

2011 Ethnicity in Ancient Amazonia. Boulder: University Press of Colorado.

Hugh-Jones, Stephen

1988 The Gun and the Bow: Myths of White Men and Indians. L'Homme 28(106):138–55.

1989 Waribi and the White Men: History and Myth in Northwest Amazonia. *In* History and Ethnicity. Elizabeth Tonkin, Maryon McDonald, and Malcolm Chapman, eds. Pp. 53–72. London: Routledge.

Kaplan, Joanna Overing

1977 Social Time and Social Space in Lowland South American Societies. Actes du XLIIe Congrès International des Américanistes 2:7–394.

Keane, Webb

2001 Voice. *In* Key Terms in Language and Culture. Alessandreo Duranti, ed. Pp. 268–71. Malden MA: Blackwell.

Kopenawa, Davi, and Bruce Albert

2010 La chute du ciel: Paroles d'un chaman Yanomami. Paris: Terre Humaine, Plon.

Kracke, Waud

1979 Force and Persuasion: Leadership in an Amazonian Society. Chicago: University of Chicago Press.

La Fontaine, J. S.

1985 Person and Individual: Some Anthropological Reflections. *In* The Category of the Person. Michael Carrithers, Steven Collins, and Steven Lukes, eds. Pp. 123–40. Cambridge: Cambridge University Press.

Langdon, E. Jean

    2007 Dialogicality, Conflict and Memory in Siona Ethnohistory. *In* Oral and Written Narratives and Cultural Identity. Francisco Cota Fagundes and Irene Maria F. Blayer, eds. Pp. 102–16. New York: Peter Lang.

Lévi-Strauss, Claude

    1966 The Savage Mind. Chicago: University of Chicago Press.

    1970 The Raw and the Cooked. London: Jonathan Cape.

Lima, Antonio Carlos de Souza

    2005 Indigenism in Brazil: The International Migration of State Policies. *In* Empires, Nations, and Natures. Benoît de L'Estoile, Federico Neiburg, and Lydia Sigaud, eds. Pp. 197–222. Durham NC: Duke University Press.

Londoño-Sulkin, Carlos D.

    2012 People of Substance: An Ethnography of Morality in the Colombian Amazon. Toronto: University of Toronto Press.

Lukes, Steven

    1973 Individualism. New York: Harper and Row.

Mauss, Marcel

    1985[1938] A Category of the Human Mind: The Notion of Person, the Notion of "Self." W. D. Halls, trans. *In* The Category of the Person. Michael Carrithers, Steven Collins, and Steven Lukes, eds. Cambridge: Cambridge University Press.

Muratorio, Blanca

    1991 The Life and Times of Grandfather Alonso. New Brunswick NJ: Rutgers University Press.

Nuckolls, Janis

    2010 Lessons from a Quechua Strongwoman: Ideophony, Dialogue, and Perspective. Tucson: University of Arizona Press.

Oakdale, Suzanne

    2002 Creating a Continuity between Self and Other: First-Person Narration in an Amazonian Ritual Context. Ethos 30(1–2):158–75.

    2005 I Foresee My Life: The Ritual Performance of Autobiography in an Amazonian Community. Lincoln: University of Nebraska Press.

    2009 Ritual and the Circulation of Experience. *In* Ritual Communication. Gunter Senft and Ellen Basso, eds. Pp. 153–70. New York: Berg.

Paillalef, Rosa Isolde Reuque

    2002 When a Flower Is Reborn: The Life and Times of a Mapuche Feminist. Florencia Mallon, trans. Durham NC: Duke University Press.

Rabben, Linda

    2004 Brazil's Indians and the Onslaught of Civilization. Seattle: University of Washington Press.

Radin, Paul

    1999[1926] Crashing Thunder. Ann Arbor: University of Michigan Press.

Ramos, Alcida

    1988 Indian Voices: Contact Experienced and Expressed. *In* Rethinking History and Myth: Indigenous South American Perspectives on the Past. Jonathan Hill, ed. Pp. 214–43. Champaign: University of Illinois Press.

Raoni.com

    2012 Biography. Raoni.com. http://www.raoni.com/biography.php/, accessed June 16, 2012.

Raoni, and Jean Pierre Dutilleux

    2010 Memoirs of an Indian Chief. Paris: Rocher.

Rappaport, Joanne

    2005 Intercultural Utopias: Public Intellectuals, Cultural Experimentation, and Ethnic Pluralism in Colombia. Durham NC: Duke University Press.

Rubenstein, Steven

    2002 Alejandro Tsakimp: A Shuar Healer in the Margins of History. Lincoln: University of Nebraska Press.

    2012 On the Importance of Visions among the Amazonian Shuar. Current Anthropology 53(1):39–79.

Sáez, Oscar Calavia

    2006 Autobiografia e sujeito histórico indígena: Considerações preliminaries. Novos Estudos—CEBRAP 76:179–95. http://dx.doi.org/10.1590/S0101-33002006000300009/, accessed June 17, 2012.

Sahlins, Marshall

    2004 The 2002 CSAS Distinguished Lecture, Anthropologies: From Leviathanology to Subjectology—and Vice Versa (Part II). CSAS Bulletin 39(1):7–14.

Santos-Granero, Fernando

    2009 Hybrid Bodyscapes. Current Anthropology 50(4):477–512.

Seeger, Anthony, with Roberto Da Matta and Eduardo Viveiros de Castro

    1979 A construção da pessoa nas sociedades indígenas brasileiras. Boletim do Museu Nacional 32:2–19.

Silverstein, Michael, and Greg Urban

    1996 The Natural History of Discourse. *In* Natural Histories of Discourse. Michael Silverstein and Greg Urban, eds. Pp. 1–20. Chicago: University of Chicago Press.

Strathern, Marilyn

    1988 The Gender of the Gift: Problems with Women and Problems with Society in Melanesia. Berkeley: University of California Press.

    1992 Parts and Wholes: Refiguring Relationships in a Post-Plural

World. *In* Conceptualizing Society. Adam Kuper, ed. Pp. 75–104. London: Routledge.

1996 Cutting the Network. Journal of the Royal Anthropological Institute 2(3): 517–35.

Survival International

2012 Davi Kopenawa Yanomami. Survival International. http://assets .survivalinternational.org/static/lib/downloads/source/progress cankill/davi_yanomami_bio.pdf/, accessed April 27, 2012.

Taylor, Anne-Christine

1993 Remembering to Forget: Identity, Memory and Mourning among the Jivaro. Man 28:653–78.

2007 Sick of History: Contrasting Regimes of Historicity in the Upper Amazon. *In* Time and Memory in Indigenous Amazonia: Anthropological Perspectives. Carlos Fausto and Michael Heckenberger, eds. Pp. 133–68. Gainesville: University Press of Florida.

Turner, Terence

1988 Ethno-ethnohistory: Myth and History in Native South American Representations of Contact with Western Society. *In* Rethinking History and Myth Indigenous South American Perspectives on the Past. Jonathan Hill, ed. Pp. 235–81. Champaign: University of Illinois Press.

Urban, Greg

1989 The "I" of Discourse. *In* Semiotics, Self, and Society. Bruce Less and Greg Urban, eds. Pp. 27–51. Berlin: Mouton de Gruyter.

Veber, Hanne

2007 Merits and Motivations of an Ashéninka Leader. Tipití 5(1):9–32.

2009 Historias para nuestro futuro, Yotantsi Ashí Otsipaniki, narraciones autobiográficas de líderes Asháninkas e Ashéninkas. Copenhagen: IWGIA.

Vilaça, Aparecida

2010 Strange Enemies: Indigenous Agency and Scenes of Encounters in Amazonia. Durham NC: Duke University Press.

Viveiros de Castro, Eduardo

1992 From the Enemy's Point of View: Humanity and Divinity in an Amazonian Society. Chicago: University of Chicago Press.

1998 Cosmological Deixis and Amerindian Perspectivism. Journal of the Royal Anthropological Institute 4(3):469–88.

2001 Gut Feelings about Amazonia: Potential Affinity and the Construction of Sociality. *In* Beyond the Visible and the Material: The Amerindianization of Society in the Work of Peter Riviere. Laura Rival and Neil Whitehead, eds. Pp. 19–44. Oxford: Oxford University Press.

Wagner, Roy

    1991 The Fractal Person. *In* Big Men and Great Men: Personifications of Power in Melanesia. Maurice Godelier and Marilyn Strathern, eds. Pp. 159–78. New York: Cambridge University Press.

Watson, Lawrence C.

    1968 Guajiro Personality and Urbanization. Los Angeles: UCLA Latin American Center.

    1970 Self and Ideal in a Guajiro Life History. Acta Ethnologica et Linguistica 21, Series Americana, 5.

Whitehead, Neil

    2003 Introduction. *In* Histories and Historicities in Amazonia. Neil Whitehead, ed. Pp. vii–xx. Lincoln: University of Nebraska Press.

Williams, Raymond

    1977 Marxism and Literature. Oxford: Oxford University Press.

Wright, Robin

    1998 Cosmos, Self, and History in Baniwa Religion: For Those Unborn. Austin: University of Texas Press.

    2005 Historia indigena e do indigenismo no Alto Rio Negro. Campinas SP: Fundo de Apoio ao Ensino.

    2013 Mysteries of the Jaguar Shamans of the Northwest Amazon. Lincoln: University of Nebraska Press.

Wright, Robin, and Jonathan Hill

    1986 History, Ritual, and Myth: Nineteenth Century Millenarian Movements in the Northwest Amazon. Ethnohistory 33(1):31–54.

Part One

Neither Myth nor History

1

"Like the Ancient Ones"

The Intercultural Dynamics of Personal Biography in Amazonian Ecuador

CASEY HIGH

I was born on Fish River.
Afterwards we lived well on Palm River.
We saw the high hills far off clearly.
We saw far downriver.

My big brother was Wawae.
My father was Tyaento, my mother Akawo.
Nampa my brother was a small child.
Oba my sister was still younger.
My big sister was Onaenga, my other sister, Gimari.
My mother's relatives were many.
My uncles were Wamoñi and Gikita.

Moipa and Itaeka did not do well.
Fleeing and hiding we came, far, far downriver.
We went by canoe, then we went back.

When did they spear? They speared at night.
My father escaped into the water.
They dug a grave for him and he was caused to die.
But he didn't die right away.
I didn't see it. They spoke and I heard.
My relative said, "I buried him."

Moipa and Itaeka speared.
Where did they go, did they say?

On a small stream upriver we returned.
We didn't see them.
We drank the water of maeñika fruit.
It rained, we got wet.
The jaguar growled, the monkeys called.
We climbed the trees when the jaguar came.

Then we fled.
We came at night in the moonlight.
We speared gyaegyae fish.

We were planting peanuts on Palm River.
The outsiders came with guns and shot.
Their dogs barked.
We went in the water, then fled on the other side.

    —*The Dayuma Story* (Wallis 1960:14)

This chapter considers the ways in which autobiographical narratives express indigenous Amazonian understandings of personhood, history, and relations with nonindigenous people. It looks specifically at how, in Waorani communities of Amazonian Ecuador, personal biographies of violence have become part of a broader cultural narrative in the context of changing intergenerational and intercultural relations. Ethnographies of narrative practices in lowland South America have provided examples of how indigenous regimes of myth and history evoke historical continuities and incorporate aspects of colonial history (Hugh-Jones 1988; Hill 1988; Gow 2001; High 2009a). This work, alongside the growing attention to memory in Amazonian anthropology (Fausto and Heckenberger 2007), raises important questions about the relationship between indigenous understandings of personhood and historical consciousness in lowland South America (Taylor 1993; Oakdale 2001; Course 2007). As elsewhere, Amazonian historical narratives express not only a sense of group identity and alterity but also highly individualized experiences that transcend the spatial and cultural boundaries of communities, ethnicities, and even nation-states.

In this chapter I attempt to understand how the autobiographies of certain Waorani elders, which tend to emphasize Waorani people becoming victims of violence, at the same time describe complex and enduring relations across social boundaries. Drawing on the autobiographical narrative of Dayuma, a key figure in both Waorani and missionary history, I describe how Waorani people have come to incorporate *kowori* (non-Waorani people) into a cultural narrative in which victimhood is a marker of personhood and sociality. I also examine how narratives of victimhood like these are transformed in the context of urban Amazonian Ecuador, where young Waorani men involved in indigenous politics align themselves with the biographies and imagery of famous warriors. I argue that in the case of both Dayuma's autobiography of victimhood and young men's praise for "the ancient ones," a cultural process of forgetting takes place in which personal biographies become part of a broader regime of indigenous history and political representation.

My analysis draws in part on ethnographic fieldwork in Waorani communities along the Curaray River and the surrounding areas since the late 1990s, Christian missionary texts published since the 1960s, as well as a short excerpt from Dayuma's autobiography as she told it to me in her home in 2009. My hope is that the combination of these sources, alongside the practices and commentary of young men who recently migrated to the frontier cities of Amazonian Ecuador, will illustrate the ways in which autobiographical narratives become cultural narratives and how these narratives change from one generation to another, evoking indigenous engagement with broader intercultural and political relations in Amazonia today.

Dayuma's Story

In 1960 a Christian-inspired book, *The Dayuma Story: Life under Auca Spears*, was published and distributed widely among evangelical communities in North America. Much as its author Ethel Emily Wallace anticipated, the book and the story it told became a source of inspiration for evangelical missions and Christian audiences across the world. It tells the story of Dayuma, a young Waorani woman who fled her native community in the 1940s in the wake of a series of intergroup revenge killings. She later befriended U.S. missionary Rachel Saint while living and working at a hacienda on the frontier of Amazonian Ecuador. The book's front cover claims to tell "the breathtaking story of the Ecuadorian Indian girl who escaped from—and returned to—the world's most murderous tribe." It tells how the Waorani, then referred to in Ecuador as *aucas* ("wild" Amazonian Indians), became the target of one of the most widely publicized mission campaigns of the twentieth century.

As the opening lines of Dayuma's narrative quoted at the beginning of the chapter suggest, *The Dayuma Story* tells how Dayuma's family became victims of spear-killing raids carried out by rival families and the incursions of nonindigenous people who came into contact with Waorani groups at a time when they were relatively isolated from the national society. It also describes an event in 1956 in which Rachel Saint's brother, Nathan Saint, and four other North American missionaries were killed by Waorani in a failed attempt to establish peaceful contact with Waorani people—some of whom were close relatives of Dayuma. This event, which came to be known in missionary literature and international media as the "Palm Beach" killings, became an important narrative of Christian self-sacrifice in the name of evangelism.

At the time of the killings Rachel Saint, who was affiliated with the Summer Institute of Linguistics (SIL) missionary organization, was conducting interviews and linguistic research with Dayuma, who later joined Saint in her return to Dayuma's family. Their relationship became a key platform for establishing the first Christian mission in Waorani territory. Dayuma and Saint would eventually become central figures in the mission in the 1960s, facilitating relations between Waorani groups, other indigenous communities, the Ecuadorian authorities, and petroleum companies that sought to develop oil resources on Waorani lands. Dayuma's autobiography is thus not only one of personal tragedy but also a narrative that maps the ways in which Waorani people came to establish enduring relations with *kowori*—non-Waorani people. Like Dayuma herself, by the 1970s most Waorani at the mission had converted to Christianity, and there were an increasing number of marriages between Waorani and Kichwa-speaking people (Yost 1981). Most importantly however, at least in *The Dayuma Story* and numerous other missionary books published subsequently, the mission coincided with a significant decrease in spear-killings between Waorani groups. The enduring presence of Dayuma's story in popular imagination, and that of the missionary "martyrs" killed in 1956, became evident in 2006 when a Hollywood film about Waorani history, *End of the Spear* (Hanon 2006), was released and viewed by millions of cinemagoers in the United States.

The point of this chapter is not to recount or debate the "history" told in missionary texts, movies, and more recent ethical critiques of missionary activities among the Waorani. My interest is instead to consider "Dayuma's story" as an autobiographical narrative that both exemplifies Waorani expressions of the self as victim (Rival 2002; High 2006) and points to the ways in which missionaries and other nonindigenous people have come to be part of Waorani understandings of history and sociality. Although the SIL was banned from Ecuador in the early 1980s and Rachel Saint died in 1994 after living with the Waorani for decades, Dayuma continued to live in the Waorani village of Toñampari—not far from the locations where her relatives and the missionaries were killed in past times—until her death in 2014. To outsiders who read misleading accounts of Dayuma as the "chief" or "matriarch" of her "tribe," she might have appeared to be a seemingly unremarkable elderly woman when I first met her in the mid-1990s. While few status distinctions are recognized in Waorani communities—even among elders—Dayuma was an avid and capable storyteller. On several occasions she shared with me pieces of her autobiography, sometimes at my request and sometimes on her own initiative. It wasn't until recently, however, that I began making video recordings of her narrative as part of a project to document the Waorani language. The following are short excerpts from a narrative she told to me in her home in June 2009:[1]

Dayuma: Long ago they speared my father dead, you understand? They really speared my father dead long ago, but I did not see it myself. We went to the other side and hid; then we heard that they speared my father. I ran away, all the way to the outsiders' house, but nobody was there. We went far away, but we found no outsiders. Since we were worried we returned, and when we got back Wamoñe had been speared in the leg. Despite so much killing they survived; only my father died.

Casey: What about your mother?

Dayuma: Yes, my mother, Akawo, only recently died in Tiweno; she died of sickness. My father was speared dead, and so was my brother Wawe. Other Waorani people killed Wamoñe for no reason at all; that's how he died. They speared him all over, and then [after he was dead] they speared him in the head and in the eyes, again and again. My mother told me that he was lying there dead; she said they speared him in the head.

Not long ago my mother, Akawo, died in Tiweno. My brothers and Nemo died; they cut her with a machete. My sister Onenka . . . at night the wind was blowing so much that branches were breaking from the trees . . . one went right through my sister's eye, like this [*demonstrating with her hand*]. She died . . . two of my sisters died, but two survived and are still alive today. I came to Tiweno, and we lived very well until Guimare's child had a painful birth. She died while giving birth, but her child Tomas and her other child survived. My sister Oba became sick and died of measles, so now I am alone, an old woman. I live all alone, but there are many children of Oba and Guimare. Her [Guimare's] husband already died but Oba's husband Yowe still lives.

Casey: Was Nemo [missionary Rachel Saint] like your sister?

Dayuma: Nemo was like my sister, and I lived loving her very much. She used to go to Quito and bring me food; she brought rice, noodles, and oatmeal for me to eat. Now Nemo is gone, and there is nobody to bring me food. She was very good. She also brought medicine for everyone to take when they were sick. When they found out that Nemo died they no longer listened to God's words since Nemo was gone; she was a great preacher. They live very badly; they get drunk and fight.

Don Pedro, Eduardo, Captain Nathan [missionaries] . . . five of them died. They died because Nenkiwi was angry and speared them. When they buried Guimare, they became angry among themselves and wanted to kill. They grabbed his [Nenkiwi's] spear and broke it, and then went and killed the outsiders. I am angry because they secretly speared and killed them while I was away in Quito. If I hadn't gone to Quito, I would have heard them calling and would have returned. If the outsiders had lived, they would have made a big runway and we would have lived very well. I am very angry because they did this very bad thing. Babe [missionary Steve Saint], Nathan's son, used to live here, but he doesn't come anymore. Felipe never comes anymore; I wonder who the other one was, his brother? I don't remember who it was; he used to come a lot, but he doesn't come anymore.

In this instance, Dayuma began speaking to me about how her father was killed after I asked her to tell me a story about her life. As with several other autobiographical narratives she shared with me in the past, this story focuses on the violent deaths of her close relatives and how the apparent chaos of past killings led to the suffering that comes with the absence of kin—both then and still today. The lines quoted here are part of a longer narrative she told that details the pain experienced by her relatives after they were speared. While Dayuma's experiences and personal biography are no doubt extraordinary, her emphasis on victimhood is part of a broader Waorani cultural narrative that firmly situates the self and the group as victims of aggression, be it from enemy spears or *kowori* outsiders. Ethnographies of the Waorani have given considerable weight to the idea that Waorani see themselves as "prey" to powerful outsiders, who they assumed until recently were cannibals (Rival 2002; Robarchek and Robarchek 1998). The word *kowori*, applied to all non-Waorani people, appears also to have referred to "spirits" of the dead who were contrasted to "people" (Waorani) on the basis of their assumed cannibalism. A common theme in many Waorani oral histories is the violence of *kowori* who entered their lands in the past. Still today Waorani often position themselves explicitly as victims of *kowori*, whether in reference to other Ecuadorians who colonize their lands or oil companies operating on the Waorani territorial reserve.

Killings like those narrated by Dayuma are commonly described in morally charged terms, such as *ononki*, which refers to deceptive or unjustified actions. *Ononki* can refer lightheartedly to a mistake, perhaps simply going the wrong way on a path, but it is also used to describe intentional behavior that aimed at tricking someone or lying or in reference to

Fig. 1. Dayuma in her home in 2010. (Photo by Casey High)

unjustified or unprovoked killing. In the text here Dayuma describes the killing of her uncle Wamoñe, saying, "Warani ononki ononkiponi tenonani" (others speared him for no reason at all), emphasizing his victimhood in the face of seemingly unprovoked violence. Dayuma gives particular emphasis to the word *ononki* in this phrase by repeating it and adding the intensifier suffix, *poni*. Similarly, the word for spearing, *tenonani* (they spear), is often repeated for emphasis.

Narratives like these also describe past killings as *wene* (bad, evil) or *wiwa* (bad, ugly). Like *ononki*, the term *wene* can also be highly morally charged, to the extent that Waorani people translate it as the Spanish word *diablo*, meaning "devil." They generally use this term not to talk about a specific supernatural entity (such as the Christian devil) but rather as a general concept of actions that they find to be unacceptable. In the transcription Dayuma repeats the word *wene* in describing her anger after the killing of the missionaries (*wene wene kegaranimpa* / "they did this very bad thing"). Although *The*

Dayuma Story and similar missionary texts do not provide transcriptions, it is likely that translated phrases we find in them, such as "Moipa and Itaeka did not do well," would have indicated similar usages of *ononki* or *wiwa* given the tone and content of the narrative.

An important theme of narratives like these, which appears in the excerpt transcribed here and in Rachel Saint's recording in the 1950s, is a focus on loss, displacement, and separation from kin as a result of spear-killings. Both narratives focus on how Dayuma and her surviving relatives are forced to flee long distances through the forest to escape the attacks of enemy Waorani, culminating in her eventual arrival to *kowori onko* (the outsider's house). These narratives convey a powerful sense not just of personal loss but also of large groups of kin being depleted and dispersed through violence, leaving the narrator with few remaining kin. Dayuma's autobiographical account in *The Dayuma Story* begins with a list of her family members and the comment, "My mother's relatives were many"—a prelude to her story of loss in the lines that follow. Similarly, the stories that I recorded with Dayuma often begin with a list of kin and explanations of how they died, followed by her commenting on the absence of her closest family members today. This state of affairs poses an explicit contrast to the frequently stated Waorani ideal of living in large and growing households, full of close kin and children.

Civilized Victims

In some ways Waorani narratives of violence, like oral traditions described elsewhere in Amazonia, tend to draw out social boundaries, emphasizing a strict conceptualization of alterity between the group and "others." This can be seen in Waorani narratives about ancestors who encountered dangerous *kowori* in the past, as well as stories like those told by Dayuma, which distinguish between her kin (*girinani*) becoming victims and Waorani "others" (*warani*) who carried out spear-killing raids against her household group. And yet this same narrative genre of violence and victimhood allows us to begin considering how various "others" are incorporated into indigenous notions of personhood and group identity.

We can see in Dayuma's 2009 narrative that the missionaries killed in 1956 have become part of a broader Waorani narrative of victimhood and loss by which Waorani elders describe their own kin being killed in the past. These accounts lament particularly the cutting off of past and potential sociality and sources of support. For example, at the end of her narrative, Dayuma speculates that, had Waorani people not killed the missionaries, they would have built a "big runway" for airplanes, providing further links with the outside world. This is followed by Dayuma regretting how the missionaries and their kin no longer visit her village. Similarly, in talking about her family history Dayuma laments the absence of Rachel Saint much in the same way that she describes her own family. A common theme in many stories like these is how past violence deprived the narrator of his or her potential kinship relations, whether these are ancestors or missionaries. These narratives thus provide a strong contrast to the Waorani ideal of one's group of kin increasing its number and expanding its potential sources of sociality.

This emphasis on social growth and expansion can be seen most clearly in narratives of what Waorani people call the time of "civilization" (*civilización*), which refers to the period between the 1960s and the 1980s when the majority of Waorani people came to live with Dayuma, Rachel Saint, and other missionaries at the mission settlement of Tiweno in the western part of the Waorani territory. Although a considerable amount of useful historical material exists from the writings of missionaries who lived in Tiweno and observed Waorani converting to Christianity, less attention has been given to the prominent place of Waorani concepts of *civilización* in contemporary autobiographical narratives and historical imagination.

This notion of *civilización* constitutes an important point of historical reference in Waorani narratives despite the fact that, thirty years after the official closure of the mission, few Waorani today call themselves *cristianos* or take serious interest in biblical teachings, as Dayuma notes in her story. The idea of having become *civilizado* (civilized) is a central theme by which Waorani people define their present mode of sociality. Waorani adults today contrast themselves to their ancestors on the basis that they or their parents became "civilized." Laura Rival (2002) has described how, in the 1980s, many Waorani were attracted to formal schooling because they saw it as an opportunity to become *civilizado*. The Spanish term *civilizado* is to some extent still used in reference to living in villages and in contrast to revenge killings and conflicts with outsiders.

Being *civilizado* is also expressed in contrast to the few Waorani groups who refuse peaceful contact with Waorani villages and Ecuadorian society more generally. For Waorani today, becoming "civilized" marked an important beginning of the current period of relative peace, the remaking of lost alliances, and the growth and expansion of their population. Narratives of *civilización* provide a strong contrast to the image of group depletion and separation in Dayuma's autobiographical narratives. Adults often say that families should grow large and fill the Waorani territory with more people. The notion of becoming *civilizado* and living peacefully in a *comunidad* (community) is highly valued and often contrasted to the hardships of displacement suffered in the past. Accounts of becoming *civilizado* are thus not only a way of relating the past but also one that attributes a moral value to the present state of village relations and an imagined future of growth.

Discourses of *civilización* are a particular form of historical representation that not only departs from but also complements the emphasis on violence in much of Waorani narrative. As we shall see in the following story that a Waorani man told me in Spanish about how his family became "civilized," these accounts often build directly on narratives of violence and victimhood like those told by Dayuma:

My family came from far downriver. There were no missionaries then, and people killed a lot. My father's family speared many people from the upriver group and took my mother away with them when she was a young girl. My father married her. Later my mother's brother Toña went with the missionaries to find my mother and civilize my father's group. They flew overhead making noise and talking from the airplane with a loudspeaker. Then they landed along the river, and Toña brought my mother's sister to help find my mother. They met my father's group, and Toña and five missionaries stayed with them for two months. They wanted to civilize my father's group so they would no longer kill. But my father's group threatened Toña, thinking that the missionaries wanted to take my mother back to where she came from. They thought Toña was a *kowori* [non-Waorani], so they lied to him. They told Toña to cut down *chonta* trees to make spears and said that they were for him to take and sell. But Toña already knew they wanted to kill him, because he had dreamed of a jaguar eating his head. My mother overheard the men planning to kill Toña, and she went to warn him. He was a *cristiano*, so he was not afraid. Early in the morning, they took Toña to a hill to kill him. They had waited for him there without spears the day before. They told Toña to chop down a tree to make spears. While he was chopping, the other men speared him in the back. With spears in his body, Toña said that he had no problems with the men who had speared him [forgiving them], saying that he was a real Waorani person. He said, "Don't kill" and "I die so that you should no longer kill." Then they speared him more, and Toña cried.

My father did not approve of the other men killing Toña. The others chopped up Toña's body "like meat," thinking he was a *kowori*. Just before they cut off the head, my father said, "Don't cut up my brother-in-law like an animal!" Then one of the men threatened to kill my father. He wanted to take my father's sister for his third wife. My father went home to tell his family about the killing, but they couldn't stop the killers taking his sister away. The next day my father went with his family to the burial site of Toña. Later he went with his brothers to live on the Tiputini River, where I was born. We lived there for five years. My mother wanted to return to her family upriver. My father did not want to go but did not want my mother to leave. Later they went to hide next to an airstrip near the river, and the missionaries took them all to a Kichwa town by plane. They stayed there, next to Kichwas, for fifteen days. Then they were flown to Tiweno (the mission), and my mother was reunited with her relatives there. Everyone cried because they were so happy, having thought one another were dead. They lived there with Toña's wife, the missionaries, Dayuma, and several other families in one big *comunidad*. We lived there for four years. We were very happy, and we became civilized in Tiweno. But then many diseases came, and more than twenty people died. Dayuma and some others decided to leave and found Toñampari. My family went too. That's why we live here now.

What becomes clear in this narrative is the attention given to a transition from intergroup violence to living together in one place. In addition to criticizing the killing of Toña, the narrator emphasizes how the large mission settlement led to his family's "civilization" and ultimately its escape from intergroup conflict. Although his father's group is implicated in a series of killings, the story also represents the narrator's closest kin as victims. His mother was taken captive as her relatives were killed, and his father only narrowly escaped being killed after opposing the killing of Toña. Since the man who told this story was a small boy when his family relocated to the mission, it appears that he was both reproducing a historical narrative of victimhood told by members of his family and defining himself as "civilized." Although he does not identify himself as a *cristiano*, the story reflects a biblical perspective on the apparent martyrdom of Toña, who forgives his killers after being speared. It suggests that this narrative of martyrdom has had some resonance for the Waorani, even for those who do not identify today as "Christians" (High 2009b). The idea of forgiving or not avenging past killings is an important part of how my adult informants envision the process they call *civilización*. The notion of becoming *civilizado* and *cristiano* is valued precisely because these terms refer to the conditions by which the most intense period of past revenge killings was transcended and rival groups began living in closer proximity at the mission settlement.

Waorani narratives of "civilization" also establish a sense of shared history with *kowori* people, namely, the missionaries. While it is clear from Waorani ethnography that the mission settlement had profound impacts on Waorani social life and cosmology, their relations with the missionaries can be understood in terms of a cultural narrative of victimhood evident in the autobiographies of Dayuma and other elders. In the missionary texts Dayuma's acceptance of Christianity through Rachel Saint's teachings is presented as having a pivotal role in making possible the mission at Tiweno. Part of what makes the narrative in *The Dayuma Story* so compelling for Christian readers is how relatives of the missionaries who were killed at Palm Beach, particularly Rachel Saint and Elizabeth Elliott, joined Dayuma to establish the mission among some of the same Waorani who killed the missionaries in 1956. While for Christians in the United States this became an ideal narrative of Christian martyrdom and forgiving, the notion that Saint's and Elliott's close kin were victims of violence appears to have also resonated strongly with many Waorani. The missionaries enter Waorani historical narratives as people whose kin were speared "wrongly" (*ononki*). In contrast to stories about aggressive *kowori* outsiders, these missionaries are described much in line with Waorani ideals of personhood and sociality: they are remembered as members of the convivial group, generous providers of food, and, perhaps most importantly, kin of people who were killed violently. Elders like Dayuma thus narrate stories about the missionaries within a similar genre of victimhood that they use in telling how their kin were killed in the past.

In this way Waorani narratives of victimhood not only express strict social boundaries between "Waorani" and "kowori" but also point to the porous nature of group identity in which semi-human *kowori* outsiders come to be understood as "persons" by virtue of their association with victimhood. In contrast to the five missionaries killed at Palm Beach, who were assumed to be cannibals invading Waorani lands, Dayuma later introduced her missionary companions to other Waorani as the kin of people who were speared years earlier. This understanding likely had a crucial role in the making of enduring relations between Waorani people and the missionaries. That is, from the perspective of Waorani historical narrative, it was not only Waorani people who were "civilized" during the missionization process but also the missionaries, who came to be accepted as real "persons" like Waorani by virtue of their association with victimhood.

Generational Narratives and Intercultural Relations

I hope to have demonstrated that Waorani narratives of victimhood and "civilization" express not only how individuals remember remarkable past events but also how these memories are linked to a wider cultural narrative that incorporates people from beyond the boundaries of Waorani society. Despite the enduring importance of victimhood in Waorani cultural identity, narratives like these also change across generations and in new contexts. In urban interethnic relations, young Waorani men construct a contrasting narrative that embraces the killer's point of view, evoking an idealized future of Waorani autonomy in relation to other Ecuadorians.

This becomes particularly clear in the historical narratives and embodied memory performed by men in their twenties and thirties who find themselves at the interface of Waorani and *kowori* worlds. As a result of involvement in the Waorani political organization in the regional capital and employment with oil companies, these men spend an increasing amount of time in the frontier towns of Amazonian Ecuador. In contrast to the autobiographies of elders, their narratives tend to emphasize the strength and bravery of their ancestors in defending Waorani lands from *kowori* invaders with spears. In some contexts they identify with this historical imagery in conveying the importance of Waorani autonomy in political relations, whether in negotiating contracts with oil companies or engaging with the wider Ecuadorian population at regional folklore festivals (High 2009a). To some extent young men embody the popular Ecuadorian stereotype of the "wild" *auca* warrior when they appear in front of these audiences seminude and carrying spears. While this imagery is no doubt strategic and individualized, I suggest that it is also part of a generational and gendered narrative that engages increasingly expansive relations across distant social spheres.

Even as this image of the "wild" Amazonian Indian appears to invert the narrative of victimhood expressed in the autobiographies of many elders, people like Dayuma approve of young men embracing historical imagery of fierceness and warriorhood. They often help to produce spears, necklaces, and feather headdresses to be used by young people in protests and urban festivals. There are, however, key differences in how the victim's and the killer's points of view are expressed in Waorani historical narrative. Whereas victimhood is most commonly narrated explicitly in autobiographical narratives of personal loss and suffering, a cultural narrative of warriorhood is expressed most clearly by nonverbal means. Accounts that glorify male ancestors as killers are rare even among younger men. The killer's point of view is instead conveyed through bodily imagery, gesture, and embodied performances that young men describe as *durani bai* (like the ancient ones). Their identification with warriorhood is thus generally expressed not through the biographies of individual men who killed in the past but instead as a broader sense of ethnic identity as Waorani people.

For many young men *durani bai* has come to acquire a specific reference to their ancestors' strength, independence, and resistance to outsiders by which they distinguish themselves from *kowori*. Like the indigenous historical genres described by Ellen Basso (1995), it is as much a statement about their vision of the future as it is a way of understanding the past. Whether in embodying memories of their ancestors or claiming to be like the "uncontacted" groups of today, this imagery of past warriorhood and autonomy has become an important part of an emerging masculine fantasy for a new generation of Waorani men (High 2010).

Forgetting: From Autobiography to History

The ideas expressed by young Waorani men in urban inter-ethnic contexts clearly depart from the narrative of victimhood described in the first half of this chapter. However, it is important to note that their embodied performances of the killer's point of view are also built out of the autobiographical narratives of victimhood told by Dayuma and other women and men of her generation. Young people are familiar with the life histories of people like Dayuma and come to know about their ancestors through similar narratives of how they were killed in the past. Elders tell these stories frequently in the home, often in extraordinary detail and in the presence of children of all ages. Young people tend to know the most famous of these stories even if they seldom narrate them. And yet it appears that for many young men today, these biographies of how specific people who died are collapsed into an emerging cultural narrative that celebrates spear-killing as an expression of what it means to be Waorani. While this generational narrative appears in some ways to invert that of elders, young men are in no way restricted to a single mode of historical consciousness. They too explain that Waorani people have been and continue to be victims of powerful *kowori*, even if it is not the central expression of cultural identity within the increasingly intercultural contexts in which they live.

The differences between Dayuma's autobiographical narrative and the notion of *durani bai* expressed by young men raises questions about how new forms of "historical consciousness" emerge at the interface of indigenous people and national societies in lowland South America. As Terence Turner (1993) has argued, the emergence of ethnopolitics has coincided not only with the transformation of indigenous cosmology but also with a profound change in historical and political consciousness. His characterization of the process by which the Kayapó previously envisioned themselves to be a unique mythical creation, in contrast to seeing themselves today as agents of their own history, has a certain resonance with the contrasting Waorani historical narratives that I have described. Young Waorani people have come to see themselves and their society in a radically different way than their grandparents, who distinguished themselves as the exclusive realm of real persons—against semihuman *kowori* cannibals. However, instead of positing a trajectory in which a mythic register of alterity is replaced by a more "historical" consciousness, I suggest that we might be open to a reverse view of contemporary relations in Amazonia, one that recognizes the ongoing process in which seemingly "mythical" shared cultural narratives are made out of the autobiographies of specific people.

The tendency of young Waorani men to embody a generalized killer's point of view resonates with descriptions of Amazonian societies that structure history in a way that excludes or minimizes the agency of nonindigenous people. In contrast to people who define themselves as a product of periodized historical processes of ethnogenesis and "civilization" (Whitten 1976; Gow 1991; Muratorio 1991), Anne-Christine Taylor characterizes Jivaroan historicity as one in which "individual memory is redistributed to build up a collective memory of adversarial relations" (2007:150). Taylor (2007) points to the ways in which particular regimes of historicity are closely linked to indigenous concepts of personhood. Historically, in Amazonian Ecuador indigenous people have moved between colonial social categorizations such as *auca* (wild) and *manso* (tame) not just by converting to Christianity, but also by embracing a new kind of historical discourse that contrasts past times of "wildness" to a present state of "civilization." So are we then to view Waorani narratives of "civilization" as a recent example of this ongoing process, or do the embodied performances of urban Waorani youth indicate a return to an *auca* regime of historicity? I suggest that Waorani autobiographies and embodied forms of memory demonstrate multiple modes of historical consciousness that contrast and build on one another. This is to say that being a Waorani person in some contexts means embracing a shared narrative of becoming victims and *civilizados*, while in others this same cultural identity is expressed in terms of group autonomy and adversarial relations with *kowori*.

Although narratives of victimhood and civilization can be seen to incorporate nonindigenous people—namely, *kowori* missionaries—into Waorani understandings of sociality and being, the narrative of "wild" *auca* killers embraced by male youth is oriented specifically toward relations of difference between Waorani and *kowori*, even as this notion of difference departs significantly from ideas about *kowori* cannibals expressed in previous times. Like the Jivaroan shamans described by Taylor and the generation of young "cultural brokers" described in much of Amazonia, young Waorani men today also have an important role as "managers of alterity." They occupy this role of engaging in relations with other Ecuadorians not by dismissing the narrative of victimhood with which they are so familiar but instead by building a new cultural narrative out of the intersection of colonial imagination and the autobiographical narratives of Waorani elders. In this sense what I have described is how autobiographies become "history" in new social and political spheres, even if this history has many of the characteristics of "myth."

I suggest that this multiplicity of Waorani historical consciousness can be understood in terms of not only what is "remembered" in autobiographical accounts and wider cultural narratives but also what is "forgotten." Ethnographies of Amazonia have described the cultural importance of forgetting in mortuary rituals and song (Oakdale 2001), a process that in some contexts is vital for the production of new persons (Taylor 1993). Suzanne Oakdale in particular draws on Raymond Fogelson's (1989) concept of "nonevents" to describe how Kawaiwete (Kayabi) mortuary songs "depersonalize and 'de-eventualize' individual deaths by submerging them into a more all-encompassing process" (Oakdale 2001:382). In the case of Waorani elders, stories about how their kin became victims of past violence tend to "forget" how these events were part of a wider series of revenge killings in which their own families, and in some cases they themselves, were also involved as killers. When they describe spear killings as *ononki* (unprovoked), they collapse these events into a broader narrative of victimhood that excludes other historical processes in which the events occurred. In the narrative of *durani bai* embraced by young men, past killings become "latent events" that are depersonalized in the construction of a "wild" image in urban interethnic relations. Here they "forget," albeit temporarily, the narrative of victimhood that has such an important place in the autobiographies of their parents and grandparents.

To some extent these seemingly conflicting narratives support Turner's (1988) claim that "cultures" have not only "multiple pasts" but also "multiple presents." However, I suggest that they also constitute different visions of the future. Narratives of victimhood and "civilization" embrace an idealized future in which relations across social boundaries are transcended to allow new and productive forms of sociality. This future orientation suggests an openness to the "other" familiar to studies of indigenous Amazonian sociocosmology (Lévi-Strauss 1995; Viveiros de Castro 1992). And yet young men also manage their present alterity through historical narratives that promote a sense of closure and difference in the face of outsiders. The future they envision with their current political relations is one of strict differentiation, even as, or perhaps especially because, they become increasingly part of the wider cultural politics of Ecuador.

Appendix

TEXT 1

(1) bo-to menpo bo-to menpo in-gan-te teno-nani wen-gan-tapa, iñi-mi?

(1-pn) (father) (1-pn) (father) (be-3-ing) (spear-3p.) (die-3-past-assert.) (hear-2-?)

"Long ago they speared my father dead, you understand?"

(2) bo-to menpo teno-nani wen-ga-kai-mpa bo-to ara-mai in-ta-bo-pa

(1-pn) (father) (spear-3p.) (die-3-cert.-assert.) (1-pn) (see-neg.) (be-past-1-assert.)

bo-to

(1-pn)

"They really speared my father dead long ago, but I did not see it myself."

(3) nanene go-bo awemo teno-nani moni-to wori
wino-ta-moni-pa

(away?) (go-1) (secretly) (spear-3p.) (1p-inclus.-pn) (quickly)
(hide-past-1p-inc-assert)

menpo in-gan-te teno-nani iñen-te werin-ke

(father) (be-3-ing) (spear-3p.) (hear-ing) (perceive-incip.)

*"We went to the other side and hid, then we heard that they speared
my father."*

(4) wori yewa ino kowori onko-ne woro go-ta-bo-pa

(quickly) (down) (there) (outsider) (house-at) (nearly)
(go-past-1-assert.)

go-yo-mo dee aa

(go-when-I) (not) (exist)

"I ran away, all the way to the outsiders' house, but nobody was there."

(5) go-ta-moni-pa go-yo-moni kowori dee aa werin-ke

(go-past-3p-incl.-assert.) (go-when-3p-incl.) (outsider) (not)
(exist) (perceive-incip.)

oke emen-te pon-ta-moni-pa oke emen-te poo aye

(move) (return-ing) (come-past-3p-incl-assert.) (move)
(return-ing) (come) (again)

Wamoñe wori mani-ñomo tapa ko-tin-ta ononti

(Wamoñe) (deceased) (this-here) (spear) (pierce-infer.-past)
(leg)

*"We went far away, but we found no outsiders. Since we were wor-
ried we returned, and when we returned Wamoñe had been speared
in the leg."*

(6) teno-nani woro wee woro wee ke-te kewe-nani-ta-pa bo-to

(spear-3p) (nearly) (die) (nearly) (die) (do-ing) (live-3p-
past-assert.) (1-pn)

menpo-ke wen-ga-kai

(father-only) (die-3-past.)

"Despite so much killing they survived; only my father died."

(7) Casey: bi-to bara diye?

(2-pn) (mother) (what about?)

"What about your mother?"

(8) oo bo-to bara Akawo ñowo wen-ga-ta-pa Tiweno

(affirm.) (1-pn) (mother) (Akawo) (now/recently) (die-3-past-assert.) (Tiweno)

wen-ga-ta-pa daikawo gawen-te

(die-3-past-assert.) (illness) (sick-ing)

"Yes, my mother, Akawo, only recently died in Tiweno; she died of sickness."

(9) bo-to menpo teno-nani wen-ga-tapa, bo-to toniñaka Wawe in-gan-te

(1-pn) (father) (spear-3p) (die-3-past-assert.) (1-pn) (brother) (Wawe) (be-3-ing)

teno-nani wen-gan-tapa

(spear-3p) (die-3-past-assert.)

"My father was speared dead, and so was my brother Wawe."

(10) wa-rani ononki ononki-poni teno-nani Wamoñe tono ina-te

(other-pl.) (wrongly) (wrongly-emph.) (spear-3p) (Wamoñe) (with) (3p.excl.-ing)

teno-nani-ta-pa wa-rani teno-nani wen-ga-rim-pa

(spear-3p-past-assert.) (other-pl.) (spear-3p) (die-3-infer.-assert.)

"Other Waorani people killed Wamoñe for no reason at all; that's how he died."

(11) mani tomaa mani ba-o teno-nin-ke awinka tomaa

(that.one) (all) (that.one) (become-?) (spear-infer.-incip.)
(eye) (all)

tenon-te okamo watii watii watii watii

(spear-ing) (head) (again) (again) (again) (again)

*"They speared him all over, and then [after he was dead] they
speared him in the head and in they eyes, again and again."*

(12) teno-nani aa oño-ga-kam-pa ante bo-to bara

(spear-3p) (say) (lay/there-3-distant.past-assert.) (say-ing) (1-
pn) (mother)

wori an-te wen-ga-kam-pa okamo ti-ka

(deceased) (saying) (die-3-distant.past-assert.) (head) (stuck.
inside-with.instrum.)

teno-nani-ta-pa a-ga-kam-pa

(spear-3p-past-assert.) (say-3-distant.past-assert)

*"My mother told me that he was lying there dead; she said they
speared him in the head."*

TEXT 2

(13) ñowo Tiweno wen-ga-ta-pa bo-to bara Akawo

(now/recently) (Tiweno) (die-3-past-assert.) (1-pn) (mother)
(Akawo)

"Not long ago my mother, Akawo, died in Tiweno."

(14) bo-to toniya-rani Nemo-wori wen-gan-ta-pa yeémen-ka

(1-pn) (brother-pl.) (Nemo-deceased) (die-3-past-assert.)
(machete-with.instrum.)

yi-rani wen-gan-ta-pa

(cut.w.machete-3p) (die-3-past-assert.)

"My brothers and Nemo died; they cut her with a machete."

(15) bo-to toniyaka Onenka-wori awe woyowote awe pemente

(1-pn) (sister) (Onenka-deceased) (tree) (night) (tree) (shake-ing)

uboye pemente nangui pemente awe tobee

(wind) (shake-ing) (much) (shake-ing) (tree) (break)

"My sister Onenka . . . at night the wind was blowing so much that branches were breaking from the trees."

(16) awinka pereic ino mani-no ko-te awinka pereic

(eye) (perforate) (over.there) (this-here) (pierce-ing) (eye) (perforate)

mano-mai to-menga awinka mano-mai tat-in-ta-pa

(this-like) (pn-3) (eye) (this-like) (stick. through-infer.-past-assert.)

bo-to toniñaka in-gan-te Onenka in-gan-te

(1-pn) (sister) (be-3ing) (Onenka) (be-3ing)

"One went right through my sister's eye, like this."

(17) wen-ga-ta-pa mea bo-to toniyara we-na aye mea

(die-3-past-assert.) (two) (1-pn) (sister) (die-3p.excl.) (still) (two)

kewe-na-ta-pa kewen-te ñowo

(live-3p.excl.-past-assert.) (live-ing) (now)

"She died . . . two of my sisters died, but two survived and are still alive today."

(18) bo-to po-mo Tiweno kewen-te waa kewen-te waa kewen-te

(1-pn) (come-1) (Tiweno) (live-ing) (good) (live-ing) (good) (live-ing)

waa kewen-te kiwi-nin-ke kiwi-nin-ke Guimare wori wiíñe

(good) (live-ing) (live-??-incip.) (live-??-ke) (Guimare) (deceased) (child) man-te wiíñe nan-ta-ka

(have-ing) (child) (hurt-past-3)

"I came to Tiweno, and we lived very well until Guimare's child had a painful birth."

(19) eñarin-ke nañe wen-ta-pa ñowo to-menga wiíñe aye

(giving.birth-incip.) (in pain?) (die-past-assert.) (now) (pn-3) (child) (still/then)

kewen-ga Tomas aye waka

(live-3) (Tomas) (then/also) (another)

"She died while giving birth, but her child Tomas and her other child survived."

(20) Oba-wori tanampiyo baá-te wen-ga-ta-pa bo-to toniñaka

(Oba-deceased) (measles) (become-ing) (die-past-assert.) (1-pn) (sister)

to-menga dee am-pa ñowo bo-to aro-bo-ke kewe-mo i-mo pike-mo

(pn-3) (not) (exist-assert.) (now) (1-pn) (one-1-only) (live-1) (be-1) (old-1)

"My sister Oba became sick and died of measles, so now I am alone, an old woman."

(21) aro-bo-ke aro-bo-ke kewe-mo i-mo Oba wiñe-nani bakoo

(one-1-only) (one-1-only) (live-1) (be-1) (Oba) (child-pl.) (many)

i-nani Guimare wiñe-nani bakoo i-nani

(be-pl.) (Guimare) (child-pl.) (many) (be-3p)

"I live all alone, but there are many children of Oba and Guimare."

(22) to-menga nanogenga doóbe wen-ga-ta-pa Oba nano-genga aye

(pn-3) (spouse) (before) (die-3-past-assert.) (Oba) (spouse) (still) kewen-ga Yowe

(live-3) (Yowe)

"Her [Guimare's] husband already died, but Oba's husband, Yowe, still lives."

(23) Casey: kowore Nemo bi-to toniñaka bay?

(outsider) (Nemo/RachelSaint) (2-pn) (sister) (like)?

"Was Nemo [missionary Rachel Saint] like your sister?"

(24) Nemo bo-to toniñaka bay in-gan-ta-pa nangui bo-to

(Nemo) (1-pn) (sister) (like) (be-3-past-assert.) (much) (1-pn)

toniñaka an-te kewen-ta-bo-pa

(sister) (see/want-ing) (live-past-1-assert.)

"Nemo was like my sister, and I lived loving her very much."

(25) to-menga Quito go-te kengui en-te pon-ga-ta-pa arroz

(pn-3) (Quito) (go-ing) (food) bring/take-ing) (come-3-past-assert.) (rice)

pon-ga, fideo en-te pon-ga . . .

(come-3) (noodles) (bring-ing) (come-3)

"She used to go to Quito and brought me food; she brought rice, noodles, . . ."

(26) avena en-te poo bo-to ken-te kewen-ta-bo-pa ñowo Nemo

(oatmeal) (bring-ing) (come) (1-pn) (eat-ing) (live-past-1-assert.) (now) (Nemo)

dee am-pa ekano en-te pon-gui kengui, Nemo wa-poni

(not) (exist-assert.) (who) (bring-ing) (come-infer.) (food) (Nemo) (good-emph.)

ke-ka Nemo waa ke-ka in-ga-ta-pa

(do-3) (Nemo) (good) (do-3) (be-3-past-assert.)

"and oatmeal she brought for me to eat; now Nemo is gone, and there is nobody to bring me food. Nemo was very good."

(27) biímo aro-bai en-te po-gan-ta-pa toma-nani daikawo

(medicine) (one-like) (bring-ing) (come-3-past-assert.) (all-pl) (illness)

gawe-nani to-menga goron-ga be-rani-ta-pa

(sick-3p) (pn-3) (bring/take-3) (drink-3p-past-assert.)

"She also brought medicine for everyone to take when they were sick."

(28) Nemo wen-ga a-te iña-nani . . .

(Nemo) (die-3) (see-ing) (hear-3p)

"When they found out that Nemo died . . ."

(29) wegongui yewemonga wii iñente kerani Nemo-wori waá-poni

(god) (words/writing) (not) (hear-ing) (do-3p) (Nemo-deceased)(good-emph.)

wegongui yewemonga apene-ka iñe-nani-ta-pa ñowo Nemo dee am-pa

(god) (words) (call-3) (hear-3p-past-assert.) (now) (Nemo) (not) (exist-assert.)

"They no longer listened to God's words since Nemo was gone; she was a great preacher."

(30) wene wene ke-rani kewe-nani tiname birin-ke yewen-te

(bad) (bad) (do-3p) (live-3p) (alcohol) (drink-incip.) (crazy-ing)

tamon-te we-rani

(fight-ing) feel/react-3p)

"They live very badly; they get drunk and fight."

(31) Don Pedro, Eduardo, capitan Natanael mani-nani we-nani-ta-pa

(Don Pedro) (Eduardo) (captain) (Natanael) (that-pl)
(die-3p-past-assert.)

ononpo emepoke

(hand) (five)

*"Don Pedro, Eduardo, Captain Nathan [missionaries] . . . five of
them died."*

(32) i-nani teno-ga-rani-mpa Nenkiwi wene wene ke-ka

(be-3p) (spear-distant.past-3p-assert.) (Nenkiwi) (bad) (bad)
(do-3)

beye teno-nani wen-ga-ta-pa

(this is why) (spear-3p) (die-3-past-assert.)

"They died because Nenkiwi was angry and speared them."

(33) we-nani-ta-pa Guimare-wori in-te wen-ke-te an-te ke-te

(bury-3p-past-assert.) (Guimare-dead) (be-ing) (bury-incip.-
ing) (want-ing) (do-ing)

tapa teno-ke-te an-te ke-ka ta ta ta mee-po-te ke-te

(spear) (spear-incip.-ing) (want-ing) (do-3) (break) (grasp.
spear-come-ing) (do-ing)

engui ba-te po-te kowore-iri i-nani teno-nani-ta-pa

(angry) (become-ing) (come-ing) (outsider-pl) (be-3p)
(spear-3p-past-assert.)

*"When they buried Guimare, they became angry among themselves
and wanted to kill. They grabbed his [Nenkiwi's] spear and broke it,
and then went and killed the outsiders."*

(34) nangui pií-mo bo-to Quito kiwi-ño-mo-te teno-nani-ta-pa

(much) (angry-1) (1-pn) (Quito) (live-when-1-ing)
(spear-3p-past-assert.)

awemo teno-nani we-nani-ta-pa

(secretly) (spear-3p) (die-3p-past-assert.)

"I am very angry because they secretly speared and killed them while I was away in Quito."

(35) bo-to wii go-te bay Quito wii go-bo bay bo-to e-mo-wo

(1-pn) (not) (go-ing) (like) (Quito) (not) (go-1) (like) (1-pn) (hear-1-spec)

aape-yo-nani bo-to doóbe pon-ke-ro-mo-in-pa po-mo bay

(call-when-3p) (1-pn) (before) (come-incip.-caus.-1-inf.-assert.) (come-1) (like)

"If I hadn't gone to Quito, I would have heard them calling and would have returned."

(36) aye kewen-ke-ro-nanim-pa kowori-iri mani-ñomo tomaa ñene

(still) (live-conject.-3p-assert.) (outsider-pl) (that-there/here) (all) (big)

ebopanka ba-ron-kero-nanim-pa mani ebopanka ba-ron-te

(airstrip) (become-caus.conj.past.pl.assert.) (that) (airstrip) (become-caus.-ing)

waá-poni ke-te kewen-kero-nim-pa

(good-emph.) (do-ing) (live-conj.past.pl.inf.assert.)

"If the outsiders had lived, they would have made a big runway, and we would have lived very well."

(37) iña-nani wene wene ke-ga-ranim-pa bo-to nangui pií-mo-pa íi

(these-3p) (bad) (bad) (do-distant.past-3p-assert.) (1-pn) (much)(angry-1-assert.) (this)

"I am very angry because they did this very bad thing."

(38) Babe tome-gano wenga Natanael wenga iñomo kewen-ga-ta-pa

(Babe) (that-place) (son) (Natanael) (son) (here)
(live-3-past-past-assert.)

ñowo dee po-namai inga

(now) (not) (come-neg.) (be-3)

*"Babe [missionary Steve Saint], Nathan's son, used to live here, but
he doesn't come anymore."*

(39) Felipe po-namai kowe iñ-anga ekano emogano

(Felipe) (come-neg.) (always/never) (this-3) (who) (what.name)

in-ga-ta-wo waka nano-toniñaka

(be-3-past-dubative) (other) (other-brother)

*"Felipe never comes anymore; I wonder who the other one was, his
brother?"*

(40) wii ponewe ekame in-ta-pa mani-nga poo poo

(not) (remember) (whoever) (be-past-assert.) (that-3)
(come) (come)

ke-te ñowo dee po-namai in-ga

(do-ing) (now) (not) (come-neg.) (be-3)

*"I don't remember who it was; he used to come a lot, but he doesn't
come anymore."*

Notes

1. I thank Ramon Gaba for transcribing and translating an early version of the recording of which this text is part. While Connie Dickinson
also provided technical training and support to Ramon and myself, any
errors in the transcription and translation are my own.

Bibliography

Basso, Ellen B.
    1995 The Last Cannibals: A South American Oral History. Austin:
    University of Texas Press.
Course, Magnus
    2007 Death, Biography, and the Mapuche Person. Ethnos 72(1):
    77–101.

Fausto, Carlos, and Michael Heckenberger, eds.

    2007 Time and Memory in Indigenous Amazonia: Anthropological Perspectives. Gainesville: University Press of Florida.

Fogelson, Raymond

    1989 The Ethnohistory of Events and Nonevents. Ethnohistory 36(2):133–47.

Gow, Peter

    1991 Of Mixed Blood. Oxford: Clarendon Press.

    2001 An Amazonian Myth and Its History. Oxford: Oxford University Press.

Hanon, Jim, dir.

    2006 End of the Spear. 16 mm, 111 min. Every Tribe Entertainment, Studio City CA.

High, Casey

    2006 From Enemies to Affines: Conflict and Community among the Huaorani of Amazonian Ecuador. PhD dissertation, London School of Economics, University of London.

    2009a Remembering the Auca: Violence and Generational Memory in Amazonian Ecuador. Journal of the Royal Anthropological Institute 15:719–36.

    2009b Victims and Martyrs: Converging Histories of Violence in Amazonian Anthropology and U.S. Cinema. Anthropology and Humanism 34(1):41–50.

    2010 Warriors, Hunters, and Bruce Lee: Gendered Agency and the Transformation of Amazonian Masculinity. American Ethnologist 37(4):753–70.

Hill, Jonathan

    1988 Introduction: Myth and History. *In* Rethinking History and Myth: Indigenous South American Perspectives on the Past. Jonathan Hill, ed. Pp. 1–17. Champaign: University of Illinois Press.

Hugh-Jones, Stephen

    1988 The Gun and the Bow: Myths of White Men and Indians. L'Homme 28(106):138–55.

Lévi-Strauss, Claude

    1995 The Story of Lynx. Chicago: University of Chicago Press.

Muratorio, Blanca

    1991 The Life and Times of Grandfather Alonso. New Brunswick NJ: Rutgers University Press.

Oakdale, Suzanne

    2001 History and Forgetting in an Amazonian Community. Ethnohistory 48(3):381–401.

Rival, Laura

    2002 Trekking through History: The Huaorani of Amazonian Ecuador. New York: Columbia University Press.

Robarchek, Carole Jeanne, and Clayton Robarchek

1998. Waorani: The Contexts of Violence and War. Fort Worth: Harcourt Brace.

Taylor, Anne-Christine

1993 Remembering to Forget: Identity, Memory and Mourning among the Jivaro. Man 28:653–78.

2007 Sick of History: Contrasting Regimes of Historicity in the Upper Amazon. In Time and Memory in Indigenous Amazonia: Anthropological Perspectives. Carlos Fausto and Michael Heckenberger, eds. Pp. 133–68. Gainesville: University Press of Florida.

Turner, Terence

1988 History, Myth and Social Consciousness among the Kayapó of Central Brazil. In Rethinking History and Myth: Indigenous South American Perspectives on the Past. Jonathan Hill, ed. Pp. 195–213. Champaign: University of Illinois Press.

1993 De cosmologia a história: Resistência, adaptação e consiência social entre of Kayapó. In Amazonia: Etnologia e história indigena. Eduardo Viveiros de Castro and Manuela Carneiro da Cunha, eds. Pp. 43–66. São Paulo: Fundação de Amparo a Pesquisa do Estado de São Paulo.

Viveiros de Castro, Eduardo

1992 From the Enemy's Point of View: Humanity and Divinity in an Amazonian Society. Chicago: University of Chicago Press.

Wallis, Ethel E.

1960 The Dayuma Story: Life under Auca Spears. New York: Harper and Brothers.

Whitten, Norman

1976 Sacha Runa: Ethnicity and Adaptation of Ecuadorian Jungle Quichua. Urbana: University of Illinois Press.

Yost, James

1981 Twenty Years of Contact: The Mechanisms of Change in Wao (Auca) Culture. In Cultural Transformations and Ethnicity in Modern Ecuador. Norman Whitten, ed. Pp. 677–704. Urbana: University of Illinois Press.

2

"This Happened to Me"

*Exemplary Personal Experience Narratives among
the Piro (Yine) People of Peruvian Amazonia*

Peter Gow

The Piro (Yine) people of the Bajo Urubamba River in Peruvian Amazonia have a distinct genre of exemplary personal
experience narratives that deal with very unusual and emotionally charged life events, such as flight from a murderous
boss or a lone encounter with a jaguar. These narratives are
explicitly tied to a particular person, as his or her story, and
are ideally told by their "experiencer/owner." They focus attention on the uniqueness of individual experience, and on its
multiplication through the act of telling the story to others,
multiplicity being the key definition of the person for Piro
people. As such, they differ dramatically from Euro-American
genres of autobiography and biography, which focus attention
on the individual as a unique singularity. Every Western person has a biography, by dint of being a singularity. Piro people, by contrast, have such singularity imposed on their basic
multiplicity by the world.

I here call these narratives "exemplary personal experience
narratives," but I do not intend by this name that Piro people
consider there to be anything heroic or laudable about the situations they describe. At best they are admirable because the
narrator survived the experience. Rather, I consider these stories to be "exemplary" in the sense of being "singled out," which
is not necessarily a positive experience for any given person.

My interest in Piro exemplary personal experience narratives derives from two distinct sources. The first is a general interest in American linguistic anthropology and analyses of linguistic genre and what these reveal about my ethnography of Piro people. The second is more specific, for over the years I have used such narratives as historical evidence. In light of the present analysis, I now consider this use of these narratives to have been rather uncritical, given that it assumed that the focus of the tellers' interest was the historical event experienced, rather than other aspects of the event in which it was narrated.

That my original interest in exemplary personal experience narratives was as historical evidence has two further implications for my argument here. First, it critically affected my analytical "angle of entry" to the topic, as I explain later in the chapter. Second, my interest in these narratives continues to be primarily as historical evidence, for the elucidation of the history of indigenous people in southwestern Amazonia since the nineteenth century from their perspective. As such these exemplary personal experience narratives provide fascinating insight into how indigenous people experienced the transformations of their worlds from their own point of view. Most of what is known about the local history is known through the accounts of literate outsiders, usually state officials, missionaries, or travelers, who necessarily only register what exactly interests them. Even accounts from rubber bosses are remarkably few, and those that do exist provide a picture very different from the mass of archival sources. Indigenous accounts are currently proliferating, but in order to use them, we need to know more about what exactly motivates such narratives.

Piro Discourse Genres

Over the years I have discussed a number of verbal genres among the Piro (Yine) people of the Bajo Urubamba River in Peruvian Amazonia, such as personal experience narratives, historical narratives, "stories about ancient people," "ancient people's stories," and a number of sung discursive forms. I should stress that while I have studied linguistics, I do not think of myself as a linguistic anthropologist, far less as a cultural anthropologist. I am a social anthropologist and am trying to follow a program described several years ago by Joanna Overing as follows: "Our task is to combine the best of American cultural anthropology with the best of European social anthropology. The cultural anthropologists are great at analysing what people say, but we also need to look at the relation between who is talking and who is listening, which is what the social anthropologists do well" (Overing, personal communication; see also Gow 2001). This is, of course, the path that many linguistic anthropologists have followed.

Here I want to look briefly at a subset of personal experience narratives that I call exemplary personal experience narratives. By this term I mean stories of personal experiences for which the teller is well renowned because they tell of extraordinary experiences, usually life threatening, that the teller survived and hence lived to tell the tale. These extraordinary experiences of emotional intensity become narrativized and are told in a largely monological fashion, such that the speaker is heard out until near the end of the story. Listeners "whatsay," to use Basso's important discovery (1985), and may ask questions for clarification, but do not change the topic until the story comes to an end.

In order to give a flavor of the genre, let us consider an example that I have discussed before (Gow 2001): *"Nato Yonisyani Ginkakle Tenyapachro Pirana,"* "Our Late Mother Dionisia's Story about the Aeroplane," from the Summer Institute of Linguistics school reader *Muchikawa Kewenni Pirana ga wa Pimri Ginkaklukaka* (Nies 1972). Dionisia García's story goes as follows and refers to events in the early 1930s after the narrator and her kinspeople had fled from their boss, Francisco "Pancho" Vargas, far downriver to the Bajo Ucayali:

We saw the first aeroplane a long time ago. I was still a young woman and my daughter Ana María was too, while Miguel, Felipe and the other little girl were still very little. Before that time, our boss Pancho had told us that a man with wings and shoes would come, flying through the air, and it was said that this was how God would come.

And that day when it came, we were living downriver from Contamana in Inahuaya village at the mouth of the Cachiyacu river. We were alone, just sitting around, Ana María, the children and me, when we suddenly heard a noise coming from the big straight stretch of the Cachiyacu: hlalalalalalalala. Ana María said, "Mother, what is that noise, hlalalalalalalala? Maybe it's a jaguar." "Who knows what it is?" I replied to her, "A jaguar? Perhaps it is black jaguars who have come out onto the big straight stretch of the Cachiyacu." We went to look, but we saw nothing. All we heard was the sound, hlalalalalalala.

I said, "Take the axe to kill the jaguar!" I grabbed the machete and Ana María the axe and we ran off to find out what it was. As we looked around, Ana María looked up and saw the aeroplane. We saw it as a person with wings and shoes, just as we had heard in the stories. "Ay! Perhaps it is truly God, for they said that he will come with wings to carry his children into heaven." We looked up, thinking we saw his open arms, when in fact it was an aeroplane.

Then we shouted, saying, "Father, we are here! Take us with you!" We thought the pilot was God, but he wasn't. "Father, here we are, your children!" As we watched the aeroplane went on, and we said to each other sadly, "It seems he didn't see us. If he had seen us, he would have come down to take us away."

We were wrong to imagine that it was God, when it was just the pilot, a white man. This happened when we lived on the Cachiyacu river. That is the story. (Nies 1972:21–27)

As I discussed earlier, this story is freighted with meaning for the narrator, including the fraught relation with the boss

Vargas, the millenarian expectations being disseminated by Adventist missionaries, the transforming transport systems of the area, and the importance of the SIL and their airplanes in her life and in the lives of her kinspeople. Beyond all that, however, it is a very funny story about ignorance and self-deception. Dionisia García had no reason to know what an airplane was, and her interpretation of the sound of the engine in terms of a jaguar's roaring is perfectly reasonable. But what is funny, from a Piro perspective, is her mistaking the airplane for God and her credulity with regard to her former boss Pancho's idiosyncratic vision of the Second Coming.

Exemplary Personal Experience Narratives as Social Experiences

I first became aware of Piro exemplary personal experience narratives as a specific genre through my late compadre Pablo Rodriguez. Following our return from a remarkable, and at times terrifying, journey up the Urubamba River from the village of Santa Clara to the village of Miaría in 1988, Pablo insisted that we go to his home village of Huau, just across the river, to record "the story" of his maternal grandfather, Jorge Manchinari. I had assumed that Pablo meant that we should record Don Jorge's life story, but "his story" turned out to be something very different. It was not an autobiography but an intense and dramatic account of an episode from his young manhood, which detailed the events of his flight up the Juruá River from an abusive Brazilian boss who wanted to kill him and his kinspeople.

At the time I noticed the mismatch between my expectations of what this story might be and what it actually was, but only when I thought about Don Jorge's story in the context of writing this chapter did I realize its deeper significance. Pablo did not simply want me to hear his grandfather's story; he wanted to tape-record it. I never much liked using the tape recorder and had over the years relinquished this task to Pablo, who did enjoy using it. Indeed, the journey to Miaría, which I intended to be about Piro visual art, subtly transformed, at Pablo's insistence, into a fascinating piece of research on women's songs and other sung discourse forms. Piro visual art is an exclusively female concern, and women seldom found it easy to discuss it with me. But they were always happy to sing, because their songs are about men, often men of outlandish origins such as myself. Pablo was quite explicit that he did not want the tape recorder and that the tapes were for me to take to my country so that my kinspeople could hear them.

Some aspects of the journey to Miaría were extremely frightening, for this was the "hot year" of the civil war in Peru. While not under effective Sendero Luminoso control, most of the Bajo Urubamba River had been abandoned by government forces, and followers of Sendero operated fairly openly. As I have discussed elsewhere (Gow 2008), I nearly managed to get Pablo, his nephew Juan, and myself shot by two very nervous men convinced that we were *senderistas*. That was the worst moment, but there were a whole string of intense encounters and events. Because of this, I think, Pablo wanted to record his grandfather's story about his own terrifying journey, and he wanted me to hear it and take it back to my country.

Don Jorge's story was not simply about a terrifying journey fleeing from a murderous Brazilian boss; it was also, like Dionisia García's story, a story about delusion. Don Jorge began his story with his decision as a youth to flee to the lower Ucayali River, far to the north, to escape the oppressive behavior of his boss, Pancho Vargas, the "big boss of the Piro people." Vargas treated the young Don Jorge badly, so he fled. This was a biographical detail among many others. But it gave remarkable meaning to his subsequent experiences on the Juruá River, where he found himself working for a boss who did not simply mistreat him but then sought to kill him. In search of a solution to his initial problem with Vargas, Don Jorge found a solution that actually proved to be very much worse. Vargas was certainly abusive, but he did not kill his workers; on the other hand, Brazilians are feared by people in Peruvian Amazonia for their violence.

It is possible that Pablo realized that the journey to Miaría had the makings of an exemplary personal experience narrative like his grandfather's story of the flight up the Juruá River. His untimely death prevents me from knowing if that was true. What is certain is that aspects of that journey became an exemplary personal experience narrative for our young companion, Juan Mosombite, Pablo's nephew. Many years later I visited Juan, who is a reluctant talker, and I was amazed when he started to remember the most terrifying part of that journey: "Remember when we were stuck on that beach. Remember how you said, 'We must go to that house!' Remember how we went to the house and heard the bullet going into the chamber, trak, trak! How afraid I was, oh, how afraid! Then we slept in the outhouse, and the rain fell on us. How much we suffered, remember!" His voice was straining with emotion, and I had never heard Juan talk so animatedly and at such length. He said to me, "Often, in the evening, I tell my children about that journey with my late uncle Pablo and with you. And my children listen to me and ask me, 'What happened next?' I will never forget that journey! Never!" The story of that journey has become Juan's exemplary personal experience narrative for the audience of his children.

A Personal Context for Don Jorge's Story

Some sense of the remarkable nonsalience for me of Piro exemplary personal experience narratives comes from my memories of Don Jorge's narration and the actual record of my note keeping of that event.

When writing of this chapter, I looked for my notes on Don Jorge's story and turned first to an article that I wrote in Iquitos a couple of months later that was published in 1990 and where I thought I had published his story. Given the extraordinary political circumstances in which I found the Bajo Urubamba and Peru in general, I wanted to write something about Piro people that might, just might, reach the various armed groups involved. I was aware that armed insurrectionist forces are not amenable to classical liberal political pressure, but I thought that they might respond to a Clastrean take on Piro history. I thought of Don Jorge's story as particularly apposite, since it dealt with survival completely outside any appeal to state mechanisms. In my memory the article and its unusual intended audience involved my reflections of Don Jorge's story. But when I reread "Learning to Defend Yourself," what I found there was not Don Jorge's story as such, but rather what I thought was more interesting and probably significant than this story, namely, his reply to my questions about his life.

My records of Don Jorge's story itself consist only of the taped original in Piro, and the following very brief note in my field notes based on his untaped Spanish translation. I wrote, "Taped a story of how he was nearly killed in Brazil, because a Peruvian sold a collared peccary skin to another man. The boss had him killed then wanted to kill all the others too. They had great difficulty escaping. They finally came back to Peru, to the Tamaya, via Huacapishtea."

These notes do not refer to one of the most important features of my actual memories of Don Jorge's story. This was Don Jorge's meticulous description of the flight up the Juruá River. He and his companions were terrified of meeting other people, so they traveled by night and hid during the day, and they had very little food. However, Don Jorge described each day of the flight, and exactly what they ate each day, if anything, and exactly where they did or did not eat. At the time I was impressed by how all this detail, especially the exact specification of meals eaten half a century earlier, conflicted with Euro-American narrative conventions: meals and their locations are not a common focus of our own genre of escape dramas.

I do, of course, have the taped Piro original of the story,

but I would be very hesitant to transcribe, far less translate, Don Jorge's story in Piro without help from a competent native speaker. This is certainly a potential project for the future, but whether it would be possible, and under what conditions, I do not know. However, even my very inadequate documentation and analysis of Don Jorge's story contain their own data, albeit primarily about my own growing understanding of the Piro lived world, and what I was beginning to realize I did not know about it.

Following the summary of the story given earlier in the chapter, I wrote, "[Don Jorge] went to the Juruá with Enrique Cobos and with Oscar Manchineri, his brother (Monsín's F), his own wife was also there, and Pablo Rodriguez's mother was born in Brazil. If it hadn't been for the boss trying to kill them, they would have stayed in Brazil." This is followed by a little genealogical diagram specifying the relations between Don Jorge, his daughter, his grandson Pablo, his brother Oscar and his son Monsín, and his brother-in-law Enrique Cobos, a white man kidnapped as a child by Don Jorge's oldest sibling, Amelia, who later took the captive for her husband, in a long and happy marriage. Further, the bulk of the notes from that visit consist of answers to questions that I asked Don Jorge about his story and about his life, which I clearly considered much more relevant to my concerns as an ethnographer than his story itself.

This confession embarrasses me, obviously enough, but I think it contains an important reflection on ethnography. At the time of writing the notes, I was struggling to understand the twentieth-century history of Piro people as they understood it themselves. Vivid though it was, Don Jorge's story struck me as very restricted in scope for my project, since it only dealt with a relatively short period of time over fifty years earlier. I was more concerned with what I needed to know in order to interpret it, that is, to set it within a wider history of kinship ties, of relations with white bosses, and of a much wider world of known places than the Bajo Urubamba. In this I was undoubtedly helped by my personal knowledge of the other people involved, and by my travels, the previous year, to the Juruá River in Brazil. My personal experience of the Juruá River, and of Don Jorge's kinspeople, co-implicated me in his story from his point of view (see Gow 1995), but clearly not in ways that I understood at the time.

For Don Jorge, and for the usual audiences of his story, none of this would apply. For them relations with kinspeople and with bosses are a massive experiential given, the ground on which the figure of the story takes shape. Piro people know these things, while their ethnographers do not, and it requires a major effort on the part of the latter to bring to conscious-ness the full implications of what Piro people know for the interpretation of what they say. Elsewhere I have discussed the remarkable implications of a Piro sung historical narra-tive, "Purús Song," and what we can learn about what we, as anthropologists, consider important in its "historical context," and about the social production of that "historical context" in complex interactions between Piro people and bosses in a specific colonial setting (2006).

The Meaning of Piro Exemplary Personal Experience Narratives

Euro-Americans would have no difficulty recognizing Piro exemplary personal experience narratives as biographical, and indeed autobiographical. Euro-American conception pos-its any individual human as a person and hence as the con-scious liver of a human life. Any person necessarily has a life story and hence a potential biography, and more importantly a potential autobiography. Don Jorge's story, like that of Juan, was clearly autobiographical in this sense, but I do not think that their clear interest for Piro people rests there. Indeed, as I have noted, I was disappointed that Don Jorge's story was *not* autobiographical in the Euro-American sense, and I rudely pestered him for further details, in a vain attempt to "round out," or still worse "contextualize," what he told me. Don Jorge's story was about his life, but not an account of his life as a whole. Imagined as a Euro-American-style autobiography, it reduced his long and successful life as a Piro man to two juxtaposed moments of emotionally intense flight from abusive bosses.

I do not want here to debate the importance of life history, biography, and autobiography in the development of a very fertile strand of American cultural, and in particular linguistic, anthropology. As Eduardo Viveiros de Castro once said to me, "Cultural anthropologists are interested in something completely different than you are. They are interested in the relation between culture and the individual. You are interested in social relations." Viveiros de Castro's point was liberating for me, since I could never understand why different genres of anthropology were so keen on either asserting their differences in a triumphalist, hierarchical mode, or simply denying them. Surely, I reasoned, the science of human diversity should be able to deal with such diversity within itself. If anthropologists could be so diverse, then our object was established as real.

As I have argued elsewhere, I think that Piro people conceive of themselves, in a nontrivial way, as a multiplicity (Gow 2000). The word that they use for themselves, *yine*, is extremely unusual in the Piro language in being intrinsically plural. The word *yine* has no plural and can only be singularized as *yineru*, "male human, male person, Piro man," or *yinero*, "female human, female person, Piro woman." The Piro person is a precipitate out of an a priori multiplicity. By this I mean that the Piro people, the *yine*, are not a collectivity made out of the sum of Piro people but rather the ongoing multiplicity out of which Piro people emerge as persons. I mean this quite literally, and I believe it is very close to how Piro people conceive of themselves as a people and as individuals. Piro people, *yine*, are made not by sexual acts but by the intricately orchestrated relations of *nshinikanchi*, "memory, thought, love, respect," between older and younger kinspeople. Indeed, people along the Bajo Urubamba continue to refer to themselves habitually as "Piro," and not "Yine," the term that has been adopted by some NGOs to refer to the group as a whole. If they want to refer to themselves as a collectivity, they call themselves *wumolene*, "our kinspeople."

As an ongoing multiplicity, all Piro people have the same biography/autobiography in the Euro-American sense, for it is the history of the Piro people and primarily the mythic origins of their current way of life. For example, Piro people are interested in where they were born and grew up, but not in the characteristic Euro-American way. A Piro person's "homeland" (Piro: *nochiji*, "my land, my place") is not the stage on which his or her birth and childhood was enacted but rather the specific place in which his or her parents and other older kinspeople were living, making houses and gardens, at that specific time. For Urubamba Piro, each person's specific "homeland" becomes more or less subsumed into the Bajo Urubamba River area, such that they are all *Gorowampa gwachine*, "dwellers on the Bajo Urubamba river." This same river was the site of their mythic creation.

In my original research among Piro people, I was able to elicit fairly detailed residential histories for some Piro people that I knew well (1991). For one man, my late compadre Artemio Fasabi, I was able to connect that residential history to what I knew about the recent general history of the Bajo Urubamba (2001). For none of these people, however, do I think that my reconstructed biographical accounts would have been meaningful as narratives. For example, I have absolutely no confidence that my biography of Artemio Fasabi would have had any real salience for him as an account of his life. Artemio would tell of some periods of his life with intense detail, of others with relative indifference, and about others he was completely silent, and I had to fill in the details from other sources.

Residential autobiographies do seem to have a salience for indigenous Amazonian people, as confirmed by some impressive studies by Peter Rivière (1969), Gustaaf Verswijver (1992), and particularly by Aparecida Vilaça (2006). The ability of indigenous Amazonian people to recall their lives in terms of places of residence and constellations of coresident kinspeople has been used by social anthropologists to produce detailed accounts of social structures, but they have not, to my knowledge, explicitly reflected *why* this method is so productive. I suspect that such accounts are the local equivalent of Euro-American biography/autobiography and might deserve fuller exploration.

Except when they are thinking about their residence histories, biography or autobiography do not seem to come easily to Piro people. Piro people's lives are kinship lives, constantly lived with and for other people who stand as kinspeople to them. As such it does not occur to them to single themselves out as the unique focus or the viewpoint from which to see the ongoing facts of living.

In this light I think it is possible to treat exemplary personal experience narratives as a special case of self-singularization. These stories refer to dramatic events that could potentially be experienced by any Piro person but which are not, for they are experienced only by a very few. The narrator is literally the tragicomic hero of an often life-threatening experience, such as flight from a murderous boss. He or she has experienced firsthand a genuinely terrifying threat that looms virtually in the lives of all Piro people and has, as we say, "lived to tell the tale." A central narrative driver of these stories is the two-leveled evidentialities that they contain. Exemplary personal experience narratives necessarily have a reassuring outcome, for the listeners knows that the teller survived, since the teller is sitting in front of them, talking to them. But the teller's story allows them to vicariously experience the life-threatening events from the open-ended resolution of the teller's experience *at the time.*

Significantly, exemplary personal experience narratives do not seem to survive their tellers' deaths. I can think of no exemplary personal experience narrative told from the perspective of a dead person by a surviving kinsperson. This is slightly surprising given that Piro people will necessarily know a lot about the exemplary personal experience narratives of their close kinspeople, including dead ones. Pablo, after all, knew his grandfather's story well enough for him to want me to hear it. But these stories do not seem to survive death, presumably because the dead do not lose their agency through death but rather radically change their perspective. Dead kinspeople, as dead people, become malignly disposed toward their living kinspeople and must be radically distantiated from the interests of the living. Exemplary personal experience narratives are treated like any other personal possession of the dead, such as houses, gardens, and clothes, and are destroyed. Piro people certainly talk about their dead kinspeople, but they do so in a very generic way. The remembered lived actions of dead people tend to be in habitual mode, as reflected in a comment by Pablo's wife, Sara: "My late grandfather would put tobacco juice in his ears and nose when he went fishing at night, to frighten demons." These stories never take the form of "One night, when he went fishing, my late grandfather . . ."

There are certain kinds of emotionally extreme experiences that cannot, it seems, form the basis for exemplary personal experience narratives. These include, rather surprisingly, at least to me, experiences of illnesses and experiences of becoming shamans. People will certainly tell about such experiences, often in vivid detail, but they are never viewed as "X's story about Y." Although it bears further consideration, I suspect that experiences of illness or of becoming shamans are not amenable to "socialization." People who are ill or becoming shamans are not deluded in the manner discussed here, for they are being subjected to irrationalities far beyond their commonsense control, such that their experiences become fragmented and incoherent as powerful beings manifest themselves in their lives. The resolution to emotionally intense personal experiences such as these lies not in personal experience narratives but in the dynamics of shamanic curing sessions, which are dialogical transactions with powerful beings.

"This Happened to Me"

Because of their form, Piro exemplary personal experience narratives are very easy to record and to publish. Many of the texts collected by SIL missionary linguists take this form, and indeed the first published extended text in Piro spoken by a Piro person is an exemplary personal experience narrative, Virgilio Gavino's story about his childhood encounter with a jaguar (Matteson 1955). Further, many of the bilingual school texts produced by the SIL take the form of exemplary personal experience narratives: they are fairly short, with a clear narrative structure, and are less religiously problematic than mythology. They are also of known interest to Piro people.

The textbooks published under the auspices of the SIL for classroom usage in Piro bilingual schools constitute a fascinating problem in their own right, full of intriguing linguistic intertextualities, and I hope to study this issue more deeply in the future. Here I want to briefly discuss one interesting aspect of this problem, which is that SIL missionaries and others have often been completely unaware of the meaning of the exemplary personal experience narratives that they have published.

A good example of this would be *Nato Krara Ginkakle Mgenoklu Pirana*, "Mother Clara's Story about the Jaguar," published in the same school reader as Dionisia García's story (Nies 1972:38–46). Clara Flores was a resident in Pablo's home village of Huau and was closely related to his family. She was also the mother of Manuel Zapata, who had been married to Luisa, the eldest sister of Pablo's wife, Sara, and who is currently married to her older sister, Lidia. Her story goes as follows:

One day my husband was weeding. I said to him,

Now I am going to get manioc from the garden on the ridge.

He said to me,

Who are you going with?

I am going alone. What is there to be afraid of there? There isn't anything.

Aren't you afraid?

No. I'm not afraid. What would I be afraid of?

In those days I was not old like I am now, and I went upriver, poling the canoe from the stern. Arriving at the mouth of the stream, I left the canoe and then I went up the ridge until I arrived at the garden. First I dug up manioc, then I cut sugar cane, and then I dug up sweet potatoes.

Then I thought, "I'll carry the manioc first, then I'll come back for the sugar cane." Then, putting the manioc in the basket, I carried it to the low ground, when a jaguar surprised me. I heard his footfall, trac, trac, toc, and then I looked behind me and saw his spotted skin, he was ready to pounce and his ears were moving.

In fear, I let the basket drop to the ground and I started to scold the jaguar, as if I was not afraid,

Grandfather, where are you going? What do you want here? Did you used to eat the flesh of our grandmothers? Now I am going to push you away.

I did not give him a chance, but continued to scold him, as I began to climb up the branch of a fallen tree.

Grandfather, what are you doing here? Go right away. Did you used to eat the flesh of our grandmothers? Now I am going to push you away. With that, the jaguar began to leave, walking very slowly then it looked back at me once more.

And shaking with fear, I said to him,

What are you doing here? Go right away. Do you think that I am your kinswoman that you should come to visit me?

Finally he obeyed me and he went off waving his tail, shac, shac, as he disappeared into the forest.

Still terrified, I tried to put the basket on my back, but I couldn't do it. I got down on my hands and knees and carried the basket to the low ground. There I heard a guan flying: clalalan!

Oh! What's that? I screamed in fear.

It seemed to me a long way to the riverbank, and when I got to the canoe, I loosed it and went back downriver without returning to the garden to get the sugar cane and sweet potatoes.

When I got back to the village, my husband came to the canoe to meet me, and he greeted me.

When I didn't reply, he asked me,

What's wrong?

With that I began to cry. He tried to console me, but I just went on crying.

Again he asked me:

What happened to you?

I didn't reply. I just went on crying.

I put on the basket and carried it to the kitchen.

What happened to you?

A jaguar frightened me.

Then why didn't you tell me that before?

Clara Flores's story describes a lone encounter with a jaguar in the forest while visiting a garden far from her village. Her husband had explicitly advised her against going alone, but she scoffed and asked what there was to be afraid of. She then tells of her terrifying encounter with a jaguar and of her extreme fear. Initially the story reads as a simple yet terrifying encounter that luckily ended well. I will return to her resourceful verbal response to the jaguar later.

The story seems simple enough. However, any Piro listening to Clara Flores's story who was in any way familiar with its teller would have known that her husband was generally suspected of regularly turning into a jaguar. Her husband, Manuel Zapata Sr., was a respected and feared Piro shaman who, it was said, had a jaguar wife and who transformed into a jaguar himself. In the story her husband, who was much older than she, tells her not to go alone, and it is when she returns to him that she bursts into tears. It seems extremely unlikely to me that had the SIL compiler known this, this story would have been published in a school textbook.

Experiences with Others

Reviewing the materials I have dealt with so far, we can discern here a pattern familiar from current themes in Amazonianist literature. Piro exemplary personal experience narratives tend to deal with noncollective and often solitary encounters with key others: jaguars and white people. Piro people's understandings of their collective experiences could, without undue violence, be described as their various experiences with jaguars, *mgenoklu*, and white people, *kajine*. One of the two most often told Piro myths, the one about the demiurge Tsla, begins as a lethal jaguar experience event of the mythic woman called Yakonero and ends with the origin of white people.

It is to this mythic narrative, I think, that Clara Flores was alluding in her extraordinary conversation with the jaguar. She told it, "Grandfather, where are you going? What do you want here? Did you used to eat the flesh of our grandmothers?"

I am certain that Piro listeners would hear this as an allusion to the marital relationship between Yakonero and the mythic-time jaguars and its subsequent disastrous breakdown. This cosmogonic encounter would be personally disastrous if repeated in the present world. Clara Flores continued, "Do you think that I am your kinswoman that you should come to visit me?"

Clara Flores was locally renowned for the fact that, as a very young woman, she had married a much older man, an important leader and jaguar shaman. In her exemplary personal experience narrative, she shows herself as brave enough to deal with her husband in her lone encounter with his jaguar form but also as profoundly human: initially dismissive of his solicitude for her and then incoherently grateful when she returns to his human form.

To expand on this point, I reiterate an argument about the relation between myths and personal experience narratives from *An Amazonian Myth and Its History* (Gow 2001:290–91). I there argued that Piro myths and personal experience narratives have some remarkable qualities in common. The myths, like the one about Yakonero and Tsla, are the personal experiences of the mythic beings, insofar as they describe what happens to these beings over relatively short periods of their lives. But in no sense can the myths be imaged as autobiographies of the mythic beings in the Euro-American sense, for we are not told, for example, who Yakonero's parents were nor what happened to Tsla after his abrupt decision to go downriver. Such anterior and posterior sets of events are simply not parts of the myth as known and told, and it would be pointless to ask about them.

But if the myths are narratives about the personal experiences of mythic beings, it is most definitely not the mythic beings who tell them. The myths are *tsrunnini ginkakle*, "ancient dead people's stories," the stories once told by long-dead Piro ancestors and now repeated by living old people to their young grandchildren. But the beings in these stories, the mythic beings, are emphatically not "ancient dead people" or ancestors. They are of a completely different order. A mark of this difference is that no attempt is made to specify witness in mythic narratives. If the exemplary personal experience narratives discussed here drew their dramatic force from the fact that their narrator, here in front of you now, is the main character in the story, there is an absolute disconnect between the mythic beings and the narrator of a myth. The narrator of the former is the direct witness of what he or she tells, while in the latter case he or she could not possibly be such a witness.

Indeed, the myths never posit witness in the sense of a continuity from an original witness through a chain of tellers over time down to the present narrator. As Nancy Munn has observed of the Walbiri case from Central Australia, the mythic action is simply going on, oblivious of how exactly this action could be memorialized (1973:112–18). This feature of myths apparently conflicts with a central feature of Piro narrative epistemology, that if the narrator is not the witness to the events described, this fact must be grammatically marked by the use of a quotative modifier specifying that this story is the repetition of something told originally by someone else. In the case of myths, the ultimate original source of the telling is the "ancient dead people," who originally told these stories, but the "ancient dead people" are never posited as witnesses to mythic events. This is because mythic events logically preceded the existence of the "ancient dead people," who did not yet exist when these events occurred.

There is, therefore, a temporal disconnect between mythic times and Piro people. The "ancient dead people" are unquestionably ancestral to contemporary living people, for it was they who, in their activities of building houses and making gardens and raising children, ultimately gave rise to the oldest living generation of Piro people, who in turn, through the same actions, gave rise to all younger Piro people. As I have argued at length in other publications (1991, 2001), kinship for Piro people is identified with history, because history is the process by which contemporary kin relations were made. Mythic events lie beyond history, because they belong to an anterior prehistorical period. This explains the narrative disconnect noted earlier between mythical events, on the one hand, and kinship and history, on the other, in the absence of posited witness. Claude

Lévi-Strauss's statement that a myth is "a message that, properly speaking, is coming from nowhere" (1970:18) would find precise phenomenological coordinates in the Piro lived world.

My present analysis expands my earlier analysis in *An Amazonian Myth and Its History*. The exemplary personal experience narratives are characterized by virtually no use of the quotative mode, which is obligatory in every phrase of myth telling. In myth telling the narrator explicitly denies being a witness to the action, for mythic action took place at the beginning of history, before human kinship existed: as noted the original authorities of the mythic narratives are the post-mythic "ancient dead people." In the exemplary personal experience narrative, the whole force of the action is that every aspect of the experience was directly and personally experienced by the teller. Any reported speech of others is quoted as personal experience, using the verb *china* with pronominal inflection (he/she/they said), rather than the pronominally uninflected quotative verb *gima*, "it is said."

In their intense detail and heightened emotional power, the exemplary personal experience narratives and myths are remarkably similar, but they differ markedly in witness: the former draw their power from the identity of narrator and witness, while the latter posit no original witness. This is unquestionably connected to their very divergent temporal trajectories. As noted, the former die with their narrator/experiencer/witness, while the latter, where no witness is posited, are precisely "ancient dead people's stories," the ideal narratives to transmit from generation to generation.

If mythic narratives are the personal experience narratives of mythic beings, and indeed their exemplary personal experience narratives, then Piro people's exemplary personal experience narratives could be defined as their personal myths.

The idea of personal myth is hardly alien to anthropology, since it is familiar from the psychoanalytic understanding of dreams and more especially of neurosis. In Piro terms, however, myths and exemplary personal experience narratives seem much closer to each other than either is to dreaming or to illness. The subjects of myths and exemplary personal experience narratives are very different from the subjects of dreaming and illness: the former subjects act rationally, the latter irrationally. It might be interesting to explore myths more generally from this Piro perspective, rather than from the psychoanalytic perspective that links them to dreams and neurosis much more strongly than to everyday life. Munn makes a similar point about the Walbiri, and the everydayness of myth is at the heart of Lévi-Strauss's *Mythologiques*.

There is, of course, an obvious difference between the subjects of myths and of exemplary personal experience narratives, for the former are cosmogonic while the latter merely survive to tell the tale. Mythic subjects, through their experiences, generate the basic cosmic frames of contemporary life; exemplary personal experience narrative subjects generate the constituent subjects of everyday life simply by surviving their experiences and then going on to do the humdrum stuff of Piro lives, making houses and gardens, and raising new generations of Piro people. But the present analysis may go some way toward explaining a fairly strange feature of Piro mythic narratives, namely, that whatever else they are, the mythic beings are clearly *yine*, people in the most strongly marked sense of Piro people.

Acknowledgments

My fieldwork on the Bajo Urubamba between 1980 and 2008 was funded by the Social Science Research Council, the British Museum, the Nuffield Foundation, the British Academy, the London School of Economics, and the University of St Andrews. I would like to thank Suzanne Oakdale and Magnus Course for the invitation to participate and the other participants for their comments on the original presentation. I would also like to thank Juan Pablo Sarmiento for sharing with me aspects of his own ethnography of the Bajo Urubamba.

Bibliography

Basso, Ellen
   1985 A Musical View of the Universe: Kalapalo Myth and Ritual Performance. Philadelphia: University of Pennsylvania Press.
Gow, Peter
   1990 "Aprendiendo a defenderse": La historia oral y el parentesco en el Bajo Urubamba. Amazonía Indígena 11:10–16.
   1991 Of Mixed Blood: Kinship and History in Peruvian Amazonia. Oxford: Oxford University Press.
   1995 Land, People and Paper in Western Amazonia. In The Anthropology of Landscape. Eric Hirsch, ed. Pp. 43–63. Oxford: Oxford University Press.
   2000 Helpless: The Affective Preconditions of Piro Social Life. In The Anthropology of Love and Anger. Joanna Overing and Alan Passes, eds. Pp. 46–63. New York: Routledge.
   2001 An Amazonian Myth and Its History. Oxford: Oxford University Press.
   2006 "Purús Song": Nationalization and Tribalization in Southwestern Amazonia. Tipití 4(1 and 2):271–94.
   2008 The Tempest: Anthropology and Human Development. In Human Development in the Twenty-First Century: Visionary Ideas from Systems Scientists. Alan Fogel, Barbara J. King, and Stuart G. Shanker, eds. Pp. 91–103. Cambridge: Cambridge University Press.
Lévi-Strauss, Claude
   1970 The Raw and the Cooked. London: Jonathan Cape.
Matteson, Esther
   1955 Analyzed Piro Text: A Boy and a Jaguar. Kroeber Anthropological Society Papers 12:22–44.
Munn, Nancy D.
   1973 Walbiri Iconography: Graphic Representation and Cultural Symbolism in a Central Australian Society. Ithaca NY: Cornell University Press.
Nies, Joyce
   1972 Muchikawa kewenni pirana ga wa pimri ginkaklukaka (Los antiguos perros y otros cuentos: Cartilla de lectura 10). Lima: Ministerio de Educación.

Rivière, Peter

1969 Marriage among the Trio. Oxford: Oxford University Press.

Verswijver, Gustaaf

1992 The Club-Fighters of the Amazon: Warfare among the Kaiapo Indians of Central Brazil. Ghent: Rijksuniversiteit, Gent.

Vilaça, Aparecida

2006 Quem somos nós: Os Wari' encontram os Brancos. Rio de Janeiro: Editora UFRJ.

3

Memories of the Ucayali

The Asháninka Story Line

HANNE VEBER

Stories of a shared past supposedly afford a sense of belonging to a larger collectivity, real or imagined (Anderson 1991).
Researchers tend to agree that a shared past is created when
the same stories are told and retold over and again in a process that allows some events and circumstances to be selec-
tively recalled while others are left silenced and forgotten. It
is also commonly agreed that such (hi)story is rarely a one-
to-one reflection of "what really happened," but neither is it
entirely invented. The stories that make history must to some
extent correspond to experiences that their audience may recognize as their own. The stories achieve credibility because
they echo a collective framework of reference that contributes
to the sense of community (Jackson 2002). Yet the nature of
the collective framework of reference easily escapes attention when research is focused on memories and preoccupied
with "what really happened," rather than with the ways stories are told, and the ways some features rather than others
are highlighted in the telling (Veber 2007a). As demonstrated
by Maurice Halbwachs (1992) and others, collective memory
is not a mechanical appendage to a group or a community
of people; indeed, human memories are social and socially
constructed in interaction. Similarly, historical consciousness
develops in continuation of, or synchronous with, the formation of political consciousness in contexts of action directed

at securing the collectivity in circumstances of the present (Turner 1988). Hence, it is no coincidence that the concept of collective memory has been defined as "those parts of the past which remain in the present life of groups or indeed what these groups make of the past" (Hoffmann 2002:135n1). Yet Mary-Elizabeth Reeve's work on Curaray Runa histories of the Amazon rubber boom (1988) and Terence S. Turner's synthesizing review of native South American representation of contact with Western society in particular (1988) indicate that indigenous memories of the "colonial situation" tend to represent contradictory relations and patterns of action (e.g., resistance, adaptation, withdrawal, transculturation) that comprise the indigenous group's differential relation to the colonial situation.[1] Indeed, comparative studies of indigenous forms of historical consciousness show that homogeneity in indigenous formulations of their contact experiences cannot be taken for granted (Turner 1988). First of all, indigenous narratives of the past vary according to the cultural genre and dialogic context of its expression; second, interlocutors may convey different perspectives on the past. The Asháninka of Peru's central Amazon, Selva Central, present a case in point.

This chapter considers the different kinds of stories told by Asháninka people and pays particular attention to how they are told. The stories offer insight into the different perceptions of the past and the ways specific episodes are narratively ordered to reflect not only the past but also the problems and potentials for action relevant to the storytellers in the present (Veber 2007b). From these stories the Asháninka actors emerge, not as victims of abuse or as heroes of resistance, but as personifications of a pragmatic adaptability and resilience that appears to have sustained their survival through four centuries of violent and episodic colonization.

The focus here is on memories from the Ucayali, the region around the major river that flows north and then east through Peru's tropical lowlands before it unites with other major tributaries to eventually become the mighty Amazon. The Ucayali was previously a regional center of the rubber trade, accommodating several merchants' trading stations where rubber was handed in, reloaded, and eventually shipped to the larger trading ports downriver on the Amazon.

Historicity and Family Memories

Since colonial times the Asháninka have been known to live scattered across the *montaña* of eastern central Peru, la Selva Central, between the rivers Pachitea to the north, the Apurimac to the south, the Chanchamayo to the west, and the Tambo-Ucayali to the east. Today their population is more than ninety thousand, making the Asháninka one of the largest, if not *the* largest, surviving indigenous people of the Amazon. The Asháninka subgroups share traditional culture, language, and cosmology, but they hardly constitute a homogenous population (Hvalkof and Veber 2005). Highly varied and discontinuous processes of colonization have resulted in divergent living conditions from one subregion to the next. Some Asháninka have relatively easy access to the small towns and colonized areas that progressively invaded the rain forest during the twentieth century. Others continue to live in isolated areas difficult of access. Some are monolingual Asháninka speakers, but many more are bilingual in Spanish and Asháninka. Some Asháninka survive from subsistence production, while some grow cash crops and/or take on paid work for mestizo landowners, in the lumber industry, or in other types of casual labor. A few are educated, most often as bilingual schoolteachers or health workers.

The Asháninka qualify as "people without history" in the sense that their historical past has been depicted primarily by outsiders who often portrayed the Asháninka as savages and killers of scores of Franciscan missionaries before they forced all missionaries, settlers, and colonial authorities out of the entire Selva Central by 1742 (see Valcarcel 1946; Veber

2003). Following Peru's independence, the region was gradually recolonized, and the depiction of the Asháninka shifted from that of rebellious savages to one of subordinate characters and obstacles to progress but otherwise undeserving of historical attention.

Asháninka stories about the recent past form an oral tradition of historical tales and family memories that relate to events in local subregions and in the personal lives of parents and grandparents. They deal with incidents and relations that in many cases may be verified by other types of records. Apart from family memories and local tales, a rich mythology explains the creation of the world and describes the relations between humans, animals, plants, spiritual beings, and natural phenomena such as rocks and rivers. These myths also depict transformations between the different forms of appearance that all living beings, humans included, may take on.

While myths appear to be shared among all Asháninka, family memories and local tales tend to circulate primarily in the subregions where the events of the tales unfold. So a shared Asháninka "history" is not inherent to the indigenous universe—if by "Asháninka history" we refer to a common discourse that records historical events recognized as shared by *all* Asháninka. This does not mean that Asháninka historical consciousness rests solely in myths, leaving family memories and local tales as discrete individualized reminiscences. Indeed these constitute the components of what may soon enough transform into a common Asháninka history. The family memories that form the subject of this chapter relate to the Ucayali, a zone of economic and exploitative ventures that at all times appear to animate the less attractive proclivities of human beings (cf. Santos-Granero and Barclay 2000; Hvalkof 1998). Indeed, the Ucayali is not simply a river and the name of a region in eastern Peru; it is a set of circumstances in native memory, as revealed in the following recollections of the Ucayali past and interpreted by specific Asháninka family memories. This chapter considers the extent to which these recollections correspond to the historical perspectives brought out by academic analyses of written records, and it contemplates the ways indigenous recollections are made significant to Asháninka lives in modes that resonate with indigenous cosmology.

The discussion revolves around selected excerpts from two autobiographical narratives recounting experiences of parents and grandparents in the early twentieth century. Collected by the author in 2004 and 2005, the excerpts represent differing perspectives on a particular type of colonial situation. The excerpts are not exhaustive representations of Asháninka historical consciousness; rather they serve to illustrate analytical points emerging from current research on the poetics and hermeneutics of history, myth, and indigenous identity in Latin America (see essays in Hill 1988, 1996; Rappaport 1998; Veber 2007a, 2007b, 2009; Gow 1991; Hoffmann 2002; Whitehead 2003). Let us take a look at the way in which one particular family memory is recalled:

> My grandfather on my mother's side was Mokatzari, an Ashéninka from Mankoite, now a *comunidad nativa*.[2] My grandfather had many holes in his lower lip where he would put feathers, empty cartridges, or small sticks for decoration. This is why they gave him the name Mokatzari. It means "little holes." . . . Around 1920 my grandfather Mokatzari . . . [came to] . . . the Tambo River and . . . stayed in Cushireni because he had fallen in love with my grandmother, Shiná. . . . They had four children, Iroisa Lucía, who became my mother, Berta, Eliseo, and Nicolás.
>
> Some other people from the area invited him to go and harvest rubber and wood, so he traveled to Masisea. A cousin of his was in touch with some mestizos who bought and sold children, and he encouraged my grandfather to work for them. . . . And so with my grandmother and their four children, my grandfa-

ther went down river on a raft . . . [and] arrived in a small village called Masisea. They stayed there for several months along with the others, who formed a group of Ashéninka.

At a drinking party they got into an arrow fight, and my grandfather won. The argument had been about work, and later on they set a trap for my grandfather. Some child-trafficking mestizo thugs who were in league with some bad Asháninka accused . . . the little Eliseo of being a child witch, and they told my grandfather to sell him to the traffickers. If not he would be killed and burned as a true witch. My grandfather argued and wanted to kill the trafficker, but his thugs were too many for him and they captured him . . . [and] . . . left him tied to a tree. Then they took the little boy away, his hands tied to the boat, and poor Eliseo was never seen again. (Veber 2009:262–63, my translation from Spanish)

With this tale Bernardo Silva Loayza initiates the story of his life. He goes on to tell how his grandfather escaped from Masisea with his wife and the three remaining children. Masisea is located on the right bank of the Ucayali a good distance below the mouth of the Pachitea River. By the early 1900s Masisea was a haunt of raiders and traders, buyers and sellers of rubber and of native captives, most often women and children.

The escape of Mokatzari and his family evolves dramatically. Afraid of persecution, the fugitives dare not follow the river and make their way through swamps teaming with caimans, electric eel, snapping turtles, and poisonous reptiles. Later they cross over land to reach their home on the Tambo River. In the mountains they face hungry predators, poisonous snakes, and other dangers. Yet they find themselves in familiar areas, and after four months of cutting through dense forest they reach Cushireni. Later they venture upriver into the Perene to Sutziki, where an Adventist mission has been established, and here they stay. Then another disaster strikes.

Mokatzari's wife is bitten by a poisonous snake and shortly afterward dies. Mokatzari falls into a deep depression and occasionally launches into fits of madness, shooting arrows at random. His fellow Asháninka are terrified and see no remedy other than getting rid of the man in order to restore peace to the community.

> One day when he was in a moment of good humor, a group of men came and invited him to come along and bathe in the Perené River in the heat of the day. And on the way there they jumped on him and strung him up from a tree with a liana. But before he died, he cursed his captors with these words: "You can kill me, but one day you too will die, cowards!" This he said to his captors, and they killed him. (Veber 2009:262–63)

The three children are now left on their own. Lucia, the oldest of them, eventually meets a man in the Upper Perené with whom she stays, and in 1947 she gives birth to Bernardo, her firstborn son. He grows up learning the use of bows and arrows and the practices of horticulture according to Asháninka tradition. But with time Bernardo changes his way of life. Circumstances lead him to move to the Ucayali, where he becomes actively engaged in indigenous politics. His story permits a glimpse into the past of one particular family but supplies little information on the context in which it unfolded. Some historical background for interpreting his story may be established by taking a brief look at the region's past, the major features of which have been illuminated through studies based on written records.

The Economic Frontiers of Colonization

Current historical writing points to two economic frontiers that conditioned the development of the regional economic systems in Peru's central Amazon. One is characteristic of the *montaña* zones, where an agro-pastoral economy is directed at producing fruit, coffee, and cattle; the other system is basically one of shifting extractive economies prevalent in the Ucayali and the Amazon lowlands to the east (Santos-Granero and Barclay 1998, 2000). Asháninka territories extend across both regions, and from the middle nineteenth century onward the Asháninka were pressured from both frontiers, one approaching from the west and the other from the east (Brown and Fernández 1991; Hvalkof 2004).

Historical memories among the groups in the areas in the Upper Perené closest to the Andes emphasize a glorious past of successful fighting against Spanish colonial powers and detail the ways in which the Peruvian army lured the Indians into laying down their arms by offering them abundant gifts of attractive merchandise. By contrast Asháninka indigenous people living in the eastern zones of the Selva Central appear less interested in colonial history. The historical accounts that circulate here deal with colonization in the twentieth century. They are accounts of specific named settlers and specific Asháninka individuals or families, not of settlers or Asháninka in general. The same goes for the memories of the Ucayali, previously a frontier zone on the periphery of Asháninka territories, a space where men would go to trade but not an area where many Asháninka settled prior to the so-called rubber boom.

In the colonial past the Ucayali was dominated by the Yine (Piro), Shipibo, and Conibo. In the late nineteenth and early twentieth centuries, the region became a center for the rubber boom, a significant epoch in the history of extractive economies. It came to involve considerable numbers of Asháninka who were recruited for work in rubber tapping, voluntarily or involuntarily. The conventional history of the rubber boom reflects the global economy and the demand for raw latex beginning in the latter part of the nineteenth century and ending around World War I when the British had succeeded in smuggling rubber plants from the Amazon to their overseas colonies in Southeast Asia. This ended the large-scale export of Amazonian rubber, which had been a lucrative business for the select few who controlled the trade.

Collection of rubber in Peru was organized through hierarchies of investors, buyers, and rubber tappers with the Indian tappers at the bottom. Local Indians were hired against payment in goods such as metal tools, guns, and ammunition. They knew how to locate the valuable trees and were inexpensive to outfit.[3] There were few alternative sources of labor for rubber tapping, so indigenous labor was crucial to the trade (see Oakdale's chapter this volume for a similar situation in Brazil). The rubber patrons made sure the Indian workers were kept indebted so they could be forced to continue working. The system was known as *habilitación* and constituted a form of debt slavery. To ensure that the indebted tappers would not escape, a regime of terror was instituted comprising all sorts of cruelties and intimidations to keep the indigenous peoples subjugated.

Additionally, a labor supply system was developed as a separate economic venture in which the rubber patron commissioned raiding parties to capture women and children from indigenous settlements. The captured children would grow up as part of the patron's household, where they would become the loyal labor of the future. Indigenous persons entered all sectors of these labor supply chains, whether as victims or as perpetrators of raids. The story of Bernardo's grandfather reflects the intricacy of the system. For the Indians choices were limited: to defend themselves they needed access to firearms; and the only way firearms could be acquired was by working for rubber patrons, as tappers or as "procurers" of labor.

Eyewitness accounts of the victimization of the indigenous people were recorded by explorers, missionaries, and others who traveled the Ucayali and its tributaries during the rubber boom (for examples see Sala 1925; Samanez y Ocampo 1980). They reflect the restrained distance of the outsiders. We have few records documenting the indigenous perspective. So what kind of story is Bernardo's grandfather account of the world of rubber gatherers? Is it the story of a victim? Or the opposite, the story of a heroic escape? Or is it yet something different?

On Victims and Heroes

When Bernardo relates the story of his grandfather, he is not simply recounting family history; he is using it to validate his own moving of his entire family from heavily colonized Perené to the Ucayali. In the Ucayali, he says, there were empty lands open for settlement and plenty of game in the forest and fish in the rivers. "I heard people saying that there was an abundance of fish in Atalaya, and I remembered . . . the one that some bad mestizo and Asháninka thugs had sold, which my mother had told me of as a child" (Veber 2009:269).

The story suggests the presence of family in the Ucayali in the person of the small boy who had been taken from his parents and never heard of again. Nevertheless, he is assumed to linger somewhere in the Ucayali. The story of Mokatzari and the lost child is not simply a story of victimization. Mokatzari himself was asking for trouble. He was rowdy and willingly joined up with bandits. The image of the belligerent grandfather is retained in the description of Mokatzari's madness following his wife's sudden death: "My grandfather . . . began to shoot arrows like he used to when he was fit, when he used to lead the raiding ambushes, as a powerful warrior" (Veber 2009:265). Even after his murder Mokatzari continues to haunt those around him: "People said they could hear noises at night as if he were still alive. And so they burned him, and once he was gone the nights became peaceful once more, as they had been before they killed my grandfather" (Veber 2009:265).

Mokatzari's rowdiness defied even death. But he was not *only* a troublemaker, and his strength was not merely physical; it was also mental and spiritual. He demonstrated willpower and spoke up against his enemies. Moreover, he is presented as a responsible and caring head of his family, ideals that Bernardo appreciates. Mokatzari is hardly a prototypical victim, and his story mirrors the paradox of violence as simultaneously inappropriate and indispensable. Mokatzari is a violent man in a time of violence; yet violence, that is, his murder, is also the remedy that restores peace and order.

The story might have been told differently, perhaps as a more clear-cut story about Mokatzari the "great warrior." This possibility would seem likely considering the existence of a narrative "war story" genre among the Asháninka.[4] Lately Asháninka commonly refer to their cultural heritage with remarks such as "in the past we were warriors" or even "after all, we *are* warriors!" This kind of talk was never heard in the 1980s.[5] Back then even old men with reputations as former raiders would swear that war was something they would never even dream of participating in. War was something their ancestors carried on, they would say, and add with a wily smile: "Now we are very, very peaceful!" Today, after twenty years and a war with two seditious movements, nobody refers to the Asháninka as "peaceful."[6] By 2004 the chairman of a meeting in a village on the Tambo announced the election of four security officers with the words: "We all know that we are not as peaceful as we used to say!" The security officers would maintain order during the meeting. They were equipped with automatic weapons and kept guard day and night at the entrances to the village.

The important thing among the Asháninka is to control tempers. Doing so involves manifestations of strength and readiness for action while at the same time avoiding its use. Maintaining a convincing display of this kind takes nerve. One elderly Asháninka illustrated the attitude with words he claimed he had said to a patron on an occasion when he and another Asháninka had been upset with the man. He had threatened to kill the patron, fully aware that he would probably lose his own life in the process: "Let's see! Who will die first? You or me? I think you'd better die first!" In this specific situation the patron had yielded to the Asháninka, knowing that the words were no empty threat.

Yet there are other types of memories of the Ucayali. The story of Mokatzari has a parallel in family memories that form part of the life story of Adolfo Gutierrez, an elderly Asháninka leader from the central Perené. He had gained a reputation as the best boatman on the Perené River, a rather unusual occupation for an Asháninka. Adolfo had also been actively involved in the struggle for land and indigenous organization in the 1960s and 1970s, the era of massive settler invasions in the area. Of his father Adolfo tells the following:

> My father's name was Andrés Gutiérrez Shimuncama. . . . He was from Atalaya. He grew up with a patron called Jaime Morón and worked for him during most of his life. My father had a wife, but they never had any children. The patron made my father responsible for obtaining people in different places. But they did not come with him freely; he had to make exchanges, trade, in order to obtain persons. So he brought the patron girls, boys, and even adults. . . . The trade took him to the zone of Perené, and he passed through the Upper Yurinaki. Here he had a client, so to speak, to whom he delivered guns so the other would procure people for him.
>
> My mother was still a little girl. She lived in Yurinaki. One day some men came . . . to steal my mother. They carried her off together with her twin sister, Maria, whom they would sell to some German settlers. . . . My mother came to stay in Atalaya with my father. . . . When they first arrived there, my father's wife said to him: "You know what, Andrés, don't hand this girl over to the patron! We'd better have her stay with us. . . . I think she might help us with certain things." My father obeyed. . . .
>
> After some time, when she had grown up, my father's wife said to him: "Andrés, perhaps you should start living with our . . . girl. Perhaps she'll bear you children!" My father . . . began to want to live with my mother, if I may put it this way. At the beginning

VEBER

my mother did not want it, she told me, . . . but little by little, she got used to my father. My father was already old and gray haired when my mother became pregnant. She gave birth to a little girl, her first born, but she died after a month.

Then what happened? My father was a retainer of the patron . . . , but if anything was lost my father was blamed for it. And then he was punished. They took him to the stocks and punished him, and they adjusted the stocks to find out what had happened to the things that were missing. If a canoe went missing, he was punished. It was nothing but punishment. . . . Then my father got tired of it all and said: "We'd better go somewhere else!" At the time a missionary had arrived, . . . a cousin of my mother's or father's. He was not a legitimate Asháninka, but mixed with the Piro, a son of the Piro. His name was Abel Fieta.[7] He had come with another uncle, also a Piro, named Ulises. They were carrying the message of the gospel, the word of God. Then my father said: "We'd better go! Let's follow the cousins to where they live." (Veber 2009:244–46)

Andrés and his wives run away and end up in the Adventist mission in Sutziki, where they settle down. In 1935 Adolfo is born. His father dies, presumably from tuberculosis, when Adolfo is five years old. The family is convinced that the disease is the result of the constant punishments at the hands of the patron. Adolfo grows up in the mission, goes to school, and learns Spanish well. A few years later his mother wishes to leave with another man and return to Atalaya. She wants the boy to come with her. But he refuses: "I thought of my father's account with the patron. If he were to discover that I am the son of Andrés, he would carry me off and make me pay my father's debts. . . . For this reason I did not want to go" (Veber 2009:246–47). He is nine years old and terrified at the idea of coming to Atalaya. He prefers to remain in the mission and work to support himself.

Adolfo at no time uses terms such as "slave," "slavery," or

"raiding." These terms have been applied to the phenomenon by posterity. At the time of the rubber boom nobody, neither patrons nor the indigenous people, perceived the systems of *habilitación* and "procured" domestic labor as "slavery." Strictly speaking the patron did not own the worker; he owned his debt. In theory the women and children "procured" for the patron became part of the patron's workforce, not as slaves but as members of his household (Santos-Granero and Barclay 2000:34–55). Adolfo's father had clearly been "procured" for the patron as a child and then brought up to become the patron's henchman who made contact with raiders and supplied them with firearms in return for the human merchandise they "procured." Grotesquely, Adolfo's mother had been abducted from her home as a little girl by man hunters whom Adolfo's father paid on behalf of the patron. Andrés himself was subject to the patron's cruel methods of control and only managed to escape when a place of refuge became available in the form of the Adventist mission in Sutziki. At the time thousands of Indians, including Bernardo's grandfather Mokatzari, congregated here.

Adolfo's account of his parents' fate seems more a victimization story than does Bernardo's story of grandfather Mokatzari. Yet from the way Adolfo constructs his biography, the story of his parents serves primarily to demonstrate his roots in the Adventist mission. He highlights his relations to particular named missionaries and fondly recalls what they meant to him as he grew up. He remains an Adventist after leaving Sutziki, and rather than looking east toward the Ucayali, he prefers to look to the west, toward the Andes and Lima, the country's capital and the progress and change it represents. Fitting in with his orientation to independent self-preservation, Adolfo becomes active in the struggle for indigenous land rights.

The Poetics of Narrated Experience

Bernardo's and Adolfo's stories permit insight into indigenous perceptions of the past and the meaning of the narrated experiences of parents and grandparents. They provide a sense of the way the rubber boom is differently interpreted not only because the storytellers are different persons but because the experiences they recount are founded on very different subject positions relative to the historical parameters. Beyond this, three questions present themselves: First of all, do memories of the rubber boom matter at all to today's indigenous peoples, be it in relation to their formation of identity or their perception of contemporary situations? Second, does the rubber boom constitute a shared framework of historicity for the region's indigenous peoples whose ancestors have been victims as well as perpetrators of violence and abuses? Are there regularities in the ways the positions are narrated? And if so, what is the nature of the regularities? Third, in what ways, if at all, do rubber boom memories touch on something of concern to all Asháninka? And how may the diverse memories actually be tied together analytically and empirically within an optic that goes beyond the local or private family perspective?

As Kirsten Hastrup has pointed out, experiences that become stories are not simply private experiences. They are social relations: "When singular experiences are lifted from the motley collection of experiences and events we bump into, meanings are attributed to them that cannot be private. Meaning is always established with reference to a context in relation to which relative significance is determined" (1999:271, my translation into English). The same applies to memories; their most important characteristic is actually their nonfortuitousness. Their meanings are not merely retrospective but reflect the significance of memory in the context of its recitation.

Peter Gow has described how the Piro (Yine) Indians of the Ucayali and the Lower Urubamba talk of the rubber boom as a time of slavery that they have now put behind them. Today they perceive of themselves as civilized in the sense of people previously attached to large haciendas and therefore educated and able to speak Spanish, unlike people such as the Asháninka, whom they perceive of as uncivilized "forest people" (1991:6, 86, 101). The Asháninka present a more variegated picture. To them the question of being civilized is irrelevant to indigenous identity (Veber 1992). Memories of the rubber boom may be relevant to the formation of the identities of families who were involved in the rubber trade, but the rubber boom appears to have had little impact so far on the emerging collective identity as Asháninka.

On the other hand, the contemporary political situation is clearly relevant to the ways in which Asháninka construct their stories. For even though the rubber trade collapsed, the stealing of women and children continued into the 1950s, and debt slavery was common in the Ucayali into the 1980s and 1990s tied to other extractive industries (see essays in Parellada and Hvalkof 1998). The situation did not change until the early 1990s, when AIDESEP, the umbrella organization uniting Peru's Amazonian groups, intervened.[8] AIDESEP brought in the so-called Multi-Sectoral Commission reporting to the Ministry of Justice and the Council of Ministers, and many Indians stepped forward and testified against patrons and regional authorities responsible for maintaining the system of debt slavery. The patrons falsely accused several indigenous leaders of terrorism but to no avail, and eventually all public officials in Atalaya were forced to step down. It was decided by ministerial resolution that former hacienda lands should be titled to the indigenous populations who lived there (Parellada and Hvalkof 1998). In practical terms this was equal to a revolution in Atalaya: It had been made clear that Indians have legal rights, including the right to territory and the right to vote and run for public office. Given their sheer numbers, these facts do make a difference in local politics, and the Indians are very much aware of it.

That things change, however, does not mean that the past disappears from collective discourse; quite the contrary. The indigenous people have not forgotten what abuse means, and discourse about abuses on the part of patrons continues to have political significance. For one thing the stories of Adolfo's and Bernardo's parents and grandparents might not have been told as frankly had it still been highly dangerous to criticize the patrons. The question is, *what* is remembered, and for what purposes is it used when told?

We still need to take the influence of the particular narrative genre of storytelling into account. We know that memories are made from far more than simply a "photocopying" of "what really happened." The Asháninka stories emerge from a native storytelling tradition that nourishes attention to details and drama and invites the continuous updating of the elements of the stories in accordance with the situation of their telling and with a native audience that actively contributes to it. Bernardo is a good storyteller and likes to elaborate on details to make the stories entertaining. What parts of the story about grandfather Mokatzari have been provided by Bernardo himself? The year ("around 1920") of Mokatzari's adventure in Masisea is probably supplied by Bernardo. The details about the dangerous predators and the poisonous swamps are self-evident to anyone familiar with the zone and furnish an authentic picture of the environment of the Upper Ucayali. These details are certainly not rendered less dramatic by being recounted. Then, if much of the story is illustrative of "stuffing," what message remains from the story?

As we have seen, an important context of interpretation is the contemporary political situation. The power established by the patrons during the rubber boom has only recently been curbed as a result of the political organizing by the indigenous peoples themselves. Moreover, with the formation of self-defense militias against the Sendero Luminoso in the 1990s, collective Asháninka self-consciousness gained new momentum. From the point of view of the Asháninka, *they*, and not the Yine, the Shipibo, or others, made the active driving force in the resistance. The energy and will to act presented by these

Asháninka are very much part of their image of who they are. In the memories presented here, it emerges most clearly when we pay attention to the story line that may be summarized as follows: Man travels to a distant place in search of resources. He gets into trouble and suffers much hardship before he returns home safely. Indeed, dangerous travel to foreign spaces appears to be a culturally prescribed plot also common in Asháninka mythology. To the protagonists effects of their adventures range from gains in knowledge to transformative changes, through dramatic death or the remaking of man into animal or other nonhuman being—sometimes followed by a return home with rewards acquired from the dangerous and/or powerful "others." The rewards invariably prove crucial to the continuing reproduction of native society.

Then how does it come about that so many Asháninka appear resigned to being objects of abuse from patrons for long periods of time? Nothing seems to point to their perceiving inequity as "natural," and they have in no way internalized a subordinate mentality. Yet important forces for life in the Amazonian world, crucial to the production and reproduction of social life, have their origin in dangerous and violent exterior domains. The operating principles of this cultural logic prioritize acquisition of the exterior resources and their inclusion or assimilation as a means of neutralizing the ontological insecurity presented by the "other" (see also Taussig 1993; Overing and Passes 2000:6). This logic may help to make sense of the ambiguities in Asháninka people's openness to involvement with patrons as well as their conservatism in maintaining their ethnic and cultural identity.

Even so we also need to note that it takes very little for the Asháninka to rise up and get on the move. It may happen when some fiery soul, a missionary, or a rebel leader, be he Asháninka or not, inspires action. Then the words resound: "*Aate, thame aate!*"—"Let's go! Come on, let's get going!" These words are a signal for action in daily life. In Adolfo's story his father speaks the words: "Let's go!—and the entire family travels far away from the place where they have lived for most of their lives. For years Adolfo's father had traveled around trading firearms for captives on behalf of his patron, all the while faithfully serving the abusive patron even if he, technically speaking, would have had plenty of opportunities to escape. Similarly, Bernardo's grandfather willingly seeks patrons in the Ucayali and offers to work for them. Why? The storyteller provides the answer: a cousin invited Mokatzari to come along to the Ucayali: "*Aate, thame aate!*" Like most Asháninka, Bernardo's grandfather desired a gun and other merchandise available from the mestizo patrons, and when the opportunity arose, he went for it.

Men who have the courage to face the dangers of close contact with strangers are not perceived as victims by the Asháninka. They are fighters who may turn into heroes or bandits as they venture into foreign territory to acquire resources that will optimize social reproduction amongst their own. This logic emerges from a colonial situation in which tribal self-sufficiency ceased to be a viable option long ago. Daring the encounters with violence and death, however, has a price, and the fates of Mokatzari and Andrés Gutierrez testify to this. In this way the family memories become personalized allegories of the general situation in which the Asháninka find themselves. Yet they are also reflections of the storytellers' self-images as leaders and as enterprising men who take charge of the organization of their communities and manage their foreign relations. They carry history along and they act on it.

It is hardly a coincidence that our storytellers construct their stories the way they do. They arrange their narratives into sequences of events—events that "mean" something in relation to topics such as venture into unknown territories, exchange, escape, abduction, fights, and death or the threat of dying as a precondition to the restoration of peace and tranquility so that society may continue to reproduce itself.

At the most elementary level, the narrative structure is one in which one action is followed by the next and focus is on the Asháninka as actors, reflecting the ways in which the Asháninka codify the role of males within the reproductive structures of native society.

The stories may be read as orientations for action in the colonial—and postcolonial—situation. As such both stories put a premium on risk taking and involvement with potentially dangerous spheres. This permits the mavericks of native society to participate in the structure of domination *as low-level dominators* who in some perverted sense become the vicarious authors of their own subordination. By identifying indigenous agents as active producers of their own subordination, they assert a measure of control over the situation as submission and resistance are rendered simultaneously possible. Patrons are presented as accessible and, by implication, vulnerable to manipulation by the indigenous actor. As we have seen, appropriating space and exterior resources is highly valued, and the notion of keeping the channels open to subvert—if not in some sense "cannibalize"—the life force of the "other" is part of the plot. The Asháninka actors emerge as embodiments of a pragmatic flexibility that appears to have sustained indigenous survival through four centuries of violent and unpredictable colonization and resistance. Narrative codification to this effect permeates the form as well as the content of the stories.

It is here, in their narrative, that Asháninka memories of the Ucayali differ most significantly from the conventional academic expositions of the rubber boom. As presented by historians and anthropologists, the Ucayali rubber boom concerns the amount and distribution of foreign investments, the quantity of exports, fluctuations of the market, the networks and mutual relations of the patrons, the organization of labor, and the economic structures of debt slavery (Santos-Granero and Barclay 1998, 2000). In this "dominant" history the indigenous peoples are acted on and with, literally speaking. In the Asháninka stories they themselves are the active characters who establish spaces for themselves. The appropriation of space for collective self-realization in the present calls for parallel appropriation of the past. Therefore, autonomous interpretations of history are important to the emergent collective indigenous identities that regularly accompany processes of decolonization. From this perspective, Asháninka narratives assert that the world was not created by patrons or gringos who fell from the sky. It was created by Asháninka who took matters into their own hands. As such the biographical narratives are statements that the present and the future lie open to further action by those who have the will to act. By their telling the narratives enter collective memory, and the people take their place in history—and take possession of their world.

Notes

1. Terence Turner employs the expression "colonial situation" to contexts of domination where ethnically and culturally different populations coexist within an analytic field "united" by diametrically opposed although interdependent interests (Turner 1988:239–40).

2. During the reform-oriented government of army general Juan Velasco Alvarado (1968–75) special legislation concerning indigenous rights in the Amazon, Ley de Comunidades Nativas y de Promoción Agropecuaria de las Regiones de Selva y Ceja de la Selva (D.L. 20653), was promulgated in 1974 as the first of its kind in Peru. The law was reformulated in 1978 as the Ley de Comunidades Nativas y de Desarrollo Agrario de las Regiones de Selva y Ceja de Selva (D.L. 22175) to facilitate business investments in the Amazon lowlands and the *montaña*. The law established the concept of the *comunidad nativa*, "native community," as a social and political collective of indigenous persons legally recognized as forming a separate community. *Comunidades nativas* may hold collective titles to land and run their internal affairs with a high degree of autonomy.

3. *Hevea* and *castilloa* are the more important tree species (Santos-Granero and Barclay 2000:23).

4. On the face of it, it seems that stories about "great" warriors tend to revolve around the murder of the "great" warrior at the hands of a "lesser" warrior who then becomes "great." For examples see the stories edited by Eduardo Fernández (1986).

5. The author carried out fieldwork among the Ashéninka of the Gran Pajonal and in the Ucayali for almost two years, 1985–87. The study was supported by the Council for Development Research (RUF) of the Danish International Development Agency (DANIDA) and the Danish Research Council for the Humanities (Veber 1989). The project was titled "Campa Cultural Identity and the Frontier of Development."

6. During the 1990s the indigenous populations of the Selva Central faced armed conflicts and terrorist acts resulting from the presence of two rebel movements, the Sendero Luminoso, and the Movimiento Revolucionario Túpac Amaru (MRTA) in the zone. Some AshániNka groups organized self-defense militias of their own, while others joined or were forcibly recruited into one or the other of the rebel movements. An estimated six thousand AshániNka lost their lives in the conflicts, and upward of thirty native communities ceased to exist (Comisión de la Verdad y Reconciliación 2003:241).

7. According to Alejandro Bullón Páucar, a certain Catosho Machari arrived at Metraro after having walked for fifteen days. He had heard that Pava (Father) or God was there. He spoke Spanish and became Stahl's guide. He converted and changed his name to Abel Fieta (Páucar 1976: 117–19).

8. AIDESEP, Asociación Interétnica del Desarrollo de la Selva Peruana, was founded in 1979.

Bibliography

Anderson, Benedict
    1991 Imagined Communities: Reflections on the Origin and Spread
    of Nationalism. London: Verso.
Brown, Michael F., and Eduardo Fernández
    1991 War of Shadows: The Struggle for Utopia in the Peruvian Ama-
    zon. Berkeley: University of California Press.
Comisión de la Verdad y Reconciliación
    2003 Informe Final de la Comisión de la Verdad y Reconciliación,
    vol. 5. Lima: Oficina de Comunicaciones e Impacto Público.
Fernández, Eduardo
    1986 Para que nuestra Historia no se pierda. Testimonios de los
    Asháninca y Nomatsiguenga sobre la Colonización de la región
    Satipo-Pangoa. CIPA. Documento 7. Lima: Centro de Investigación y
    Promoción Amazônica.
Gow, Peter
    1991 Of Mixed Blood: Kinship and History in Peruvian Amazonia.
    Oxford: Clarendon Press.
Halbwachs, Maurice
    1992 On Collective Memory. Chicago: University of Chicago Press.

Hastrup, Kirsten
  1999 Viljen til Viden: En humanistisk Grundbog. Copenhagen: Gyldendal.
Hill, Jonathan D.
  1988 Introduction. *In* Rethinking History and Myth: Indigenous South American Perspectives on the Past. Jonathan D. Hill, ed. Pp. 1–17. Urbana: University of Illinois Press.
Hill, Jonathan D., ed.
  1988 Rethinking History and Myth: Indigenous South American Perspectives on the Past. Jonathan D. Hill, ed. Pp. 1–17. Urbana: University of Illinois Press.
  1996 History, Power, and Identity: Ethnogenesis in the Americas, 1492–1992. Iowa City: University of Iowa Press.
Hoffmann, Odile
  2002 Collective Memory and Ethnic Identities in the Colombian Pacific. Journal of Latin American Anthropology 7(2):118–38.
Hvalkof, Søren
  1998 From Slavery to Democracy: The Indigenous Process of Upper Ucayali and Gran Pajonal. *In* Liberation through Land Rights in the Peruvian Amazon. IWGIA Document No. 90, October. Alejandro Parellada and Søren Hvalkof, eds. Pp. 83–162. Copenhagen: IWGIA.
  2004 Place, People and History. *In* Dreams Coming True . . . An Indigenous Health Programme in the Peruvian Amazon. Chap. 2. Context. Søren Hvalkof, ed. Pp. 36–87. Copenhagen: Nordeco.
Hvalkof, Søren, and Hanne Veber
  2005 Los Ashéninka del Gran Pajonal. *In* Guía etnográfica de la Alta Amazonia, vol. 5. Frederica Barclay and Fernando Santos-Granero, eds. Pp. 75–281. Lima: Smithsonian Tropical Research Institute and Instituto Francés de Estudios Andinos.
Jackson, Michael
  2002 The Politics of Storytelling: Violence, Transgression and Intersubjectivity. Copenhagen: Museum Tusculanum Press.
Overing, Joanna, and Alan Passes
  2000 Introduction: Conviviality and the Opening Up of Amazonian Anthropology. *In* The Anthropology of Love and Anger: The Aesthetics of Conviviality in Native Amazonia. Johanna Overing and Alan Passes, eds. Pp. 1–30. London: Routledge.
Parellada, Alejandro, and Søren Hvalkof, eds.
  1998 Liberation through Land Rights in the Peruvian Amazon. IWGIA Document No. 90. Copenhagen: IWGIA.
Páucar, Alejandro Bullón
  1976 Él nos amaba: La aventura misionera de Stahl entre los campas. Lima: Asociación peruana Central de la Iglesia Adventista del Séptimo Día.

Rappaport, Joanne
  1998 The Politics of Memory: Native Historical Interpretation in the Colombian Andes. Durham NC: Duke University Press.
Reeve, Mary-Elizabeth
  1988 Cauchu Uras: Lowland Quichua Histories of the Amazon Rubber Boom. *In* Rethinking History and Myth: Indigenous South American Perspectives on the Past. Jonathan D. Hill, ed. Pp. 19–34. Urbana: University of Illinois Press.
Sala, P. Fr. Gabriel
  1925 Apuntes de Viaje del P. Fr. Gabriel Sala: Exploracion de los Rios Pichis, Pachitea y Alto Ucayali y de la Region del Gran Pajonal 1897. *In* Historia de las misiones franciscanas 1619–1921, vol. 10, pt. 3. Bernardino Ispizua Izaguirre, ed. Pp. 405–601. Lima: Talleres Tipográficos de la Penitenciaria.
Samanez y Ocampo, Jose B.
  1980 Exploracion de los Rios Peruanos Apurimac, Eni, Tambo, Ucayali y Urubamba hecha en 1883 y 1884: Diario de la expedicion y Anexos. Lima: SESATOR.
Santos-Granero, Fernando, and Frederica Barclay
  1998 Selva Central: History, Economy, and Land Use in Peruvian Amazonia. Washington DC: Smithsonian Institution Press.
  2000 Tamed Frontiers: Economy, Society, and Civil Rights in Upper Amazonia. Boulder CO: Westview Press.
Taussig, Michael
  1993 Mimesis and Alterity: A Particular History of the Senses. New York: Routledge.
Turner, Terence
  1988 Ethno-Ethnohistory: Myth and History in Native South American Representations of Contact with Western Society. *In* Rethinking History and Myth: Indigenous South American Perspectives on the Past. Jonathan D. Hill, ed. Pp. 235–81. Urbana: University of Illinois Press.
Valcarcel, Daniel
  1946 Rebeliones indígenas. Lima: Editorial PTCM.
Veber, Hanne
  1989 Campa Cultural Identity and the Frontier of Development. Field Report submitted to the Danish Council for Development Research and the Danish Research Council for the Humanities. Copenhagen.
  1992 Why Indians Wear Clothes: Managing Identity across an Ethnic Boundary. Ethnos 57(1–2):51–60.
  2003 Asháninka Messianism: The Production of a "Black Hole" in Western Amazonian Ethnography. Current Anthropology 44(2):183–211.

2007a Memories, Identity, and Indigenous/National Subjectivity in Eastern Peru. Diálogos Latinoamericanos 12:80–102.

2007b Merits and Motivations of an Ashéninka Leader. Tipití 5(1):9–31.

Veber, Hanne, ed.

2009 Historias para nuestro Futuro/Yotantsi ashí otsipaniki': Narraciones autobiográficas de líderes asháninkas e ashéninkas (Tales for our future: Biographical narratives by indigenous Amazonian leaders in Peru's Central Amazon). Copenhagen: IWGIA.

Whitehead, Neil L.

2003 Introduction. In Histories and Historicities in Amazonia. Neil Whitehead, ed. Pp. vii–xx. Lincoln: University of Nebraska Press.

Part Two

Persons within Persons

4

Multiple Biographies

Shamanism and Personhood among the Marubo of Western Amazonia

Pedro de Niemeyer Cesarino

This chapter is concerned with the relationship of the multiple person to the trajectories of shamanic transformation or initiation as evidenced in the biography of a young Marubo shaman, Robson Doles Dionísio. An analysis of several testimonies and how they articulate with ethnography allows me to offer some considerations on the relational configuration that characterizes this process of transformation and some of its many conceptual consequences. Among these, I explore the meaning of "human person" in contradistinction to what is usually translated as "spirit" and "animal," as well as the problem of the replication or reproduction of self-similar structures involved in the constitution of the person and the configuration of a virtual field of sociocosmic relations. To these issues I add certain considerations of the current dilemmas confronting the Marubo of the Upper Ituí (Vale do Javari Indigenous Reservation, Brazil), for whom the trajectory of this shaman plays a central role.

Becoming a "person" or "human being," both of which are possible translations of *yora*, involves a complex trajectory. To an extent it requires that the person gradually overcome the state of desolation that characterizes life in this world, which is suggestively called the "Dwelling of the Land-Death" (Vei

Mai Shavaya). Laziness, disease, melancholy, lust: these are some of the problems that afflict the living in the present age and which ultimately drive the machinery of ritual and narrative memory that characterize Marubo shamanism. A large part of the rituals in which the performances of *romeya* shamans are involved are, in fact, aimed at altering the constitution of the person through a series of procedures that, little by little, make her more similar to the condition characterized by the magnificent *yovevo* (which we tend to translate as "spirit"). The person thus altered (*wetsakea*, "become other") already differs from her kinspeople; she is "transformed into spirit," *yovea*. This is a condition characteristic of the *romeya* shamans but which ordinary people and pseudo-shamans can also approximate.

The counterpart to this condition is the sudden attraction of the person into the *yochī* specters, the needy and potentially aggressive doubles of the dead that infest the Death World. In these cases it is said that the person has been transformed into a specter, *yochīkea*. A specter sprints toward the forest, severs the available channels for dialogue by giving in to the appeals of the dead, and distances herself from her kinspeople by following the path opposite the path leading to the magnificent *yovevo*. This latter path is the one traveled by the *romeya* shamans, as they must avoid the harassment of the *yochīvo* specters. Through their ritual activities, the *romeya* should make the specters abandon the Death World and thus cease to manipulate the living and to cause in them a series of behaviors that mark the desolation of this world. Indeed, what we would call the "individual"—a rather inconceivable thing in Marubo ontology—is not exactly responsible for his or her moral shortcomings; rather it is the detached specters of the dead, those that have returned from the terrible Death Path and wander this earth, that "place themselves on the back" (*peshotka*) of the living and ultimately command their actions. At present many among the living (particular youngsters) are afflicted by these harassments. As a result constant fighting breaks out in the towns and villages after the consumption of alcohol, as do disagreements over women, malicious gossip, disaggregation, but, most of all, an intense melancholy that sometimes leads to a death wish.

Robson Venãpa, a young teacher and *romeya* shaman, is situated at the counterflow—or, more accurately, at the point of confluence—of these processes. It is to him that we will now turn. "I am not like you," he once said to his kinsfolk. "I am like the bird spirit. I am another person." He was actually delineating what distinguished him and also making his function clear. "I worry about my kinspeople who will have nowhere to go once the world ends," he once told me. Venãpa's discourse about the end of the world has been growing steadily stronger: he says he hears from the spirits that Kana Voã, the demiurge, will return once this earth is consumed in flames. Venãpa will have a place to go, for he is "already spiritualized," yet he still dedicates himself to his kinspeople, whose doubles (*vaká*) will be lost the minute they detach themselves from their bodies. We will now turn to the consequences and conditions of this diagnosis and of the position occupied by Robson Venãpa.

Alongside old Armando Cherãpapa, Robson is currently the most active shaman in the Upper Ituí. He conducts all the main rituals, such as the Feast for Changing the Season (Shavá Saika), the Feast for Conducting the Dead (Kenã Txitõna), among others of the Marubo ceremonial calendar. He also sees to the daily shamanic séances in which the spirits sing through his longhouse body and takes charge of the extensive initiation of the *kẽchĩtxo* prayer masters, which lasts for months on end. Furthermore, he was one of the first students and a keen participant in the Indigenous teacher training courses run by the Centro de Trabalho Indigenista, as well as in the other activities offered by the Amazonas State Secretary of Education. He was also the main collaborator in my research, which began in 2004. His daily affairs include being in charge of the school of Vida Nova village and of the ritual life of this and other longhouses of the Upper Ituí, which is often quite hectic due to the illnesses that demand his attention and that of the other shaman prayer masters who are his kin. Formerly, when he was an adolescent and did not yet act as a shaman, Robson was also the first student of the New Tribes Mission (which has been established among the Marubo since 1950) and one of the best translators of biblical fragments into the native language. It is thus important that we take a step back and consider successive autobiographical testimonies. We will read two summaries edited from disperse data and then a direct translation of a longer testimony.

> Initially narrating something that had happened to his double [vaká], the young Mana [childhood name of Venãpa] said that one time he arrived at an empty longhouse. There was cooked manioc inside pans hung on the pillars of the family sections, but no one around. He heard chanting coming from afar. From the other side of the garden he saw people approaching. They were the yovevo, who immediately said: "What are you doing here?" "I don't know how I got here," he replied. "No, you are going to die, do not come here!" "No, I'm fine; I'm not going to die, can't you see?" Venãpa said. "You will die. We are not fooling you, come and see!" said the spirits. They took him to the hospital in Tabatinga. Venãpa saw alcohol lining the shelves. He saw himself laid out on a gurney, agonizing. Then he understood. "You weren't fooling me." "Yes, in two days you will die," the yove said. He saw a nurse and a white woman crying next to his body laid on the gurney.
>
> This is when he met Isko Osho [White Oropendola, his auxiliary double], who arrived with Kana Ina [the double of a deceased shaman] and the spirits of the cãocão harpy. They brought a fruit the size of an orange that they broke on his head. The fruit went inside him. He did not know; he did not understand. His flesh

became as hard as the pillars of the longhouse with new blood. The nurses *were there* [this is all Venãpa says, but they were probably at the hospital, with the event occurring in two places at once]. The *yovevo* inserted magic darts in his celiac plexus and in his back. The nurses were angry because he had serum in his veins [Venãpa moves from the narrative of the event in the longhouse of the spirits to the narrative of what occurred in the hospital, as if it were one process unfolding in distinct planes]. The nurses spoon-fed him *cachaça*. It looked like the *nãko* substance. Some Peruvian healers/shamans had brought the *cachaça*.

The episode reveals one of the critical moments of the illness of the young Mana, who had been diagnosed with tuberculosis. The event he describes occurred when he was roughly twenty-three years old and had to be taken to Tabatinga. To be sure, it was the *body* or *carcass* of Venãpa that was ill at the hospital, while his double wandered aimlessly about. This is when he found an empty longhouse, which was situated *within his own body*, and entered: "'I' was standing up, but it was *me* lying down," he says, explaining the process derived from the fissioning of his person, from which the double event that occurred at the hospital in Tabatinga and in the empty longhouse of the spirits takes place. I asked him if his double had not left his body in a dream. Venãpa offered an apparently ambiguous reply: "This is our body; this which speaks is what we wear. Except for this, it's all a dream; thought goes altering and everything is living persons, like in a dream." Strictly speaking, the excorporification of the double is not a distinct phenomenon from "real" or "true" (*namá koĩ*) oneiric experience, which also follows from the fissioning of the person and the eventual wanderings of his double. This is what the following words make clear: "Dreaming of myself I am not myself; it is like my body, but the face is another."

In addition to this subtle difference between the double that travels and the diseased person/carcass, another configuration is at stake that needs to be explained in detail. In the episode described here, Venãpa discovers his internal longhouse (*nokẽ shovo naki nanea*, "our longhouse that is inside"), where the doubles of the person dwell. This is an internal spatial reference point, localized in the chest region of the person-carcass, which reproduces or replicates external space and all its social configurations. This reveals the ubiquity of the event in question and the recursivity of the person: the person is split between his ill body at the hospital and his detached double that enters the virtual longhouse, this duplicate spatial dimension that is inside the body-carcass. Once there he recognizes a figure that had always been bound to him: Isko Osho, his *chinã nató*, his "chest or thought double," who is his elder brother. All of this, Venãpa told me, "occurred within my chest-thought, which I did not yet have" (*ẽ chinãnamã atiã ea yama*). His phrase "did not have or did not yet know" means the process of becoming "human" (*yora*). This phrase implies, among other things, a growing conscience or a progressive familiarization of this internal longhouse and the people that inhabit it. At the extreme end of this process, the person "spiritualizes" herself; in other words, she becomes other. We can thus see how Mana ultimately comes to alter himself: *yovevo* spirits transform his body (or, to be precise, his body double) through the introduction of *nãko* fruit and *rome* projectiles; his blood is renewed; he ceases to have *vei imi*, dead blood, and comes to carry *yove imi*, spirit blood. He will soon regain his health and act as a shaman in the longhouses of the Upper Ituí. But we should retreat further, to a time before the events described here, to Mana's childhood, through the following narrative recorded, translated, and edited by me from one conversation that he had with his relatives in a Marubo longhouse.

Before he moved to Vida Nova, Mana lived at Água Branca, the uppermost village in the Ituí river. He was eight or nine years old when he went to bathe in the river; he climbed a tree trunk and jumped into the water. He fainted. At that moment Isko Osho left and began to escape his body and to travel. Isko Osho still thought that the earth was flat, as the ancient ones conceived of it. He went traveling, first west and then north and south, and found that he always arrived at the same place. He then discovered that the earth was round. But it was only when Mana was thirteen, when he dreamed, that Mana understood that Isko Osho was his brother. Up until that moment, "the double and the person were ignorant of each other" [to borrow Tânia Stolze Lima's expression for the Juruna].

Before this event, at the age of ten, already living at the village of Vida Nova, Mana was also bathing and again fainted. This time Panã, his other double/brother, "left." Sani Nawa, a Shanenawavo man, then took him to the Subaquatic Dwelling Place [Ene Shavapa]. He entered the longhouse of the anacondas [of their *vaká*]. The doubles of the anacondas [the anaconda people] told him to walk over "their things," in Venãpa's words, finishing the phrase in Marubo: "their things, their disease," little animals in which he stuck his foot up to his ankles, and which stung and bit him. These animals were the disease of the anaconda, which were teaching him about themselves or about their own disease, so that he could later cure people who were struck with "anaconda sickness" [*vẽchã ichná*]. He then walked over the body of the serpents, stretched out at the bottom of the deep end of the river, following the orders of their doubles [the anaconda people]. There were many serpents, one black, the other red, another white, and he was to walk right on top of them. If he were to fall to one side, the anacondas would devour him. He was afraid, but he did not fall. The serpents shocked his belly. For this reason, today all the anacondas are respectful and fearful of him.

In July of this year Venãpa was a guest at my house in São Paulo. I took the opportunity to arrange medical exams and doctor appointments for him, since he complained of a vague "stomach tumor" that doctors had almost operated on him to remove in Cruzeiro do Sul, in the Brazilian state of Acre. After seeing one doctor we were sent to the public hospital. Venãpa underwent an X-ray tomography to examine his intestines, a procedure for which the doctors required a blood sample. It was the second time in a few days that doctors had asked for his blood, and he became restless. He told me that he could not remove too much blood from his body since he had only a limited supply of spirit blood. He is not like the other *romeya* who do not have any spirit blood because they have not been pricked or pierced (*retea*) by the *yovevo* and who are therefore able to lose great quantities of blood. He, on the other hand, could not be repeatedly pierced by the doctors of the whites, much less could he see his blood vanish or be wasted in the city's laboratories. The pills, however, presented no problem, since they please the spirits. After some convincing he accepted the procedure, and everything was settled.

On our way back home he and his companion, Matheus Txano, told me of another episode of his life that I had not heard. When he was sixteen (before the parallel episode that occurred in Tabatinga after the encounter with the anacondas), he fell gravely ill, perhaps due to the same tuberculosis. At the village he began to lose a lot of blood from his mouth, nose, ears, and anus. His mother, seated next to his hammock, collected the blood in a ceramic vase and deposited it at the foot of a large *samaúma* tree. The next day there was no trace of the vase or any of the blood, only a large anaconda coiled in the same spot. The episode seems to suggest that, once again, his blood had been "exchanged" for spirit blood, and that his anaconda kin received it. During this time when the exchange of blood was occurring, he did not appear in photographs: a white blur or a transparency always appeared where he should have been when the photographs were developed. When his finger was pierced so that blood samples could be collected for malaria exams, there was no blood. In time the situation normalized, but his blood is now another blood, because the *yovevo* definitively inhabited his internal longhouse, finally making him into a different person.

Let us reiterate the sense of the narrative: Mana, still a child, begins to establish diverse contacts with spirits and to carry out exceptional feats. During an accident in the river, Isko Osho, this elder brother/double, "leaves" his body and begins to travel through the world. He goes to the subaquatic world and undergoes a series of trials with the anaconda people. Later, in his adolescence, following the lead of a Sani Nawa, a mediating character, he carries out yet another initiatory adventure through various geographic regions. What follows is the episode of his blood being transformed into an anaconda and the alteration of the body that converges in later adolescence, with Mana's discovery of the internal longhouse and of his various brothers/doubles. Henceforth he will frequently "shamanize," as we will see in what follows. First, let us examine the translation of a testimony offered by Venãpa concerning his trajectory. In this speech his relationship to the other shamans of the Upper Ituí becomes clear.

> **Pedro**: But Cherãpapa also saw the People Spirit of Samaúma, didn't he?
>
> **Venãpa**: He did, from far away he saw them, he saw everything.
>
> **P**: From far away?
>
> **V**: Yes, from far away, but he did not leave his *vaká*, he didn't do the thing, but the other double [*vaká*], the other double that sings the chants of the spirit, this one may have seen it.
>
> **P**: Who?
>
> **V**: The one who is also his brother, the other double of Cheõpapa, Isko Ina,
> this one is like this,

he lives together with the spirits,

but the one who takes care of his house/body [*awẽ rakati vesoyavo*] scares easily.

He is scared of the *yove*, but me, I'm not scared.

It is not only now that I see the spirits, when I was a small child I saw, saw them when I was small, I was scared and kept shouting,

I fled from them, fled from them, fled from them

I am not lying, these uncles of mine saw me grow,

I was really strange, like a son of theirs [of the spirits].

I left when I was eighteen years old, when I was sixteen I left and it stopped,

stopped, stopped, stopped, stopped, stopped,

until when I was nineteen years old it started.

Then they wanted to pierce me, but I fled, fled, fled, that's what I did but they pierced me all the same, without me seeing it.

P: The spirits wanted to pierce you [with spears to introduce the *rome* agents] in your dream?

V: Yes, yes, when I was nineteen they arrived.

Between eighteen and seventeen I was ill,

At eighteen I got better and then it started when I was nineteen.

It was like I didn't know my parents, I had not called them.

This is why I was renewed during this time.

P: Who are your parents?

V: My parents [*papavo*], the Eels Fire [Txi Koni].

That's how it happened and then, this is how it happened and then I knew my parents,

Isko Osho, Panã, were the ones that I saw, I saw all of them together.

Having met with them, there in the place where we met, right there the illness stopped.

I am for my parents to dwell in me.

P: When you say "call/telephone" do you mean "relate"?

V: Yes, to think together [*chinã txiwá*], I am for them to think together.

Now, now, when the illness is about to arrive,

When they see that they are about to arrive

they tend to come and help me, take care of the disease . . .

P: When you stayed in Atalaia . . .

V: That is when I met them, during that time I knew them, then it stopped.

This was in Tabatinga.

I died, a long time ago I died.

When I was everywhere, Shetã Vimi found me, Shetã Vimi, toucan.

Then he said to me.

he, "Hey, you're dying, you've already died," but I replied, "I am not" . . .

P: Where did you meet Shetã Vimi?

V: In another place, in the house of the other people, in the house of dead people.

That is where I found him, where I found everyone,

I found Panã, I found Isko Osho, I found Shãpei, I found Shetã Vimi, and also Kana Panã,

I found them, my father . . .

The spirit I saw in my body was in the bed, it was in bed,

They took out my disease, took out things, the disease.

That is how it is now, having met them at that time, they now tend to take care of me.

That is why I don't get ill, there is no way I can get ill now.

I can get the flu, get malaria, but the bad specters can't mess with me.

Anaconda takes care of me, they protect me, protect me when I have the flu, blow on me,

blow on me when I have a fever, they take care of everything.

P: And you [Panĩpapa], did you meet your double in the same way he [Venãpa] did?

Panĩpapa: No, my nephew grew this way, he has been like this since he was a child,

but me . . . my father was a shaman a long time ago,

he was a stronger shaman, my father,

that is how it was with this nephew of mine,

that's how it was.

Because my father was that way, I started to discover when I was a child.

Thus the people who entered into my father did,

those who fed my father

who emerged from his remains,

emerged from the remains of *ayahuasca*,

from the dust of the snuff, all of these, these I saw.

They were not exactly the doubles of my father,

some were the doubles of my father, some weren't the doubles of my father.

That is how I saw, that is how I saw,

I saw those spirits, I saw *rewepei.*

I didn't see these many spirits of which people speak,

various spirits I really did not see.

The spirits who enter, who enter into our house I didn't see,

I see like Cherõpapa sees, I see exactly as he sees.

I do not see from up close, the spirits are far.

We approach from there, but see from this distance,

from here to that house, from here to [the] house of the priest,

it is from this distance that we see, from this distance we see the spirits.

But Venãpa is not like this, he really goes in, goes into their house, Venãpa does.

So that he can enter in their longhouse/house, he does not eat bloody things,

he does not eat bloody things,

he does not hang around his wife, so that he may visit the spirits.

But Cherõpapa does not enter there, he only looks from far away, as I do.

The spirits speak, although they are far,

they speak from far, like from here to the priest's house,

but it is like you talking here, for they have a very strong voice.

The bad specters [*yochĩ ichnárasĩ*] are also this way,

the bad specters do not go into us,

do not enter me, on our houses they really do not enter,

they pass close to us.

Panĩpapa, a deceased prayer shaman who accompanied us when Venãpa was interviewed, resumes the point with which I started this presentation: the way in which the senseless specters harass our body/longhouse is structurally homologous to the relationship between the *romeya* and the *yovevo* spirits, but it is its inverse in regard to its sociocosmic goal. The entrance of the undesirable specters (into oneself) must be avoided, while the relationship with the virtual plane in which the spirits remain must be favored. Venãpa, as we have seen, is particularly prone to this relationship (the capacity to "call/telephone" or to "gather thought" with the spirits, as he says using a metaphor of the whites' technology): he discovers and comes to be cared for by his "parents," the doubles of the anaconda and the eels, and also always has the company of his three brothers, Vimi, the youngest (his double of the left side, *mechmiri vakâ*); Pei, the middle brother (and of the right side, *mekiri vakâ*); and Isko Osho, the eldest (the double of the heart, *chinã nató*). Throughout this process we can see how he "died," that is, transformed himself: this "death," which tends to be evoked during the process of shamanic initiation, is quite distinct from the final death of the "body-carcass." It is at this latter moment that the internal doubles in fact choose to abandon the old and/or ill, uninhabitable, and unpleasant longhouse/body to live elsewhere with their spirit kin. This is somewhat similar to what Panĩpapa describes: instead of showing itself as an agreeable abode for the spirits, the body/longhouse makes itself filthy and chaotic (in other words, ill) and attractive for the senseless spirits who then take power of the person. At the moment of her final dissolution, the person's doubles will have different fates, which is one of the concerns of Marubo shamans.

The spirit doubles of Venãpa have always been around: some of them grew alongside his body-carcass, even though the temporality in which the doubles and the body-carcass that shelters them grow is not the same. At the time when these narratives were collected, Venãpa was twenty-nine years old and was not yet complete like Isko Osho, who is older and has his whole body covered in the *kene* designs, which are considered his writing. Not all of Venãpa's designs are complete, but they will be soon. Earlier, at the beginning of his trajectory, he did not know the *yovevo* because he had "death eyes" (*vei vero*) — that is, eyes like ours, that have ceased to perceive what was always already there. Venãpa is now a multiple person, something that all the Marubo potentially can be. He has, however, also become able to activate and manipulate this multiplicity. His shamanic and intellectual activity is possible only through his three brothers, among whom Isko Osho stands out. Isko Osho wanders throughout the world helping the dead. He was present at a catastrophic earthquake in Bangladesh and helped people cross the Death Path. He travels everywhere on his Wekorte, a sort of spaceship exclusive to the Iskonawavo, which flies faster than the airplanes of the whites (this is why, in fact, Venãpa is not afraid of flying). Isko Osho befriended a Kapanawa shaman (the Marubo of the Ituí have never had "physical" contact with the Kapanawa) called Vari Poiya, from whom he learned many chants that are not taught to younger people during feasts.

The sociocosmic field binds the bodies of living humans to myriad collectivities of doubles and other people, dead ancestors and *yovevo* spirits. What we translate as "human" (*yora*) is not a taxonomic delimitation but a position. The term "[the] living" refers to the expression *kayakavi*, "identical to a body": something that the Marubo say of themselves in relation to the spirits and the specters, but something that any subject may potentially say of himself. To themselves the specters think that they are living, even though a Marubo can only conceive of them as specters, and so forth. Sociocosmic kinship does not exactly bind humans to animals or to supernatural entities, but rather binds people to other people who live parallel to or in spite of their bodies/carcasses (be they similar to human bodies like ours or distinct, as the bodies of animals). But they are evidently *other* people, that is, people with qualities and knowledge distinct from that of the living of this earth, the Marubo.

It is thus possible to trace parallel genealogies, which refer to a segment of the kindred of Venãpa and its projection onto the virtual plane. The kinship terminology of the cosmos is the same as that of Marubo society—or, perhaps, it is Marubo society that replicates cosmological kinship terminology. Isko Osho (Venãpa's double/brother) is the son of Txi Koni (the double of the eel) and of Kana Ina (the double of João Pajé,

Fig. 2. Prancha 5—Wekorte. (Drawing by Robson Venãpa)

a deceased shaman), whose paternal grandfather (*ochtxo*) is
Wanĩ Shãko (double of Itsãpapa, another deceased shaman).
Kana Ina is *epa* (classificatory father's brother) of Ni Sina, the
double of another *romeya* shaman who, incidentally, is the
elder brother of Isko Osho. This very same Wanĩ Shãko is *epa*
of Isko Osho. Venãpa's father was a birth brother to Ravẽpapa,
both being Kananawavo (Macaw People), and the latter raised

CESARINO

Venãpa in the villages of this earth (following the death of his father, an important chief in the Upper Ituí). Parallel to this the double Kana Koni is the classificatory brother of the double Kana Ina, since both are also Kananawavo and raised Isko Osho in the subaquatic dwelling. Kana Ina's father is a member of the Anaconda-Oropendola People (Rovo Vẽcha) and his spirit mother is of the Samaúma Spirit-People (Shono Yove Nawavo). Manãnewa, Venapã's mother, was made pregnant here on this earth by her husband. Her double, however, was made pregnant in the virtual plane of reference by Kana Koni (or Txi Koni, "Eel Fire").

This situation is common in Marubo shamanism. During her pregnancy a woman can be "enchanted" (*roá*) by spirits and have her gestation altered or replicated in the virtual dimension. When she was pregnant, Manãnewa passed through a stream in which a multitude of eels spun in the water. From then on, she came to establish a special relationship with the electric fish: one of their persons, Txi Koni, Eel Fire, impregnated the double of Venãpa's mother, thus establishing the origin of a special child and future shaman. From this moment the multiple person of Venãpa becomes ever more complex. Today Venãpa can order his eel father, who is powerful like a federal policeman, to expel the other anaconda doubles who harass the living. Isko Osho, for his part, married a spirit woman and already has a child, who is called Kana Kaso (who inherits the social segment of his paternal grandfather of the eel people, who is also a Kananawavo, which is exactly what occurs in the *socius* of the living).

If the replication of the *socius* in the virtual plane guarantees a special potency to the shamanic activity of Venãpa in his attempts at defending his kinspeople from the harassment of myriad other peoples who constitute the cosmos, it is also directly linked to the circulation of knowledge in the

Upper Ituí. As we have seen, Venãpa is responsible for introducing new knowledge into this culture, which, incidentally, has always been characterized by a progressive acquisition of knowledge from the outside, ever since the time of emergence narrated in the *saiti* chants.

In an ambivalent moment like the present, the position of Venãpa is strategic. On the one hand, we have conflicts between the genders and generations, the attraction of younger people toward the way of life of the cities, the tribulations of the ancient cycles of marriage and of the formation of the person; on the other, there is a growing and intense shamanic activity that appears not only to correspond to a more general pattern previously registered among the Marubo but also to a sort of reaction to the disaggregating and transformative effects that they and other peoples of the region are currently undergoing. It is not so much an attempt at salvaging their traditions, of elaborating neo-shamanisms or reinventing culture, as described for other Panoan peoples, that is at stake; rather the recent activation of a shamanic system peculiar to the Upper Ituí within which Venãpa occupies a central place seems to answer to a singular dynamic that has yet to be properly investigated. Many of the events that define it began in 2009 and will require a more in-depth investigation in the field, although certain considerations can be ventured at this stage.

The transformations that Venãpa underwent also occurred to his younger brother. When I was in the field in 2009, his teenage brother began to sing the chants of the spirits following a period in which he was harassed by them in his dreams. In time he too will transform into a shaman like Venãpa, although he is still at the beginning of the process. This younger brother will be followed by his youngest brother, who is still a child but who later will become a shaman. Meanwhile, his middle brother is developing his shamanism with Tepi, a Matis shaman (Panoan-speaking group, neighbors to the Marubo), who has recently begun his activities in the Ituí. The doubles of this middle brother and of Tepi have met in dreams and carried out many feats together. Their relationship is similar to the one established by Venãpa's double and Vari Poiya, the Kapanawa shaman. Marubo shamanic activity therefore unfolds through a sociocosmic web that involves, on the one hand, the multiple persons who inhabit this earth and, on the other, the connections of these persons with a myriad of collectivities that occupy other positions.

Venãpa has been giving shape to this myriad in a most intriguing way. As I mentioned previously, he is the leader of the young Marubo teachers, as well as being a shaman. Venãpa is an exception among younger Marubo, who for the most part have little interest in the rituals and cycles that transmit knowledge. Often he is the only one able to bring his contemporaries to the feasts and to mobilize them through his teachings, an activity that tends to be beyond the skills of elder people. On one occasion a young teacher was listening to the songs of the Kapanawa shaman brought by Venãpa's double on a battery-operated cassette recorder: through a medium in which we would normally expect to hear the popular Brazilian songs of Amazonia, we instead heard the speech of shamanism. For this teacher the interest lay in their novelty: the songs of the Kapanawa shaman came from the outside, just like the songs of the whites. In this and other ways, Venãpa slowly gathers around himself those kinsfolk spread out in the longhouses whom he recently called "my people": those who are in his sphere of shamanic influence. Venãpa often hears what the spirits say about Kana Voã, the Marubo demiurge, who will return when everything is engulfed in an imminent fire. In this manner Venãpa and Isko Osho have been altering Marubo eschatology itself: they have been claiming that they are opening a new Spirit Path that will act as an alternative to the risky Death Path, for which the latter-day living no longer have the relevant knowledge to traverse. They thus hope to help their kinsfolk in their future passages, preventing the earth from becoming infested with unwanted specters.

At the same time, there are those kinsfolk who are gradually forming a competing network, which is different from that of his brother, the Matis shaman, and the elder shamans. This network is taking shape through the activity of three extraordinary children who have begun to prophesy in some longhouses—precisely in those longhouses where problematic kindreds live, kindreds characterized by famous cases of fission, disagreements, and illness. These are kindreds who are part of the conglomerate denominated "Marubo" but who nonetheless are considered "other people" by some of the *nawavo* Marubo sections of the Upper Ituí. These groups have long since lost their old shamans and, for many reasons, have ended up relegated to the fringes of the active ritual system. The practices of these young shamans are very distinct from what had previously been witnessed in the region. They prophesy the end of the world and possess knowledge of certain practices responsible for deaths that appear to be distinct from older Marubo sorcery. In short they spread disaggregation, which is the polar opposite of the shamanism of Venãpa and his peers. These young and threatening shamans have the designs, which some people consider bad, traced on their bodies. While Venãpa's designs have been drawn by spirits from the moment of his birth, the new shaman-prophets are covered with death designs (*vei kene*). Designs imply differential forms of knowledge that thus correspond to distinct ethical codes and modes of action. The young and threatening shamans do not receive the *yovevo* in their bodies, and they do not cure people: they are under the influence of Kanã Mari, a collectivity of demiurgical spirits who are enemies to Kana Voã.

Venãpa says that people will soon be divided into followers of Kanã Mari and Kana Voã. Kana Voã has been heard to say that a further fifteen of these bad shamans will emerge to spread evil and to complicate the tasks of his personnel.

In a certain way the division recapitulates the myth that narrates the enmity between the two demiurges. After making the sky, the earth, and all its attributes, in a time where everything was still good, Kana Voã sees Kanã Mari, his potential rival, ruin his work. Where there was a clear and beautiful field with low-growing weeds, Kanã Mari makes the tall banks, the thorns, and the branches upon which people stumble. Where there was no disease, Kanã Mari makes the anaconda, those ambivalent entities who are capable of spreading disease among the living. Kana Voã thus decides to escape from Kanã Mari, who follows him, ruining this earth in the process. In order to block his rival, who is trying to reach him, he creates the tall mountains that rise where the sun sets. He then heads west and takes refuge in the heavens, from which he will soon descend when this world burns in flames.

There is still much to be considered about shamanic trajectories among the Marubo and the questions associated with it. Parallel kinship allows us to glimpse the complex sociocosmic regime that underwrites it and its various developments, such as those linked to the production and circulation of knowledge, and to the limits, positions, and definitions of categories such as "human," "animal," and "spirit," or, still, the relational configurations involved in recent social transformations (see Cesarino 2011). The millennialism suggested here is not something that is diffused among the present-day shamans of the Ituí, although its prophetic traces (Venãpa tends to compare himself to Jesus Christ) may be continuous with the origin of the Marubo people through the activities of João Tuxáua, an important chief and shaman (see Welper 2009 and Ruedas 2004). It is too soon to weave more definite considerations on the matter or on the developments of the division of the Marubo into those under the influence of Kanã Mari or Kana Voã. Even though it rests on a canonical mythical base, much remains to be investigated concerning the contours of this new, aggressive shamanism that is emerging after a long interval in which the practice of sorcery and other forms of ritual aggression have ceased to be expressive forces among the Marubo.

Venãpa, although he is a *romeya* of the same type as his ancestors, acts within a peculiar social configuration. He is subject to widening his tasks as a mediator to well beyond the sociocosmos in which he already moves, toward the world of the whites, who still represent a challenge for Marubo social life. His criteria for reflecting on the knowledge for which he is responsible do not stem from an idiom of "culture" and "identity" (in the sense recently employed by Carneiro da Cunha 2010). This frame of reference, unlike what occurs, for example, in the state of Acre, has not yet become consolidated among the Marubo of the Upper Ituí as a productive and constant lexicon.

His visits to the cities of São Paulo and Rio de Janeiro in 2010 were marked by a reflection aligned within parameters similar to the shamanic thought that has developed in the villages. Venãpa, for example, could "see with his own eyes" that which he only "knew through thought": the frightening factories of Cubatão (in São Paulo State, Brazil) that produced "death heat" and "death fog," the immense stones of the Corcovado, and the Rio de Janeiro landscape. Shamans have always known that such things existed through poetic formulas, transmitted and actualized through their close contact with the spirits, who convey the forms of emergence and formation of everything that exists through the structure of the long *shōki* curing songs. Nothing escapes Marubo shamanic thought and its complex system of verbal formulas, which, in association with the lived experience, expands its capacity to resolve the dilemmas and to reformulate positions through contact with the world of the great cities.

To this mediated knowledge characteristic of shamanic

CESARINO

mythopoesis—the knowledge of the origin or formation of the factories or the enormous mountains of stone—Venãpa has begun to add his own visual experience. If he establishes contact with the spirits and, through this contact, actualizes and causes to circulate knowledge suspended in the virtual plane, how will he deal with the new landscapes that are revealed to him? How will his direct confrontation with the functioning of the world of the whites—the main source, we might add, of the imminent fire that will engulf the world—be elaborated? How will he guide his kinsfolk through these challenges? These are some of the questions that must remain unanswered, waiting for the events and the categories of thought that will deal with them.

Translated from the Portuguese by Luiz Antonio Lino da Silva Costa.

Bibliography

Carneiro da Cunha, Manuela
  2010 Cultura com Aspas. São Paulo: CosacNaify.
Cesarino, Pedro
  2011 Oniska—Poética do xamanismo na Amazônia. São Paulo: Perspectiva/Fapesp.
Ruedas, Javier
  2004 History, Ethnography, and Politics in Amazonia: Implications of Diachronic and Synchronic Variability in Marubo Politics. Tipití 2(1): 23–65.
Welper, Elena
  2009 O Mundo de João Tuxaua: (Trans)formação do Povo Marubo. Master's thesis, Department of Anthropology, Museu Nacional da Universidade Federal do Rio de Janeiro.

5

The End of Me

The Role of Destiny in Mapuche Narratives of the Person

MAGNUS COURSE

In this chapter I explore what at first sight appears to be a contradiction. On the one hand, certain aspects of Mapuche life seem to assume a model of the person as constituted by a multiplicity of relationships, as necessarily contingent, multiple, fluid, and, as Mapuche people themselves say, "unfinished" (*dewmangelan*). Yet on the other hand, the model of the person emergent in certain biographical and autobiographical narratives frequently appears as singular, self-contained, and "finished" (*dewmangen*), a person quite at odds with the momentary encapsulation of other selves that constitutes the Mapuche person as practiced. While upon death this "finishing" of the person is achieved emphatically and irreversibly through *amulpüllün* funeral narratives, a lesser kind of finishing seems to occur for living people through the near-ubiquitous trope of "destiny" (*mongen*) occurring in certain biographical and autobiographical narratives. In these narratives the trope of destiny locates each person, not within the complex and ever-expanding relations of alterity in which they are embedded and through which they constitute themselves, but rather as the singular recipients of a preordained destiny fixed at birth.

There is then, at first glance, a certain incommensurability between the "finished" version of the person presented in funerary narratives and narratives of destiny and the "unfinished" version of the person underlying the most basic practices of social life. While in the actions and strategies of their lives, people engage in a project of continual self-creation through engaging in relations with a variety of "potential affines," in the narratives of destiny, which are the focus of this chapter, it appears that these life projects are already finished, fixed, and either doomed to failure or gifted to success. There would then seem to be a rather radical disjuncture between the ways rural Mapuche people give their lives narrative form and the premises underlying the ways they go about living them. Whereas the lives of the Calvinists famously described by Weber seemed to adapt and respond to their divinely ordained destinies, the Mapuche people I know constantly reiterate the idea of singular destinies yet seem to reject its implications for the projects of their lives.

Through careful consideration of both persons and the various narratives surrounding them, I suggest here that these "unfinished" and "finished" versions of the Mapuche person are neither as contradictory nor as incommensurate as they might at first seem. Indeed, I hope to demonstrate the ways in which they actually presuppose one another. Rather like Rubin's image of the vase, so fundamental to gestalt psychology, one version of the person serves as the ground from which the figure of the other emerges, meaning that the two versions cannot be perceived simultaneously (cf. Wagner 1987). Put simply, in certain contexts no Mapuche person can be perceived as a self-identical, self-contained entity, for to be a "true person" (*che*) is necessarily to have engaged in reciprocal exchange relations with nonconsanguines. Yet at the same time, this understanding of the person as created through expansive incorporation of relations with others can proceed only if, in other contexts, these others are, at least to some extent, perceived as singular forms. There is no room for "generic" others in this version of potential affinity. The singular person is thus multiple, while the multiplicity is composed of singularities. The complexities of this admittedly abstract formulation will become apparent when we turn to the heterogeneity of the narratives themselves.

I begin the chapter by exploring the model of the person emergent in actual social practices, focusing on the ways in which the Mapuche person is premised on an engagement with what Eduardo Viveiros de Castro has labeled "potential affinity" (2001). I explore how this constitution of the person maps across a variety of practices both among the Mapuche and elsewhere in lowland South America before turning to look in more detail at how this centrifugal movement outwards is represented in a variety of linguistic genres. Yet through a brief analysis of Mapuche personal songs (*ül*), it becomes clear that at a metalevel, the relations of potential affinity constituting each person become encompassed by a singular self. Thus while the content of the songs and their dialogical form relate to a "centrifugal" movement outward toward others, the process by which songs come to stand for the entire subjectivity of their composer marks a "centripetal" movement inward, allowing for the conceptualization a singular, unique, and "finished" person.[1] The second half of the chapter explores in more detail this centripetal tendency in Mapuche narratives. I look briefly at the "finishing" of the person achieved through *amulpüllün* funerary narratives, before turning to the premortem "finishing" achieved through the narrative trope of destiny and its accompanying augury practices through which each person is established as a self-sufficient singularity.

The Unfinished Person

Although my primary focus here is on the role of destiny in personal narratives and the "finished" version of the person to which it gives rise, I need first to delineate the "unfinished" version of the Mapuche person. This version bears many resemblances to conceptualizations of the person found in other lowland South American societies. For put simply, a person becomes a "true person" by virtue of his or her engagement with a variety of what Viveiros de Castro has described as "potential affines" (2001). Potential affinity refers to a symbolic principle of difference that goes far beyond those relations of actual affinity created by marriage. It refers instead to "a privileged instantiation of general ontological premises [in which] difference precedes and encompasses identity" (2001:25). According to Viveiros de Castro, indigenous South American sociality can be conceptualized as a dual movement both away from and toward such potential affines. For on the one hand, consanguineal relations are constructed out of a given background of potential affinity, which therefore constitutes "the generic mode of relatedness" (2001:20). These default relations of difference are deconstructed and reforged as relations of identity, of kinship, through practices such as commensality and conviviality, practices that create shared bodies and thus a shared perspective (Gow 1991; Overing and Passes 2000; Vilaça 2002, 2005). Yet on the other hand, potential affinity remains the paramount source of value; thus people strive to incorporate the vitality of these paradigmatic others through such diverse practices as conversion to Christianity (Vilaça 1997; Vilaça and Wright 2009; Bacigalupo 2009), cannibalism (Fausto 2007; Viveiros de Castro 1992), and the appropriation of Western trade goods (Ewart 2007; Walker 2012).

Thus while some social practices are concerned with the creation of kinship through the deconstruction of affinal difference, other social practices are concerned precisely with the engagement with and incorporation of that difference. While the former practices can be described as centripetal, that is, looking inward toward relations of identity, the latter practices can be described as centrifugal, looking outward toward relations of difference. Such a schema is clearly very abstract, but as we shall see in the remainder of this discussion, it does indeed cast light on the apparent contradiction between the "finished" and "unfinished" versions of the Mapuche persons present in biographical and autobiographical narratives.

With some modifications this framework of potential affinity proves useful for an understanding of contemporary rural Mapuche society. The particularities of Mapuche history have shaped contemporary society in such a way that the centrifugal engagement with potential affinal difference is more visible than the centripetal creation of consanguinity through the deconstruction of affinal difference (Course 2011). This is the case because, to a very large extent, this deconstruction of difference has already been carried out by the colonial project of the Chilean state. Thus people are confined with consanguines on reservations that are constituted to a large extent by a Chilean legal principle of patrilineality, which is not quite the same as the corresponding Mapuche concept of patrilineality.[2] This topic is too complex to cover here; suffice to say that the engagement with others in the realization of full personhood, rather than the creation of consanguinity through the elimination of affinal difference, is most emphasized in contemporary rural Mapuche life.

Indeed, to be considered *che*, a "true person," one must be capable of entering into productive social relations with others. Both young babies and drunk people alike are said to be "not true people" (*chengelan*) for their inability to engage in proper social relations with others. While "true people" are capable of respecting others through proper greeting, offerings of hospitality, and sharing, neither drunk people, young babies, nor in some cases white people (*winka*) are capable of these practices of mutual recognition constitutive of "true people." To create oneself as a true person, one must enter a continual process of forming relationships with others and, more specifically, with those others with whom one does not share *küpal*, a term usually translated as "descent." It is primarily through relations of friendship (*wenüywen*) that one constitutes oneself as a "true person" (Course 2010). This is most usually achieved through exchange and more specifically through the exchange of cartons of wine. I have described this model of the person in detail elsewhere, but for now it should suffice to establish that this conceptualization of personhood is clearly open ended and externally oriented toward others. Indeed, Mapuche personhood could accurately be described as centrifugal, a constant movement outward, both in metaphorical terms of genealogical proximity and in the literal meaning of geographical space. This understanding of the person, not as a fixed, self-sufficient entity, but as an emerging point of connection between multiple relations is familiar in ethnographic accounts of lowland South America and resonates with Viveiros de Castro's description of the Araweté as "beings of becoming" (1992:252).

One of the areas of social life in which these forms of engagement with potential affinity are played out is that of language. Much scholarly attention has been focused on the ways in which indigenous discursive practices resonate with the "voices" of others (see, for example, works by Graham 1995; Oakdale 2005; Uzendoski and Calapucha-Tapuy 2012; Viveiros de Castro 1992).[3] Yet it is also worth noting a point that has been rather less emphasized by scholars of indigenous narratives: the role of exemplary narratives of singular lives (cf. Basso 1989, 1995). In certain instances such singularity may even exist in a generic way. Take, for example, Anne-Christine Taylor's description of *arutam* spirits among the Achuar (1993). Or Pedro de Niemeyer Cesarino's account of tensions in Marubo fractal personhood (in this volume). It would seem that the multiple engagements with others constitutive of fluid selves runs parallel to an emergence of fixed points, a point to which we shall return.

Such engagements with others through language are also of great importance to rural Mapuche people, and most of the genres of language recognized by them are fundamentally dialogical in nature. Of course, to say that language is dialogical is rather obvious, but what is significant here is that the most salient and elaborated linguistic genres in Mapuche life are not simply dialogues with other people but rather those with those people specifically recognized and categorized as potential affines—friends (*wenüy*), enemies (*kayñe*), or actual affines (*ngillan*). Most important among these genres are *chalintun*, formalized greetings that also incorporate *pentukun*, a series of questions and answers about one's "descent" (*küpal*) and one's place of origin (*tuwun*), information that serves to locate both speakers in social space. A key point is that these *pentukun* questions about one's kin, these *chalintun* formalized greetings, and even the great *amulpüllün* funerary dialogues occur only between potential affines and never between consanguines, between those sharing *küpal*, a term translated by local people as "descent."

Even those genres that do not take the obvious form of a dialogue with a potential affine, are nevertheless fundamentally directed toward such relations. Autobiographical songs (*ül*) are usually about relations of romantic love, friendship, or conflict, but rarely, if ever, about consanguineal relations (Course 2009). There are thus no songs of maternal or fraternal love so central to the folk tradition of Europe and elsewhere. Yet despite focusing outward on relations of potential affinity, the dialogical addressee of these songs is nearly always a close consanguine, a brother or a sister.

Let us take as an example the song "Wente Kawell Mallma," "The Proud Horseman," sung for me by Teresa Painemilla in 2007 at her home in Conoco Budi, a Mapuche community sandwiched between Lago Budi and the Pacific Ocean. The song was ascribed by Teresa to her late cousin, Luz, and addresses her status as a spinster and her rationale for remaining so:

1. Ñañawen, ñaña anay, ñañawen, ñaña anay,
   Oh sister, dear sister,

2. Ñañawen, ñaña anay, ñañawen, ñaña anay, ñañawen, kaynga anay

> Oh sister, dear sister,

3. Duamfelay, duamfelay, ayifelay, ayifelay,

> It wouldn't be right, no it wouldn't be right. We should not love, no, we shouldn't love

4. Wente kawell mallma anay, wente kawell mallma anay

> Those proud horsemen.

5. Ñañawen, ñaña anay, ñañawen, ñaña anay, ñañawen, kaynga anay

> Oh sister, dear sister,

6. Feyti wente kawell mallma, nenturakilcherkeylenga

> Those proud horsemen tell the people everything

7. Ñañawen, ñaña anay, ñañawen, ñaña anay, ñañawen, ñaña anay, ñañawen, ñaña anay

> Oh sister, dear sister,

8. Kalimayta, kalimayta, kalimayta, kalimayta, miawmupe, miawmupe, mallma anay, mallma anay, ñañawen, ñaña anay, ñañawen kaynga anay

> Leave them, sister, leave them. Let them wander.

9. Trarutrekantuley maynga, trarutrekantuley maynga, mallma anay ñañawen kay, mallma anay ñañawen kay, ñañawen, ñaña anay, ñañawen kay ñañay

> They walk like a traru [*Caracara plancus*, a kind of hawk], those proud ones![4]

10. Kanintrekantuley maynga, kanintrekantuley maynga, füchakenga mallma anay, ñaña anay, ñañawen kay, ñañawen, ñaña anay, ñañawen, ñaña anay

> They walk like a *kanin* [Coragyps atratus, the black vulture], those proud ones!

11. Ayifalay kaynga ñaña, ayilayafiyu anay feychi mallma anay ñaña,

> We should not love them, sister, we should not love those proud ones

12. Kalimayta miawmupe mallma anay ñañawen anay ñañawen kay ñaña.

> Let them be, let those proud ones wander, sister, dear sister.

This song is rooted in a dialogue with a consanguine, a "dear sister," yet in terms of its referential focus, it looks outward toward potential affines, in this case the "proud horsemen." What is interesting about these kinds of songs is that despite their engagement with and openness toward potential affines, at a metalevel they constitute a self-contained or "finished" version of the person. The "finished" person emerges as personal songs come to stand metonymically for the entirety of the initial composer's life (*mongen*), the same term that in certain contexts refers to one's destiny. All personal songs are initially both improvised and autobiographical. People compose songs only about their own lives. Yet it is perfectly acceptable for people to sing other people's personal songs, and when doing so, they always identify the initial composer. After death people's personal songs are sung as a way of remembering them and, in a sense, allowing the singer to experience the initial subjectivity of the composer encapsulated in each song. In this sense personal songs themselves serve as containers for singular, self-sufficient lives to move through time and space. They are simultaneously centripetal, in that they condense a whole series of open-ended relationships into one "life" (*mongen*), and centrifugal, in both the sense that they relate the creation of relationships with potential affines that allowed full personhood to be achieved, and in the sense that they are infinitely iterable and thus expansive (see Derrida 1985).

The Finished Person

As mentioned earlier this conceptualization of the person as constituted through an engagement with a variety of potential affines through a variety of different practices has been amply described in the ethnography of lowland South America. In some cases it has even been described as a "dividual" comparable to the Melanesian understanding of the person famously described by Marilyn Strathern (1988). Yet what has received somewhat less attention is the practices that seem to move in the opposite direction, those geared precisely toward congealing these distributed relations into a unique, singular, and self-sufficient person enduring through time.[5]

The most emphatic of these centripetal practices of "finishing" the person is the *amulpüllün* funeral oratory, which I have described in detail elsewhere (Course 2007).[6] Put briefly, as described earlier, Mapuche people create themselves as *che*, as "true persons," by establishing relationships with others through various kinds of exchange. At death these relations must be severed before the "spirit" of the deceased can move on to the unspecified realm of the dead. The literal meaning of *amulpüllün* is precisely this: "making leave of the spirit." This severing of relations and thus "finishing" of the person is achieved through an incredibly detailed and thorough biography of the deceased known as *nütramtun*: every place he ever went, every person he ever met, every achievement. The biography is carried out in the form of a competitive dialogue between two *wewpife* orators, one of whom is always "affinal" in regard to the deceased. The competitive element means that no stone is left unturned in recounting the life of the deceased. The *nütramtun* biography is followed by a ritual toasting known as *mariepül*. Bottles of cider and wine are placed on top of the coffin, and at the finishing of the biography, men grab bottles and drink them down. This practice contrasts with the usual etiquette of wine drinking, which emphasizes exchange and sharing. In *mariepül* the exchange is explicitly nonreciprocal; the drink comes from the deceased and serves as a final repayment of all the symbolic debts accumulated during a lifetime. The end result is that a person who in life was enmeshed with multiple others is now congealed into a singular and fixed person, a person capable of leaving this world of *che*, of true people.

While this centripetal practice of "finishing" occurs most emphatically in the *amulpüllün* discourses carried out at death, a lesser kind of "finishing" is achieved in life through the frequent use of a trope of destiny. What I call the trope of destiny is neither a genre nor a fully realized eschatological theory, but rather a constitutive feature of a variety of narratives. The trope of destiny appears most frequently in the everyday narratives people construct about their own lives and the lives of others, and I have never heard it appear in the more formalized genres of *pentukun* greetings or *amulpüllün* funerary oratory. While such narratives do not constitute a recognized genre of speech within Mapuche metalinguistic categories, they are nevertheless a daily occurrence. At mealtimes or during drinking sessions, people reflect on their lives and on the lives of others. One's own motivations and the motivations of others come under scrutiny as salient events come under discussion. Such accounts never attempt to provide a full account of a life but rather take a particular key event as indexical of a life as a whole. At certain points during these conversations, when the possibilities of explanation seem to have been exhausted, one frequently hears people say, "It must just have been my/her/his destiny."

The words I translate here as "destiny" are *destino* in Spanish and *mongen* in the Mapuche language, Mapudungun. While *destino* is a relatively unproblematic translation of the English "destiny," the term *mongen* is slightly more complex. In most usages *mongen* means simply "life" and can be verbalized by the suffix *le* to mean "living" or "alive." Yet when accompanied by a possessive pronoun, the meaning of *mongen* shifts toward that of life as an already finished, completed object that already has an outcome. Thus, for example, *iñche ñi mongen* (literally "I my life") would in most cases be more accurately translated as "my destiny" than "my life."

Let me offer three brief examples of the kinds of everyday conversations in which the trope of destiny occurs. The first is from a minor argument I had in Spanish with my *comadre* María about my reluctance to lead an overloaded oxcart down the incredibly steep slope toward the causeway separating Conoco Budi from Isla Huapi:

Maria: Why will you never lead the oxen down the hills?

MC: Because I don't want to get squashed and killed if they panic and start running.

Maria: Nobody ever gets squashed and killed leading oxen.

MC: What about Sandalio [a man who was squashed and killed by oxen]?

Maria: Ah, but that was his destiny.

A second example comes from a discussion in Spanish with my friend Marco about marriage and about why there are so many single men in Piedra Alta. Marco's wife had left him several years previously because of his drunken violence.

MC: Why is it that some people don't marry?

Marco: If it's somebody's destiny to marry, they will marry. If it's their destiny not to marry, then they won't. There's nothing they can do about it.

MC: Why did you choose to separate from your wife?

Marco: I didn't choose. It was my destiny.

A final example comes from Rosa, the mother of a young man who had committed suicide a few years previously. The deceased man had been a close friend of mine, and after his death several theories circulated about how his suicide had been caused by others, either through witchcraft or through romantic betrayal. Rosa, however, negated the variety of theories in circulation about what had motivated him to take his own life: "It wasn't his fault; he always had that destiny [*niekefuy feyti mongen*]."

Auguring Destiny

This ubiquitous trope of destiny in Mapuche personal narratives exists alongside a variety of esoteric practices designed to uncover precisely what a specific person's destiny might be. These practices are grouped under the general term *pewtun* or *pewtuwun*, meaning simply "augury." While some practices that fall under the term *pewtun* are retrospective, the majority are prospective. Around Lago Budi, where all my fieldwork has taken place, retrospective practices are primarily geared toward ascertaining who is responsible for a witchcraft-induced illness or death. In such cases the victim breathes into the mouth of a pig, the pig is then killed, and its internal organs are examined for signs of witchcraft. The types of *pewtun* practices I wish to describe here are all of a prospective nature and geared toward the uncovering of a specific person's destiny. In all these cases, the focus of the augury is a child, and the practice is carried out by a close consanguineal relative, usually a parent or a grandparent.

The most widely practiced *pewtun* is that of accompanying a child to a crossroads (*wedan rüpü*) before dawn on St. John's Day, which is known in Mapudungun as We Tripantü or San Kwan Antü and marks the start of the Mapuche year. The child and the adult accompanying him, usually his father or paternal grandfather, wait at the crossroads for somebody to come along in the opposite direction. If the first person to appear is a man of great wealth, the child, too, will be wealthy. If the person is a notorious thief, then this will be the child's destiny.

Alfredo, a man in his early eighties, was telling me of the various struggles he had confronted in his life. One of the greatest of these was alcoholism, and he had just sung me one of his *ül*, one of his personal songs, titled "Müna Potufe," which told of the suffering to which his alcoholism had led him. I asked him why he had succumbed to alcoholism, and he responded that it had been his "destiny" and proceeded to tell me the following *pewtun*:

> I remember being woken early, early one morning by my grand-father. I was just a small boy, maybe six or seven years old. He dragged me out of bed and we walked from the *ruka* [longhouse] up to the crossroads by the school. There we waited. It was St John's Day [San Kwan Antü] and just coming up to dawn. We waited a long time. Eventually two men came into sight along the road from Trawa Trawa. It was J and D, both very drunk; they were real drunks those two. My grandfather was furious; he took me home and beat me with a big leather belt. He saw my destiny and was angry.

Another form of divining the destiny of children was *miyaya-tun*, the ingestion of the hallucinogenic *Datura stramonium*, known in Mapudungun as *miyaya*.[7] Although *miyayatun* has not been practiced around Lago Budi for many years, many older people in the area underwent the procedure when children. Seeds of the *miyaya* plant are toasted, ground, and then mixed with toasted wheat powder (*mürke*) and given to the child in a liquid form. The child then enters a trancelike state that people describe as a kind of "drunkenness" (*mollin*). By carefully observing the child's behavior while under the influence of *miyaya*, it is possible to perceive his or her future destiny. If the child grabs for a bottle, he or she will be a drunk. If they find money on the floor, then he or she will be wealthy, and so on. However, in every account of *miyaya-tun* I have heard, the predicted destiny is negative and unde-sirable. Perhaps not surprisingly, then, accounts of *miyayatun* always come from third parties, rather than from those who underwent the practice themselves.

I once rode out with one of my "uncles" to discover the whereabouts of some missing sheep. On our way back we stopped at the house of a man whom I shall refer to only by his nickname of Fücha Ñua, "Old Devil." Fücha Ñua spoke only Mapudungun and was the only person in Piedra Alta to still live in a traditional longhouse (*ruka*). He was notoriously violent, and his wife and all his children had fled from him many years earlier. Upon our return home, my friend Sergio provided a biographical account of his life.

> That man's mother was a shaman [*machi*], but a shaman of the worst kind. She was really just a witch [*kalku*]; all she did was kill people. It was he [Fücha Ñua] who killed her in the end. He'd always defended her from the rumors that she was a witch, but when he found out that it was true, he was so angry that he pushed her into the fire. She died from her burns a couple of days later. He was in prison in Nueva Imperial for eleven years for that. She'd always known that this would happen. When he was a child, she'd given him *miyaya*, and as soon as he became "drunk," he ran at her and pushed her over. That was his destiny and she knew it.

Most accounts of destiny in both biographical and autobiographical narratives do not rely on what has been established through *pewtun*, yet nevertheless these practices provide people with tangible instances of the reality and truth of destiny as an idea.

Singularity and Multiplicity

In this chapter I have provided examples of moments in which the Mapuche person is represented as a fluid entity, a transient conjunction of relations, or as Mapuche people say "unfinished." I have also provided examples of moments in which the Mapuche person is presented as fundamentally self-contained, singular, and as Mapuche people say, "finished." Careful consideration of the ethnography of personal narratives in lowland South America reveals this tension to be a widespread feature, perhaps even a necessary one.

In the practice of kinship, many indigenous South American peoples are simultaneously engaging with relations of difference and forging consanguinity through the eradication of such relations, both opening up and closing off. As this and other chapters in this volume demonstrate, this dual aspect of indigenous personhood, its simultaneous centrifugal and centripetal aspects, is reflected in the representation of person in both biography and autobiography. *Pentukun* greeting narratives present each person as a conjunction of relations. Indeed, each speaker demonstrates himself or herself to be a "true person," to be *che*, precisely by virtue of his or her multiple engagements with others, and more specifically with potential affines, those others beyond whom those sharing *küpal*, descent. The biographical presentations of the deceased in *amulpüllün* funerary oratory are, at first glance, remarkably similar to the autobiographical presentation of the self in *pentukun*. They can be read as a simple listing of all the relations the deceased entered into, both the relations of descent from which the deceased person emerged, and the relations of potential affinity into which he or she entered through friendship throughout life. Yet rather than emphasizing the openness of the person, these funerary accounts serve a very different purpose: the establishment of a fixed representation of a singular, unique person. In this chapter I have described how the trope of destiny serves as a kind of premortem obituary, a kind of "future pluperfect" in which each person appears in "finished" form, rather than as a continual engagement with multiple others, as "unfinished." Of course, it should be evident by now that these two versions of the person are not really contradictory but rather mutually constitutive. Multiple engagements with others are the means by which true persons emerge, yet these persons represented as the singular possessors of fixed destinies are the concrete means by which the intangible fluidity of Mapuche personhood can be grasped; a Mapuche "science of the concrete" recast at the level of biographical and autobiographical narratives.

Notes

1. See Bialecki 2011 for an account of the "centripetal" and "centrifugal" versions of language and person in a Christian context.

2. I discuss the congruities and incongruities of "descent" and the corresponding Mapuche concept of *küpal* in Course 2011.

3. See Bacigalupo 2010 for accounts of the circulation of Mapuche shamanic biographies within and between persons.

4. This bird and the vulture mentioned in the following line, while graceful in flight, are very ungainly when walking. The song thus makes ironic reference to the fact that the proud and arrogant horsemen are rather less impressive when dismounted from their steeds.

5. The model of the person achieved in this way could accurately be labeled "individual," though I hesitate to use such a term here for fear of equating it with the much-critiqued "Western individual" (Mauss 1985[1938]; Dumont 1985).

6. Recording of *amulpüllün* discourses is strictly forbidden, hence the absence of transcripts from this essay.

7. Other accounts of Mapuche use of *Datura stramonium* for revealing the destinies of children can be found in Hilger 1957 and Munizaga 1960. Although *miyaya* is no longer given to children for augury purposes, it is still occasionally used by shamans both to treat certain forms of mental illness and to enter trance (Bacigalupo 2007:55).

Bibliography

Bacigalupo, Ana Mariella
    2007 Shamans of the Foye Tree: Gender, Power, and Healing among Chilean Mapuche. Austin: University of Texas Press.
    2009 The Re-invention of Mapuche Male Shamans as Catholic Priests: Legitimizing Indigenous Co-gender Identities in Modern Chile. *In* Native Christians: Modes and Effects of Christianity among Indigenous Peoples of the Americas. Aparecida Vilaça and Robin Wright, eds. Pp. 89–108. Farnham, England: Ashgate.
    2010 The Life, Death, and Rebirth of a Mapuche Shaman: Remembering, Forgetting and the Willful Transformation of Memory. Journal of Anthropological Research 66(1): 97–119.
Basso, Ellen
    1989 Kalapalo Biography: Ideology and Identity in a South American Oral History. History of Religions 29(1):1–22.

1995 The Last Cannibals: A South American Oral History. Austin: University of Texas Press.

Bialecki, Jon

2011 No Caller ID for the Soul: Demonization, Charisms, and the Unstable Subject of Protestant Language Ideology. Anthropological Quarterly 84(3):679–703.

Course, Magnus

2007 Death, Biography, and the Mapuche Person. Ethnos 72(1): 77–101.

2009 Why Mapuche Sing. Journal of the Royal Anthropological Institute 15:295–313.

2010 Making Friends, Making Oneself: Friendship and the Mapuche Person. *In* The Ways of Friendship: Anthropological Perspectives. Amit Desai and Evan Killick, eds. Pp. 154–73. New York: Berghahn.

2011. Becoming Mapuche: Person and Ritual in Indigenous Chile. Urbana: University of Illinois Press.

Derrida, Jacques

1985 Signature, Event, Context. *In* Margins of Philosophy. Alan Bass, trans. Chicago: University of Chicago Press.

Dumont, Louis

1985 A Modified View of Our Origins: The Christian Beginnings of Modern Individualism. *In* The Category of the Person. Michael Carrithers, Steven Collins, and Steven Lukes, eds. Pp. 93–122. Cambridge: Cambridge University Press.

Ewart, Elizabeth

2007 Black Paint, Red Paint and a Wrist Watch: The Aesthetics of Modernity among the Panará of Central Brazil. *In* Body Arts and Modernity. Elizabeth Ewart and Mike O'Hanlon, eds. Pp. 36–52. Wantage, England: Sean Kingston.

Fausto, Carlos

2007 Feasting on People: Eating Animals and Humans in Amazonia. Current Anthropology 48(4):497–530.

Gow, Peter

1991 Of Mixed Blood: Kinship and History in Peruvian Amazonia. Oxford: Oxford University Press.

Graham, Laura

1995 Performing Dreams: Discourses of Immortality among the Xavante of Central Brazil. Austin: University of Texas Press.

Hilger, Inez

1957 Araucanian Child Life and Its Cultural Background. Washington DC: Smithsonian Institution Press.

Mauss, Marcel

1985[1938] A Category of the Human Mind: The Notion of Person, the Notion of "Self." W. D. Halls, trans. *In* The Category of the Per-

son. Michael Carrithers, Steven Collins, and Steven Lukes, eds. Pp.
1–25. Cambridge: Cambridge University Press.

Munizaga, Carlos
1960 Uso actual de miyaya (Datura stramonium) por los Araucanos
de Chile. Journal de la Société des Américanistes 49:37–43.

Oakdale, Suzanne.
2005 I Foresee My Life: The Ritual Performance of Autobiography in
an Amazonian Community. Lincoln: University of Nebraska Press.

Overing, Joanna, and Alan Passes
2000 The Anthropology of Love and Anger: The Aesthetics of Conviviality in Native Amazonia. London: Routledge.

Strathern, Marilyn
1988 The Gender of the Gift: Problems with Women and Problems
with Society in Melanesia. Berkeley: University of California Press.

Taylor, Anne-Christine
1993 Remembering to Forget: Identity, Mourning and Memory
among the Jivaro. Man 28(4):653–78.

Uzendoski, Michael, and Edith Felicia Calapucha-Tapuy
2012 The Ecology of the Spoken Word: Amazonian Storytelling and
Shamanism among the Napo Runa. Urbana: University of Illinois Press.

Vilaça, Aparecida
1997 Christians without Faith: Some Aspects of Conversion among
the Wari (Pakaa Nova). Ethnos 62(1):91–115.
2002 Making Kin Out of Others in Amazonia. Journal of the Royal
Anthropological Institute 8(2):347–65.
2005 Chronically Unstable Bodies: Reflections on Amazonian Corpo-
ralities. Journal of the Royal Anthropological Institute 11(3):445–64.

Vilaça, Aparecida, and Robin Wright, eds.
2009 Native Christians: Modes and Effects of Christianity among
Indigenous Peoples of the Americas. Farnham, England: Ashgate.

Viveiros de Castro, Eduardo
1992 From the Enemy's Point of View: Humanity and Divinity in an
Amazonian Society. Chicago: University of Chicago Press.
2001 GUT Feelings about Amazonia: Potential Affinity and the Construction of Sociality. In Beyond the Visible and the Material. Laura Rival and
Neil Whitehead, eds. Pp. 19–44. Oxford: Oxford University Press.

Wagner, Roy
1987 Figure-Ground Reversal among the Barok. In Assemblage of
Spirits: Idea and Image in New Ireland. Louise Lincoln, ed. Pp. 56–
63. New York: George Braziller.

Walker, Harry
2012 Demonic Trade: Debt, Materiality, and Agency in Amazonia.
Journal of the Royal Anthropological Institute 18(1):140–59.

COURSE

Part Three

Creating Sociality across Divides

6

Relieving Apprehension and Limiting Risk

The Rituals of Extraordinary Communicative Contacts

Ellen B. Basso

This chapter focuses on the "little rituals" that emerge when speakers who are strangers to one another communicate. John B. Haviland's notion of "little rituals" is an idea of ritual language in which "echoes of more thoroughly regimented, formulaic, and contextually bound ways of using language can be heard" (2009:21). One type of resource we can use to learn about these events is biographical and autobiographical narratives, in which encounters involving "little rituals" may be the very substance of the stories themselves. Though often "mythic," these narratives have a special biographical character. While focused very often on short time frames, and thus different from Eurocentric narratives, with their life-history character, these stories with their quoted conversations, describe an individual's decisions to act, the formation of motivations, and other psychological matters.

Ritual Communication during Encounters with Strangers

Kalapalo narratives regarding contact with strangers, some "historical," others "mythological," tell us a good deal about the nature of communication in these fraught situations. In these Kalapalo stories, there are examples of all kinds of ritual communication within the contexts of encounters with strangers. Even lethally violent encounters are framed in ritual discourse, from enemies' initial mocking challenges to the horrific depictions of display and mutilation of the dead. These narratives are of particular interest because they suggest how we may think about the role of the "little rituals" of everyday interaction in new and unusual contexts, when they occur frequently during interpersonal contact in situations surrounded by extreme tension. When and if these contacts were successful, the stories show us how ritual communication functions over time in important ways to help develop new kinds of longer lasting relationships.

As we have learned from studies of Amazonian welcoming rituals and other ceremonial dialogues (Erikson 2000; Fabian 1992; Franchetto 1983, 2000; Hill 1993; Passes 2004; Surrallés 2003), ritual practices have the ability to probe the sources of community, helping participants to understand how latent hostility and the participants' feelings of risk and apprehension are transformed into concrete and positive social relationships. In this regard the speech-centered epistemic and evidential features of these ritual practices are of particular interest. This lesson may also be applied to more-concrete instances of unanticipated person-person contact in which people take chances with one another, adopting some risk knowing that the relationship in formation may fail in the end because proposing that we share understandings, rather than assuming they exist, involves that we negotiate over time. Our relationships are thus emergent, constantly being tested, challenged, and reformulated. It is in these speech-centered narratives that such challenges are remembered and described in all their developmental character.

Stance and Subjectivity

A focus on stance-taking and alignment is thus a useful approach to interpersonal communication that would serve researchers well in understanding these matters. The notion of "alignment" (Goffman 1981) involves the active seeking or rejection of a shared evaluation of some event/object, an

ongoing activity "in which two participants in dialogic interaction . . . converge to varying degrees" in taking a stance (Du
Bois 2007:22–23). Thus the "individual" is not isolated from
others nor defined mainly through social position and status, but exists within a complex communicative process that
emerges from, and may modify, the social grounding of personal identity and power. Ritual communication and little rituals in particular are an important locus of such processes.

To understand this further involves looking at the micro-
details of language resources, including the choices a speaker
has (or not) regarding terms of address, kinship words, and
titles (Basso 2007); the possibilities inherent in evidential
and epistemic features (Basso 2008); a speaker's creative met-
aphorization; and more large-scale enregistered discourse
practices (Basso 2009; Beier, Michael, and Scherzer 2002).
Collectively, these have been shown to develop an "I" of discourse (Urban 1989; Rumsey 2000) involved in stance alignments between participants.

The Story of Afuseti

The story of Afuseti (a woman abducted by a stranger) was
told to me by three narrators, the late Ugaki, a woman song
leader and storyteller living at Aifa in 1980; the late Kambe,
a major leader of the Kalapalo during the sixties and seven-
ties; and Tawana, a collateral relative of Kambe who as elder
lived with his daughter's family at Tanguro in 1998. In addition to the story's overall presentation of how women were
regarded and treated by men, several important aspects of
the story pertinent to this chapter's concern with ethnogenesis require initial comment.

First, this story is a detailed description of the abduction
of a woman by a stranger, a not uncommon event in Amazonian societies (another example from the Alto Xingu involves
the Suya abduction of Waura women). Clearly the instances
of rape and abduction in Amazonian societies is a topic for

more extensive commentary. David W. Fleck's work on Matses (sometimes called Mayoruna) abduction of women, approached from both an ethnographic and a linguistic perspective, is an important exception (Fleck n.d.).

Second, in each version a good deal of the narrative concerns the search for the woman, including the travels of the male relatives to other communities in the Alto Xingu (with the thought that she was not really abducted but had left with a lover). The conversations in these contexts are of special interest. One theme that arises as the Kalapalo men visit the other Alto Xingu communities in their search is that perhaps the abductor was someone whom no woman wanted as a husband. (There was at least one such man in Aifa at the time of my initial visit.) The accumulation of clues results, however, in a picture of what actually happened. Through the use of these clues in the narrative, Afuseti is transformed from a woman who is fleeing marriage to a local man to a person who has been abducted by a stranger.

Third, when the Kalapalo men finally make contact with Afuseti's abductor, their speech changes from an informal register to what I call affinal civility (Basso 2007). But because he has been described as a foreigner (an *aŋikogo*, or "fierce person"), the question is, how were the Kalapalo able to speak with him? According to Bruna Franchetto (personal communication), the Trumai told her this man was a Tupi-speaking ancestor of the Kamaiura. If so, it would make sense that Afuseti, one of whose parents was Kamaiura, might have been able to mediate between her abductor and her brothers when they finally came together.

Fourth, the response of the abductor to the presence of the Kalapalo men, now being described as warriors, is an important moment in the story. The abductor's giving of wealth in payment for Afuseti is a key element in the narrative, as her brothers come to accept the relationship.

Fifth, in Tawana's version, the final section of the story involves the return visit of Afuseti and her husband and children to visit the Kalapalo people. There the husband teaches an impressive musical ritual to the brothers.

This story is thus one important clue to the genesis of the multilingual Alto Xingu society, a key parameter of which is the performance of ritual music originating from different communities. While much (though not all) of this performance is done by men, as in this story, a woman may have a key role in bringing the performance from her husband's community to her natal family.

Afuseti's abductor is a man who (for a reason never made clear) has left his own community in order to find a wife. After three years' search, her relatives finally find Afuseti living with her children in her husband's settlement. They must decide whether, and how, they will bring her home. After learning that his wife's brothers have arrived, the abductor, Pañeta—now described as the woman's "husband"—greets them respectfully, acknowledging that they are the uncles of his children (lines 4–7). The following segments are taken from Tawana's version of the story.

> 1. lepene tikutsegatïfïgï, kafokombefa, isinitsïgï, onca igeli-a buh!
> *Next, all painted, wearing his toucan feather headdress, his macaw feathers, and the jaguar hide, covered all over!*
>
> 2. lepene telufa, tiŋeŋeta iño telu.
> *Then he went over to them, fearing them the husband walked over to them.*
>
> 3. ñeŋetunda ifeke. atani tugipugu egeni. ŋele aksetegei ifotugu fegei. fotugupe ege. matuga feke. ŋelefa, ŋelefa, ŋelefa, iñopegele.
> *He was afraid of them. They stood lined up, he himself (whom I spoke of earlier) decided to be the first of them, the first one was Matuga, then another one, then another one, then another one, then her [first] husband as the others.*

4. uum, adyogu, nïgifeke. amagoka fegei.

"My relatives, you seem to be here," he said. "It looks to me these are their uncles."

5. eh ehta tisuge aka tsiñeta. ulimosiko itigi, ititgi.

"Yes, we've come here to you as you can see. To get the mother of our children, to get her."

6. eh dyogu. amagoka fegei idyogu, idyogu.

"Yes their uncles. These relatives of mine are their uncles, their uncles."

7. etagimbakita. ah itseta itsa iñuŋo. itsako.

And so they kept on talking. They stood there outside the house. They stood there.

8. kekigefa, Pañeta kilï kekigefa uŋati.

"Come with me," Pañeta said, "Come inside the house with me."

9. eh he nïgifeke. sinuŋgolefa uŋati.

"All right," they answered. And so they came inside the house.

Pañeta fearfully approaches the visitors in his ceremonial regalia, indicating his status as an important leader of his community (the jaguar hides and many feather ornaments). The visitors are lined up in a defensive posture, headed by their skilled war leader ("bow master") the brother Matïga. They are greeted (line 4) as "their uncles" (that is, of Pañeta's children). They in turn inform him why they are there, using a very formal affinal register (line 5). Both lines 4 and 5 are the "core" of the ceremonial greeting: including the use of the epistemic—*aka* clitic ("seem to be"). Pañeta then invites them into the house. And they agree, another subtle indication of the peaceful intentions of the visitors (line 9). Yet the narrator's description of the event and the dialogue itself involves considerable tension. This continues when the visitors see that there are many "fierce people" in the settlement, and that they are ethnically different from themselves. In what follows, there are hints of a hoped-for peaceful resolution of the problem. Though the tension escalates on the side of the residents, the visitors assert their peaceful intent.

10. aŋikogo aketsigei. aŋikogo.

They [saw] that they were fierce people. Fierce people [i.e., ethnically different].

11. boh! Kaa, kaa, kaa, kaa, ah ŋikogo kita.

So many of them, calling out [to mark visiting strangers], surely the fierce people cried out.

12. tsakefofo. uum, tak, tak, ah iñali. wefotako aŋikogo feke, Matëgako.

Listen now. I'm thinking, as the others beat their arrows on the ground, violently. The fierce people intended to shoot them, Matëga and the others.

13. afïtï afïtï afïtï afïtï afïtï. ah, kuk^{w}etïŋiko, kuk^{w}etïŋi.

"No no no no no. I assure you, we're not here to kill you, we're not here to kill you."

14. tafaku oto agoi katote tafaku oto ago. ifametigïko, Pañeta ake.

All of them were bow masters, his brothers-in-law with Pañeta.

15. ŋigeŋunipa a ŋikogo kupoitako. ah intsene.

Don't you think possibly the fierce people were all bringing fermented piqui?

16. ohsi ñafe. efïdyauiñafofo intselemeŋe alitsue, intsene aketsige. puk, alidyu ifeke iŋandsuko.

"Come over here. Right away she offered some prepared piqui porridge. "Drink this, it's intsene. Puk, their sister drank some of it."[1]

17. lepene tuma tunïgifeke, ulepe ilidyifeke.

Afterward she gave them piqui sweet, and they ate that.

18. lepene iŋatsakenïgifeke, iŋandsuko keta. ulepe ikutsa ifekeni.

Afterward their sister cut open some piqui nuts from the fruit they were eating.

19. ah, intse ekuta, kine kidyulefa ifekene iñani.

Surely, they were eating piqui *fruit with manioc flatbread she gave to them all.*

20. iŋgetsïnipa ifeke iŋitako. itaufeke, tafaku oto.

Think of what the woman gave the bow masters.

21. ah, itsako.ñalï sïŋïlïko, ñalï sïŋïlï.

Surely as they stayed there they never slept, they didn't sleep.

22. akïŋi gele igei kaiŋa. otomope, otomope. aifa.

There were still many of the community members there. That was all.

The next day at dawn, Pañeta escorts the visitors to the bathing area.

23. lepene iminïŋgo, iminïŋgo.

Afterward, when their dawning occurred, their dawning,

24. kigekefa tuwaka mitotelefa tuwaka tufametiguko ake.

"Let's all go to the water." At dawn, to the water with this brothers-in-law.

25. fugombo ekugumbege eteluko, ainene aŋikogo tiŋi tafaku oto akago.

As they walked right across the central plaza, from across the way the fierce people watched them. "They're bow masters."

[Tawana uses hand gestures to indicate they ran away in all directions when they saw the Kalapalo because they were still carrying their arrows.]

26. uwefolu kupehene, aŋikogo itsakilï, tsuk. tsuk ifïgiko, inene. tuk tuk.

"They are going to kill us," the fierce people ran away, holding their arrows as they walked tuk tuk.

27. lepe tuwakagati. añakaŋundako. ele nakaŋunda, ele ñakaŋundako, ele nakaŋunda. ah sinïŋgo letï. sinïŋgolefa, tititi uŋati.

Next at the water place, they all bathed, this one bathed, that one bathed, that one bathed, and then they all walked back to the house.

28. lepe itsako iŋandsuko kaiŋa. okogetsi, isïŋïlïko.
Then they stayed there beside their sister. And they slept another day.

29. agikaïŋko, agikaïŋko. kogetsi aketsaŋe tisiteluiŋo dyadya
nïgifeke. okogetsi.
*They began to pack up, they began to pack up. "Tomorrow we are going
to leave Older Sister, they said to her. Tomorrow."*
*[Note: In line 29 they do not include Afuseti in the group that is leav-
ing, as they use* tis-, *the pronominal "exclusive we" prefix on the verb
"go away."]*

30. eh he kiŋalï.
"May that not be so."

31. okogetsi fofo uitagiñundaini. ufidyau, nïgifeke.
*"Tomorrow first thing I'm planning on talking, my grandchildren," he
said to her.*

32. eh he nïgïdye ifeke. eh he, kogetsi tsani.
"All right," she answered him. "All right tomorrow it will happen."

At night a flock of hyacinth macaws come to eat the *piqui.*
The visitors once again go to the bathing place, where they are
able to kill all the birds, again confirming to the fierce people that they are dangerous bow masters. Upon their return
to the house, the following conversation and activity ensues:

33. lepene kogetsi fetsaŋe iŋondiluiña dyadya, okogetsi.
*Afterward, "tomorrow I've decided to return home Older Sister, tomor-
row."*

34. eh he, egetuetsapa fetsaŋe, egetue.
"All right, go then if that's what you have to do, go."

35. lepe itsako. Kupiñano tuilulefa iŋandsukofeke. Intsene tuilulefa, kine, paŋine, ah iŋandsuko.
Their sister made something for our brothers. Their sister made piqui
soup, bread, toasted starch.

36. uum, anïŋgo iño ikanïgïfeke iño feke.

They sat there as her [original] husband talked to him.

37. amago, amago. ukiŋandsukogele aketsigei efeke apitsako. ukiŋandsukogele

"My relative, my relative. You should stay married to our sister. Our sister, still."

38. uum, afïtï dyogu nïgifeke afïtï.

"I'm thinking that's not right, Uncle" he answered. "No."

39. Aña teke. ah kapohoŋo eñugu feke atehe.

"Take these for yourselves." Indeed, he brought over a huge pile of things.

40. ah tafagufofo eitue. tafa feke.

"Keep all this wealth of yours." About the wealth.

41. ule titu endifegiku, uguka, uguka. ipïgï-iŋo fegei.

That's what things like feather headdresses, shell belts, shell belts are called. This was going to be the payment.

42. lepene dududududzz, ah ñenitigi.

The next thing that happened was they were dragged over and displayed.

43. ah dyogu, igea igetue. igoko igetue. tohoŋo iña puk, tohoŋo iña puk. tohoŋo iña puk. inïgïlefa ifeke.

"Surely their uncle, keep these things. Keep these ornaments." To another (visitor), puk, to another puk, to another puk. He gave it to them.

44. agetsïkï nïgifeke, efisuko ekugufa tueluti. tifametigu eluti. akagofale ñalïfale. agetsïkïfofo nïgifeke.

"More," someone said to him, their youngest brother who still wanted to kill him. He wanted to kill their brother-in-law. But their relatives didn't want to do that. "Do more right now," he said to him.

45. ah dyogu nïgifeke.

"Surely their uncle," he answered him.

46. amagofa. ah kogetsi aketsaŋe eŋufa kukwiŋandsuko ino-
tifeke. um aña teke. atafaguŋita tumugufeke. endifegikumba
figey. ekugu. teh! uumpok', pok', pok', pok', ah fiputelï.

*"My relative. Because tomorrow you must leave our sister. I think you
should take these for yourselves. Our son is presenting your wealth."
Feather headdresses was what he was talking about that way. The best
kind. Beautiful.* Uumpok, pok, pok, pok, *really, he put them all
down in front of them, and paid them all.*

47. ataŋe gehale teŋalï iña teke. ah, tutafisufofo ita. tafisu.
tukaŋapifeke. kafokogu, teh, eh, kafokugu eleña tundi, eleña
tundi, eleña tundi, fiputega ifeke. tufitsu fiputelu.

*"There's even more that I'm going to give you to take away." He opened
up his storage mat. Looking into his mat he took out toucan feather ornaments, beautiful, yes, giving these toucan ornaments to first one and
then another and another one of them, he paid them all. Paid for his wife.*

48. aña teke. ah tafisufofeke kokafeke mbege ige ekï,
kaŋundafisugu inde fipïgï puk' puk' puk', iña teke. ah tafisu-
fofo heitsue. ah tolokuegï ogokugufeke. lepe tunïgifeke tuku-
miluiñe fundagï tunïgifeke, tupisugiñe fundagï tunïgifeke, ah
katote ekugu.

*"Take these for yourselves." From the storage mat he took out more feather
ornaments, another kind of toucan feather ornament. "Here, payment,"
puk, puk, puk, "Take this. Keep this set of feathers." About all his harpy
eagle feathers. Next he gave tail feathers of the blue one, everything he had.*

49. aifa katote ekugu tunïgifeke.
Finally he had given everything he had.

50. tufïgipe, tunïgifeke, tuñukau tunïgifeke, tugifondogupe,
tufigugiñe, ulepe.
He gave his arrows, he gave his piqui oil,

51. fitsu egete fitsu egete.
"Keep your wife, keep your wife"

52. eh he nïgifeke kupamuwïfekefa iŋgugitako. egefekefa, ugu-
kafeke, akïŋi hipi, ihipïgï.
*"All right," he answered. Our nephew is presenting wealth to them.
About this thing, the shell belt, he had many of them. Payment.*

53. inde kwiŋandsu itsa. lafa inde kwiŋandsuko itsa. aifa igey
"Our sister stays here. Let our sister stay here forever. It is finished."

54. eh he nïgifeke.
"All right," he answered.

55. apïgï igei kugumbe sataŋagï. tufufu ititë
The very last one of these things was his flute. Called tufuu . . .

56. tisetanifa, tisetanifa. muh, ah yeñikogu . . .
"We're leaving now, we're going to leave." Muh, so many things of his . . .

The loving detail in lines 39–56 with which the narrator
Tawana describes what has been remembered of the objects
given to the brothers is remarkable. Yet this is not unexpected,
for the leader's offering of "everything he had" makes sense in
this situation. Only then does the tension ease to the extent that
the brothers agree to leave their sister with Pañeta. They depart
burdened by all their newly gained wealth. In the following segment (lines 57–102), upon returning to Kanugidyafïtï, Matïga
repeats to his parents what his sister has said (about her abductor not being with "one of them"), informs them that their
daughter's abductor has told them he will bring Afuseti back
to see her family, and then gives their mother all the wealth.

57. kohotsi etimbeluko. Matïgakombegele. aooh, uum, ama, nïgifeke. apa.
*Late in the day they all arrived. Matïga and the others all did that.
aooh, uum, "Mother," he said to her. "Father"*

58. ukugefïŋïmake wãke eindisu imbini wãke. kugefïŋï. aŋikogo.
*"It turns out the person who stole your daughter long ago was not one of
our people. Not one of our people, a fierce person."*

59. aŋi endisu. igealefa idyimo (Tawana holds up three fingers) idyimo tilako.

"Your daughter is alive. She has this many, three children.

60. fonundalefa, isi founuda, isïwï fonunda.

She wept, the mother wept, the father wept.

61. uum, a nïgifeke. tisiŋitafetsofofo, tisiŋita.

"I'm thinking," he said to them. "We'll see them later on, we'll see them"

62. apadyufofo iŋitafofo, apadyu. o ifeke.

"To see dear father later on, to see dear father,"

63. eiŋilukodyati, eiŋiluko.

"She wants to see you all, to see you all,"

64. eh he nïgi-feke.

"All right," he answered.

65. ande igepe sisoanïgï isoa titseluiŋo.

"This many of their dry seasons, during the dry season we'll plan to come."

66. iñandsu-ko igeluiŋo ifeke.

He'll plan on bringing their sister.

67. eiŋilïkodyati, eïŋiluko.

"He'll want to see you, he'll see you."

68. aiŋo fegei.

"That's how it will be."

69. etimbeluko. ifipïgï tunïgï isiña ifekene uguka, endifegiku, kafokokugu.

They had all arrived. They gave the payment to her mother, shell belts, feather headdresses, toucan feather ornaments.

70. ama, ïpi akïŋigele tafaku oto ulepe Pañeta. tafako oto, aifa.

"Mother, we have so much, because this belonged to the bow master Pañeta." That's all.

71. itsakombefa. sisoanïgï.

They stayed there after that until their dry season.

72. isoa agita kwigefunda, eteluko.

During the dry season they went to the manioc fields.

73. sinïŋgo Kanugieyafïtï-na.

The others were coming to Kanugɪdyafïtï.

74. ingefa, ingefa, dyadyako eta.

"Think of it, think of it, Older Sister and her companion are coming.

75. ifakila ukʷaiŋa, ifakila.

"They're close to us, not far away."

76. lepene kohotsi inde giti atani, taŋindambegele sita.

Afterward late in the day when the sun was way over here, they were still talking about that when they came.

77. ukugemba ukuge kilu. ukugekugumba tutu ita tisata.

One of our people was doing that, one of our people spoke. One of our very own people was going to do that, very clearly was speaking while we were there.

78. kahooh koh koh. kalapalo kilï.

Kahooh koh koh, *Kalapalo spoke.*

[using the greeting call to signal a visitor]

79. kuge, ukuge enïgï, iii kïŋamukʷe

"People, some of our people have come," some little children [called out].

80. afitïnika iñandsu-o enïmbata, afïtï iñandsuko. koh, idyimo kilï.

"I don't think our sister has arrived yet, it's not our sister and her companion." "Who knows?" their children said.

81. ifakila itsitsatiti igea ifakila enïgï,

"Perhaps those who have come are very close."

82. uum, Afuseti=maki ege. Afuseti.

"I'm thinking, that must be Afuseti after all. Afuseti."

83. mah, endïfidyu, endufidyï iñoimbeke iño

Mah, *a loud greeting call, the greeting call.*

Which they did for her husband, her husband.

[Their father as settlement leader comes to meet the returning abductor,
using a kind of little greeting ritual (lines 84–90).]

84. uum, sinïgïlefa, isuwïfeke idyopenïgï isuwïfeke idyopenïgï.

I'm thinking that while they came the father went to meet him, the father
went to meet him.

85. andema ukaiŋa. eh he.

"So you are here beside me after all? All right."

86. eifametidyau sele itagiñutale.

"Those brothers-in-law of yours are also speakers."

87. iŋumbetsufa iño.

He was looking at the husband when he said that.

88. amago aka ege.

"This person seems to be my relative."

89. ande aketsaŋe tisuge. eh he.

"We've decided to be here now." "All right."

90. etimbake. kaŋa eŋelu.

"Have something to drink." They ate some fish.

91. tseta itsa. tamitsi mbedya, Pañeta.

He stayed here for a long time, Pañeta.

ñalïtsuma tuelu Kalapalo feke. tïtomima tuelu.

The Kalapalo never killed him. "Why should they want to kill him?"

92. ñunegu, ñunegu ah tilako ñunegu telu

One month, another month, surely three months passed,

93. agaifa atanini. agai. aga.

He was going to do an aga, *an* aga, aga.

94. ñaŋundambetsa, ñaŋunda ikenilefa.
Performing it, I mean, performing it with the others.

95. buh, oh hoh, tsekegï ñaŋundalefa.
Buh, oh hoh, *so big a performance.*

96. uum, aŋika iñofeke tufuti, tafaku igisï tafaku.
"I'm thinking, is it the case that the husband knows a bow song, bow?"

97. eh fitsu kilï. eh tufutifeke.
"Yes, his wife said. Yes, he knows it."

98. ah ñaŋundakefofo, kupamuwïko, kupamuwïko,
"Then surely let our nephews' father perform, our nephews' father."

99. amago, nïgifeke.
"My relative," he said to him.

100. kogetsitsaŋe upidyau kukwakiŋundatifofo tsiŋuitue, tafakui.
"Tomorrow our grandsons want to make a performance so hurry up and prepare yourself, a bow."

101. uum, eh kiŋale nïgifeke. eh kiŋale.
"I'm thinking, usually I'd agree," he answered. "Usually I'd agree."

102. andemukʷetaka ufaŋagï fesifïgï.
"For what it's worth you'll agree that what I do here is something unpleasant."

The affinal civility register can be seen again in lines (96–102). It is marked in the story by (1) triadic communication (lines 96–97) in which the father asks his daughter whether her husband knows the particular ceremonial performance (should he have asked directly there was a chance the husband would have to deny his knowledge or in some other way embarrass the older man); (2) Pañeta's use in line 102 of the two epistemic clitics =*mukʷe* and =*taka*, the first a contraspective devaluation, the second referencing agreement with someone else's description of their experience, which contribute to

(3) his humbling description of what will be a valuable performance (lines 101–2).

103. apuŋu fegei nïgi-feke.
"It's settled then," he answered.

104. kogetsi aketsaŋe Pañeta teluiŋo tafaku-ki. Kalapalo kilï.
"Tomorrow Pañeta has decided to go get a hardwood bow," the Kalapalo said.

105. boh, Pañeta.
Boh, *a big person, Pañeta.*

106. kogetsi etikutselu etikulu, katote Pañeta fege enïgï ah alitue.
The next day they painted themselves, they painted themselves, surely everyone cheered when Pañeta came back.

107. egembe tafaku igisu inïgï. [sings]
When he did that he brought the bow song [Tawana sings]

108. igiñu fege. Pañeta tuita tisi-ña. Pañeta. Pañeta igisu.
This is the singing. Pañeta did it for us. Pañeta, Pañeta's song.

109. igealefa nïgï=lefa i-feke. igisu fege. Pañeta igisu.
This way he brought it, the song, Pañeta's song.

110. Pañeta ege. lepene hale Kalapalo aŋetïfïgï.
He is Pañeta. Afterward, Kalapalo have been performing it.

In lines 107–10 Tawana performs the song for us listeners, summarizes Pañeta's identity as a bow master and a fierce person of great size. He then describes the departure of the couple.

111. titselu aketsige. eh he nïgifeke.
"We have to leave." "All right," he answered.

112. ah, kugefïŋïmakina wāke ige wāke uikedyulefa ufeke tsalefeke iñope feke.
"Surely, he turned out to not be one of us who did this to me before, she told them about this particular husband of hers.

113. afïtï aka wãke oŋofïlïti wãke ufeke. talefeke. tiñope feke.
"Surely, you can see, can't you, this was the person who wanted to carry me away before," she told them, about her husband.

114. etelulefa, etelulefa.
He went away, he went away.

115. apïŋï, finge, apïŋï fegei. apïgï aketsige.
It's over, think of it, this is done, it has to end.

Discussion

Stance taking is an overt and repeatedly asserted matter in the private ritual dialogues in stories such as the narrative of Afuseti. In this story there are at least five predications in the inventory of the epistemic-affective field. The first involves imagining "likeness" and a sharing of these relations through the use of kinship terms such as "uncles," "our nephew," "grandson," "grandpa." At least a risk is taken that there is some possibility of that sharing; despite the violent beginning, there is an openness to the otherness of the other. The second involves wishing to agree with or validate the other, through standard agreement and validation forms such as *eh he, eh he kingilu*. The third is an epistemic scale of validation (Basso 2007, 2008, 2009), using markers characteristic of affinal civility and greetings. The fourth is the ethic of sharing, either through outright exchange or more commonly through an offering of gifts for whatever the person has received in the past or may in the future be able to provide another. The story's conclusion is a fine example of this, as the foreigner ends up contributing something important in the way of a song-dance performance that was added to the Kalapalo repertoire and still performed when I visited in 1966–68. While all these stance enactments may be initiated in a situation of danger, the fact that they occur at all leads to future development of positive relationships. The fifth is the use of gestural, postural, and self-presentational features to convey all the preceding elements. The sixth involves hortative invitations for both proximate and distal activities involving a collectivity formed by the potential antagonists, members of two different communities. That such ritual communications are so carefully remembered suggests that storytellers used their narratives as metacommunicative models, repositories of speech heard in extraordinary contexts, in need of memorization for potential use in the future.

Where personal voices cannot be heard because they can't be understood and/or have been suppressed in order to achieve at least temporary harmony, people may use the body to act out hidden predications (Turner 1969). In such cases the material body and its activities serves as a safe and effective device for communicating feelings of comfort, solidarity, patience, respect, peaceful, humble demeanor (and at the same time, similarity or differences in identity, ethnic affiliation, and the like), especially if they contrast with the usual or expected behaviors of the participants indexed as potentially violent. Nonverbal media may be understandable and workable where words can't at first be shared and understood very well if at all. Not only do paralinguistic features have meaning in themselves, in John Gumperz's words they are also "context-invoking meta-messages" or "contextualization cues" (1996). With repeated use of these multimedial events in more predictable contexts, the same hidden meanings are developed further through accompanying verbal locutions, referencing ideological experiencing. With the sharing of the semantics of this acting out, meanings cumulatively pool as people continue to experiment in similar, continuously repeated contexts of interpersonal activity. As these locutions are experimented with, the semantic may come to be paraphrased and metaphorized in ways that conform to the language ideologies pertinent to these locutions. Greg Urban (2002) writes that a locution itself may in fact be a metacommunicative ideological statement as well as an index of relationship. Where language ideologies developed from the ability to metaphorize, to invert what was performed nonverbally, these processes may also contribute to a sense that language can be deceptive because it is the means through which people create and manipulate what they already know and do. In multilingual situations a common normative discourse may begin to appear, behind which lie other voices and their accompanying participant roles available for future use.

A change in stance alignments begins with subjective and objective changes in the speech-centered self-presentations of the participants. Together with special linguistic registers, synaesthetic practices (using body paint, dress, objects used in postures, postures themselves, musical performances) are crucial for presenting and performing the participant's "theatrical I." It is the moral aesthetics of these performances that enables further development of individual networking on the margins of the performances themselves.

Acknowledgments

I am grateful to the conference organizers for their invitation to participate and to all the other conference participants for their comments and suggestions. My research was supported by the National Science Foundation, the Wenner-Gren Foundation for Anthropological Research, Inc., and the Guggenheim Foundation.

Notes

1. *Puk* is one of fifty Kalapalo ideophonic expressions used when a speaker wishes to reference the action or handling of a new or unfamiliar entity. They may be iconic, imitative sound images but also reference actions that don't have sounds in themselves. See also lines 26, 43, 46, 48, 56, 95, 105.

Bibliography

Basso, Ellen B.
2007 The Kalapalo Affinal Civility Register. Journal of Linguistic Anthropology 17(2):161–83.

2008 Epistemic Deixis in Kalapalo. Pragmatics 18(2):1–38.

2009 Civility and Deception in Two Kalapalo Ritual Forms. *In* Ritual Communication. Ellen B. Basso and Gunter Senft, eds. Pp. 243–69. London: Berg.

Beier, Christine, Lev Michael, and Joel Sherzer

2002 Discourse Forms and Processes in Indigenous Lowland South America: An Areal-Typological Perspective. Annual Review of Anthropology 31:121–45.

Du Bois, John W.

2007 The Stance Triangle. *In* Stancetaking in Discourse: Subjectivity, Evaluation, Interaction. R. Englebretson, ed. Pp. 139–82. Amsterdam: Benjamins.

Erikson, Phillipe

2000 Dialogues à vif . . . notes sur les salutations en Amazonie. *In* Les rituels du dialogue. A. Monod Becquelin and Phillippe Erikson, eds. Pp. 115–38. Nanterre: Société d'Ethnologie.

Fabian, Stephen Michael

1992 Space-Time of the Bororo of Brazil. Gainesville: University Press of Florida.

Fleck, David W.

N.d. Panoan Languages and Linguistics. *In* Panoan Histories and Interethnic Identities. Javier Ruedas and David W. Fleck, eds. Unpublished essay.

Franchetto, Bruna

1983 A fala do chefe: Generos verbais entre os Kuikuru do Alto Xingu. Candernos de Estudos Linguisticos 4:4–72. Campinas, Brazil.

1986 Falar Kuikuro: Estudo etnolinguistico de um grupo karibe do Alto xingu; Tese de doutorado, PPGAS/MN/UFRJ, vol. 2.

2000 Rencontres rituelles dans le Haut-Xingu: La parole du chef. *In* Les rituelles du dialogue. Aurore Monod Becquelin and Philippe Erikson, eds. Pp. 481–510. Nanterre: Societe d'ethnologie.

Goffman, Erving

1981 Forms of Talk. Philadelphia: University of Pennsylvania Press.

Gumperz, John

1996 Introduction to Part IV. *In* Rethinking Linguistic Relativity. John J. Gumperz and Stephen C. Levinson, eds. Pp. 359–73. Cambridge: Cambridge University Press.

Haviland, John B.

2009 Little Rituals. *In* Ritual Communication. Gunter Senft and Ellen B. Basso, eds. Pp. 21–49. Oxford: Berg.

Hill, Jonathan

1993 Keepers of the Sacred Chants: The Poetics of Ritual Power in an Amazonian Society. Tucson: University of Arizona Press.

Passes, Alan

    2002 Both Omphalos and Margin: On How the Pai'ikwené (Palikur) See Themselves to Be at the Center and on the Edge at the Same Time. *In* Comparative Arawakan Histories. Jonathan D. Hill and Fernando Santos-Granero, eds. Pp. 171–95. Urbana: University of Illinois Press.

    2004 The Gathering of the Clans: The Making of the Palikur *Naoné*. Ethnohistory 51:257–29.

Rumsey, Alan

    2000 Agency, Personhood and the "I" of Discourse in the Pacific and Beyond. Journal of the Royal Anthropological Institute, n.s., 6:101–15.

Surrallés, Alexandre

    2003 Face to Face: Meaning, Feeling and Perception in Amazonian Welcoming Ceremonies. Journal of the Royal Anthropological Institute, n.s., 9:775–91.

Turner, Terence

    1969 Tchikrin: A Central Brazilian Tribe and Its Symbolic Language of Bodily Adornment. Natural History 78:50–59, 70.

Urban, Greg

    1989 The "I" of Discourse. *In* Semiotics, Self and Society. Ben Lee and Greg Urban, eds. Pp. 27–51. Berlin: Mouton de Gruyter.

    2002 Metasignaling and Language Origins. American Anthropologist 104:233–46.

7

The Lascivious Life of Gabriel Gentil

Oscar Calavia Sáez

This chapter considers how autobiographical tales can enhance our knowledge of current indigenous history in Brazil. It focuses on a kind of subject scarcely handled by Brazilian anthropology: an urban, independent, indigenous writer.

Gabriel Gentil was born in 1954. As he wrote in his autobiography, he was raised by his father, a widower who didn't have a high status in the hierarchical Tukano sib system.[1] Within his pages, Gabriel talks about the hardships that his father endured to get and keep a new wife and about his own life in a large array of different homes, among relatives, among the Maku slaves, and with his stepmother. When he was nine, he was sent to the Salesian missionary college in Sao Gabriel da Cachoeira. (Curiously, the eulogies published after his death in 2006 explicitly deny his attendance at any Salesian school, stating that Gabriel remained in his native home and obtained a degree of traditional knowledge uncommon in his generation.) This background Gabriel shares with a whole generation of Rio Negro indigenous writers, all of whom indict Salesians for their repression of Indian culture, especially of linguistic exogamy that encompassed indigenous social life; their repression of the Yurupari ritual complex; and their authoritarian ways of dealing with their indigenous students.

As a student Gabriel was a firsthand observer of a shift that was under way in the Catholic Church from an older style of missionization to the new style inspired by liberation theology. At the end of this process, Salesian missionaries also played a role in the development of the Indian movement. Salesian training in literacy is no doubt a significant factor for the very existence of a set of Indian writers in the Rio Negro region, unparalleled in other Brazilian regions.

Missionaries played an important role in Gabriel's life, likely more so than in the lives of other indigenous students. He worked a long time for them (especially for Casimiro Beksta) as an ethnographic auxiliary. His job would have been to collect the narratives from the Tukano elders, a function that no white man could have achieved, or, conversely, to transcribe the tapes that Beksta had collected. At any rate it seems that it was in such ways that Gentil accumulated more traditional wisdom than he could have acquired based on his familial background. And this, of course, heightens the doubts about his legitimacy as a traditional sort of *kumu* (a priest-like *vertical shaman,* after the expression coined by Stephen Hugh-Jones 1996). He was not recognized as such in his distant native home. Gentil, who lived in the city of Manaus nearly all his adult life, was, however, recognized as a kind of neo-shaman and expert in Indian culture, very well acknowledged by important institutions like the Fiocruz Institute, an outstanding medical research institution in Brazil, where he was admitted as an honorary fellow, having been presented by relevant scientists who had applied on his behalf.

At age forty-two, Gentil wrote a relatively long autobiography (181 pages Times Roman 12, single spaced), in which he speaks about his childhood, his coming of age, and his years as a student in the Salesian college. In these pages, Gentil writes about a variety of topics, including the following: his father's hard life and the early death of his mother; his childhood amusements; the first words (both in Tukano or the Portuguese language) that he learned; the Yurupary sacred flutes that were shown to him (when he was still a noninitiated boy) by an elder and a somewhat malicious friend; the discussions among Indians about missionary policies; his rather bitter family life and his feeling that he was ill-treated by his father and elder brother; indigenous festivals; the relationship between Tukano and Maku people; the pressures that his father placed on him to study, fast, and restrain himself in order to become a good *kumu* or a good Christian student. He pleads for the safeguarding of traditional Indian wisdom, which many associate with the devil, and laments the scarce interest in this body of knowledge among Brazilians. Though his subtitle states his life story "is a reading for the people of the Tukano tribe," most of his efforts were designed to promote it among white people.

Gentil, the author of two published books (2000, 2005) and some papers mainly on Tukano mythology, submitted his manuscript for publication to various publishers, but to no avail. The text has not been published and probably never will be, at least not in the near future. I assume the main reason for its rejection—perhaps not the sole reason but no doubt a significant reason—is clearly visible in his text. As he writes about the various events of his life, Gentil talks principally about sex. This seems to be the case in almost every page of his text, even each paragraph of each page and almost in each line of each paragraph. This description is only a bit overstated: sexual matters constitute perhaps half of the entire text from beginning to end, with very few sex-free pages. Even a hardboiled reader may be puzzled by this continuous flow of sexual material that would equal the content of any specifically pornographic writing. Sex appears something like a quotidian stream upon which the other matters are presented.

Yet this is not necessarily pornographic material. It might be considered so by Western standards, especially if we were to look at the variety of experiences Gentil tells us about—other- and same-sex relationships, sex among children or with elders, intra- and interethnic sex, intra- and interspecies sex—

and the casual way in which sex emerges, since so many significant variants from the common array of erotic delights are shown.

Nevertheless, his narrative strategies are not those of a pornographic writer. He neither uses, like most Indian writers or storytellers, the common euphemisms of Brazilian or rural Brazilian speech, nor does he use the urban euphemisms that he undoubtedly knew very well. Instead, he employs a very concrete vernacular (Tukano) vocabulary, which include the words for sexual organs and the ways or degrees of their actions (e.g., *ñoase, ñoapese, nurise, dumëase, watepese, sipe-ñoase, bëhese*). He combines this vocabulary with direct Portuguese terms, sometimes uncommon, borrowed from erudite language rather than slang. Otherwise, he doesn't seek the pornographic effect that results from the mixing of brutality and allusion, of metaphors and crude expressions, playing on the thin line between contention and obscenity. Gentil's text is wide open, explicit, and in its own way innocent. Not that this means that it is an apathetic text since desire and affections are eagerly described, but everything is expressed in a very plain fashion, and there is no will to create a narrative climax. Nevertheless, his text would incite scandal since he describes a somewhat dark sexual ambience in the missionary school and a lighter but all-pervading and premature sexual activity in the Indian village. The reason for potential publishers' lack of interest doesn't need much elucidation.

Perhaps, however, it deserves some. Sex is not currently a very popular issue in South American lowland ethnology. Indeed, it is not a very popular issue in the whole of American ethnology, or in any ethnology for that matter. Sexual matters fill very few pages in ethnographies, and they appear mainly when they can be related to matters other than sex, cosmological or shamanic, for instance. More sex-focused descriptions, I suspect, are seen as stigmatizing, exotic-biased, or sensationalist tales that should be avoided. Since ethnologists in general cannot be described as solemn moralists, they behave this way because they fear that sex issues may support unflattering views of indigenous ways of life and of Indians themselves.

However, this was not the case from the beginning of ethnological research. The topic of sexuality or sexuality as a key for Amazonian Indian social structure or cosmology was often dealt with in specialized literature. The folkloristic and somewhat literary two-volume *Moronguetá* comes to mind (Pereira 1967). This collection of Indian tales interspersed with old-fashioned ethnographical information was subtitled *Un Decameron indígena* (An Indigenous Decameron), and like the Italian *Decameron*, it is not only erotic literature but is clearly focused on sexual stories. Jacques Lizot (1976) spoke broadly on Yanomami sexual matters. Two specialists on the Tukano area, Gerardo Reichel-Dolmatoff (1973) and Patrice Bidou (2001), made sexuality, in a Freudian style, the conundrum of their descriptions, as did Thomas Gregor (1985) writing on Mehinaku. Cecilia McCallum dealt with sexuality concerning the ideas of personhood (2001) and the Indian-white relationship (1997). This catalog could be much longer, but even in this very cursory literature review we can perceive an evolution from sexual practices to sex-focused ideologies to the politics of sexuality. In fact ethnographies could focus explicitly on sex, when Amazonian peoples were distant natives, but this openness became embarrassing when ethnographies began to be read or at least commented on in Indian villages. The uneasiness that this approach has created defies some cherished liberal beliefs. For example, more-circumspect trends also exist in Indian societies, and they come to the fore when Indian societies enter into open interaction with Brazilian society, where more-Puritan ways of thinking are much stronger than foreigners like to recognize. An excessive or nonstandard sexual behavior seems to be a heavy burden in the political arena. Kadiweu Indians of Mato Grosso became angry some years ago when a Brazilian movie (*Brava Gente Brasileira,* released in 2000) briefly featured the presence among their ancestors of a sort of berdache, a feminine man whose existence attracted the attention of the eighteenth-century missionaries and chroniclers: this, the Kadiweu asserted, was an assault against their ethnic image. In short, even in such an open time and place, sexuality is perhaps an even more difficult topic than in the past.

Surely, unbridled sexual behavior was one of the main stigmas placed on the Brazilian Indians. For instance, the sixteenth-century Portuguese writer Gabriel Soares de Sousa's *Descriptive Treatise of Brazil* (1851) offers the following:

> The Tupinamba are so lascivious that there is no lascivious sin that they do not undertake. At a very young age, they still have relationships with mature women, since the old ones, disliked by men, entice these boys . . . [and they] teach them to do things that they don't know about. . . .
>
> One woman is not enough for them [the Tupinamba], so they have many. . . . Because of this there are many men who die from exhaustion . . . and in their converses they utter nothing other than these filthy matters.

Soares de Sousa indeed continues his report with a heavy burden of "filthy" matters: appalling sexual pharmacy, sodomy, prostitution, and all the vices conveyed by the enormous lust of both male and female savages. A very hell and, no less, a very paradise for Portuguese colonists.

But the image of indigenous sexuality is more ambiguous. This hypersexualized Indian—from the time when Indian people were not only valuable allies but also dangerous foes—became a sentimental and overly chaste subject in the Indianist literature of the romantic era, when Indians became the distant ancestral symbols of the new American nations. Nobody would imagine the Mohican Uncas or the Guarani Peri uttering lascivious words or even conceiving lustful thoughts about their loved ones.[2] Furthermore, sexual longing would be a waste for these characters whose destiny was to become the last of their people. Indianist literature, it is good to remember, speaks mainly of dead Indians. How could they be the national symbol otherwise? This desexualized description of Indians perhaps reaches its acme in the work of Gilberto Freyre, one of the principal authors responsible for the image that Brazilian people have about their own country. Freyre's most famous book, *Casa grande e senzala*, translated as *The Masters and the Slaves* (1964), embodies a complete theory—still an object of heated debates today—on the building of the nation, and is a book filled with sex, a bit licentious and even sadistic according to some sensibilities. But my point here is that all the sex in *Masters and Slaves* is exclusively between black and white people. Indians appear as a shy, sad, and sober people who will vanish in due time. "Thanks to God," says Freyre at one point. "African blacks save our nation from the fatal mixture of Portuguese melancholy and Indian gloominess."

In general Indians appear in the national imagery as innocently nude and reticent people. In keeping with this national imagery, nobody misses the lack of sexuality in ethnological literature. Also since ethnography must not be mixed up with indiscreet gossip about other people's lives, this is probably for the best. However, this absence can lead to misunderstanding, because in fact sex talk may be for many ethnographers the main feature of day-to-day interaction in Indian villages. Recent ethnological literature is filled with talk about corporeal substance exchange as a key to Indian social life. Child building in their mother's womb by their mother's husband and lovers is a very common topic too, but sex, as we know, is not the same thing as substance exchange or child building and remains in the shadows, at least in ethnographies, even though in many Indian villages it may be far more common talk than cosmology or shamanism.

I have explained all this because the subject of this chapter, Gabriel Gentil, talks a lot about sex. It would not be surprising that a Western autobiographer speaks about his sexual experiences, and by the last century it became unarguably one of the principal matters from which Western subjectivity is made. Sexual memories are the conundrum of famous auto-biographies like Michel Leiris's. But in general this conundrum does not appear in indigenous autobiography. Indian autobiographers often in fact align with and confirm some Western stereotypes about Indian life rather than conform to genre ideals. For instance, they are expected to express (even Gentil does not fail to do so) the longing for lost traditions; to deal with the contrast between the world known in the village and this other, darker world that they have come to know among the whites; to tell myths; and to describe ancient ceremonies, hunting expeditions, or initiation rituals. Sex, however, is not on this checklist.

Perhaps, I should restate, it is better thus. Sexual activity is in fact a fairly common occurrence. As we know very well, sexual revelations hardly reveal anything that people don't know already through their own experience or their own desires, and thus literature on sex in exotic places or by exotic fellows will hardly contribute too much more than exotic fantasies. Since indigenous writers in general seek to tell us about cultural differences, there would be no point in stressing sexuality except to satisfy idle curiosity. Gentil's autobiography, even if it were a faithful picture of the current practice—which is not our task to evaluate—is remarkable not because it brings to us a different Indian sexual practice but because of its very insistence on this issue. Sex is the main register of his story. This is the issue at stake.

Let me focus on an interesting fact. I have pointed out, in an article concerning autobiographical tales (Sáez 2006), that autobiography is an almost unknown genre in Brazilian indigenous literature. Indian authors write and publish, increasingly, on indigenous history, mythology, and cosmology, but they almost never indulge in autobiographical tales. This is perhaps the product of sheer disinterest on the part of ethnographers and other white allies of the Indian movement, which in Brazil—in contrast to the opposite trend in North American ethnology (Brumble 1981)—has promoted the Indian voices attributable to *collective* subjects but never the *individual* ones. This trend may be changing now. Davi Kopenawa (Kopenawa 2000) and Raoni Txucahamãe (Raoni and Dutilleux 2010), two well-known Indian leaders, have published autobiographical tales, and in general such materials have begun to multiply as Indian political subjects appeared in the global scene. However, Gentil's autobiography is an outstanding case since he wrote it on his own (with a micro-computer), without any demand or incentive from outside. Moreover, he tried to publish it, and in fact distributed a number of copies among his white friends. Also, and I refer to the copy that I have in hand, he accompanied it with an emotional pronouncement against Brazilian indifference to Indian cultures. Thus Gentil's text could be considered a milestone of Brazilian Indian autobiographical literature, the first case in which a Brazilian Indian struggled to make his own life widely known. This *opera prima* is, to our surprise, a writing dealing mainly with sexual matters.

Talking about sex Gentil manages to talk about a lot of other things. He speaks about the way Indians receive the Christian message, translating it into known patterns. The holy characters are all grouped in couples and have sexual relationships, Indian children play Holy Family using a stone as their child, and priests and nuns are seen as a collective of husbands and wives. He speaks about father-and-son relationships: he reports the lectures and chastisements imposed by his father because of Gabriel's sexual amusements, till the moment when Gentil finds his father having intercourse with his new wife in his hammock—from then on, Gentil says in the title of this chapter, "my father let me live." He speaks about the whites' greed, exemplified by the figures of the missionaries who deny others access to the women in schools. He speaks about white domination, describing the way in which a Brazilian trader bought the sexual favors of Indian girls. Or the way in which the whites repress Indian sexuality, such as when missionaries put pressure on Indian fathers to beat their daughters who have made *ñoase*. He speaks about the ambiguous resistance of the Tukano people, who partly agreed to these repressive measures and partly opposed them, on the grounds that their "people always practiced *ñoase*." He speaks about relationships between humans and animals, which are seen as active partners in sex with humans (animals love the humans too, Gentil says). He writes about his own cultural dilemma, when he surrenders to Catholic injunctions and decides to restrain his sexual longings in order to be able to learn.

However, talking about sex Gentil speaks above all about the sex itself. "*Ñoase* is our life," shouts a character, a statement Gentil could shout with the same fervor about his own life in particular. He portrays himself not as a native hunter nor as a native politician nor as a shaman, that is, he doesn't stress, as is very common in shamanic tales, his own apprenticing.

Let us look with care at these excluded themes. Gentil's memories are not an exotic tale. He doesn't describe his childhood in primitivist terms that he could afterward compare with the white people's world. His childhood memories are not—as is so common in Indian memories—a sort of ethnographic account. In fact they are a bit messy, focused on individual events, without very much information about the Tukano way of life or discourses about Tukano cultural differences. They are written perhaps, as the tale's subtitle reads, "for the Tukano people," and not for a foreign audience (at least, they don't deal with the sorts of issues that interest foreign audiences). Without doubt Gabriel speaks about rituals—indeed, ancient lost rituals—stressing female agency and the sexual content of many of them.

In general Gentil doesn't speak in the common idiom of

Indian politics. He makes few, if any, statements about colonialism, dominance, or genocide, and he indulges in homiletic speech only at the beginning and the end of his work. The Indian movement, Indian rights, land claims, or conflicts are not part of his account. Indeed his descriptions may in fact be dangerous with respect to the political arena and the public image of indigenous Amazonians that he puts forward. In his account of Indian prostitution, for example, he depicts indigenous women's participation as fairly voluntary.

However, the authorized accounts of his life that have appeared, for instance, in his Internet necrologies, present him as one of the main leaders of Amazonian Indians. In a conversation with an ethnographer (Souza 2003), Gentil preferred the generic Brazilian term *pajé* to the vernacular *kumu* on the grounds that *kumu* is a simple healer, while *pajé* is also a leader (*liderança*) whose opinions are heard by his people. However, *liderança* (leadership) is a term that must be handled with care, since it designates not a chief sensu stricto but a much wider category of people with a significant voice in Indian affairs, internally but also interethnically. In many contexts any indigenous leader speaking to nonindigenous society at large in the name of Indian people can be considered a *liderança*. However, Gentil is by no means a conventional *liderança*; indeed he holds a very critical view of current Indian politics: "Democratic Indian communities, making elections, more elections, elections, elections, they only worry about elections. Thus is our present world. We are not creating new *pajés*; the Indian midwives don't exist anymore" (Gentil 2007:251).

His preoccupation is neither native culture nor Indian politics but rather sex. Sex, of course, is by no means a matter devoid of culture or politics, especially in the Tukano world. If one looks closely at his focus on sex in this narrative, one can understand it as a novel way of construing himself as a traditional shaman in an urban, literate, highly interethnic context. To understand exactly how this is so, one needs to understand the role sex played in the Tukano cosmos. To do so we return to earlier ethnographic descriptions.

The late Austrian Colombian anthropologist Gerardo Reichel-Dolmatoff was an author who didn't avoid sexuality in his descriptions. On the contrary he stressed it. In his book about the Desana (Reichel-Dolmatoff 1973), he depicts a society nearly obsessed with sex, highly repressive and projecting its own sexual fantasies on the neighboring and to some degree subaltern Maku people, their "slaves." Reichel-Dolmatoff can be blamed for a Freudian-biased focus, but such a theoretical sin would be tempting for anyone familiar with Tukano cosmology. The renowned Yurupary ritual and mythical complex, or the complex of the sacred flutes, is crucial to this cosmological vision. These flutes, not mere instruments but legitimate holy persons, are played at very important ceremonies, and it is absolutely forbidden for women (and noninitiated boys) to see them. Many myths in the Rio Negro region (in many variants from both Tukano and Arawak people) tell in spite of this that these very flutes were formerly female property. They turned into male property when men stole them from the women, upturning the earlier female dominancy into a male one. These gender-shifting flutes, both phallic and hollow, act as a blueprint for a series of myths in which the male body shifts into a container or pregnant-like condition, as in the story told by Panlon Kumu and Tolaman Kenhiri (1980) in which an ever-jealous father conceals his sons inside his rectum. Male encompasses the female (as the male sibling group in the traditional household encompasses the foreign wives). In his essay about the Tatuyo myth on the origins of death (Bidou 1979), Patrice Bidou speaks about a dreamed society founded on homosexual reproduction. An identical pattern of linguistic exogamy and clear patrilineal descent is to be found in the entire Rio Negro area, where patri-sibs perpetuate themselves from the body fragments of the Great Anaconda, avoiding all reference to the strangeness of alli-

ance, and to the perturbations accompanying sexual reproduction.[3] Hierarchical Tukano order is based even now on
such an undisturbed line.

In a lengthy article about the Tukano traditional house and
its symbolic values, Gabriel Gentil (2007) offers his own version
of that story. It is the same article in which he refers despon-
dently to the current democratic Indian world. In ancient
times Tukano life was a sacral one in which power was con-
centrated in the hands of the priests. The main event in this
era was the ritual focused on making shamans. Gentil stresses,
no less than ten times in forty-four pages, that this ritual had
a sexual dimension. Sex was performed *in public* (he never
fails to stress this detail) as part of the creation of new *pajés*.
The heterosexual (albeit not exclusively human) copula is the
ultimate origin of power:

> When Doétiro, the Tukano, went into the Heaven's House
> Ëmësewii did the ritual to open the door. He kept standing in
> front of the door, with his head lowered, doing circular signs
> with a ritual spear. He said these ceremonial words: "Oh God of
> the White Quartz Stone, I am here standing; I came here to beg
> your help. In my World in the Earth, we, the Tukano people, are
> hungry. I need fire, food, ceremonies, wisdom, *ipadu* seeds, man-
> ioc and all kind of goods and valuables. In exchange I brought
> my two pretty virgin daughters, for you to get them pregnant, to
> make children with them. Here they are! . . .
>
> Stone God answered: "Hummmmmmm, há, há, há, aaaaaaaaa!
> . . ." He took the girls and said, smiling: "Now you are mine. Make
> yourselves comfortable; we are in my Heaven's House. Here is
> Pleasure's House; the pleasures and the joys are the origins of life.
> Here is a power center. I am White Quartz Stone God. Keep your
> eyes closed; we ourselves go to enjoy making love; I go to blow
> from afar. You have beautiful thighs, you have beautiful bodies."
>
> The girls smiling answered: "Ah!!! . . . Our White Quartz Stone
> God, you turn us crazy; we are feeling pleasures." Thus saying

they lay on the floor, opening their thighs. And they said together at the same time: "Come above us. Blow us, enjoy us, we want more." After that they kept standing. Stone God caressed their breasts, touched their genital organs. The girls were virgins; they were deflowered by means of sacred positions blown from afar. They laughed feeling the tickles of the pleasures.

After the sacred sex, Stone God gave in exchange the cultural goods, the valuable objects to Doétiro the Tukano. If somebody would laugh at him, Stone God would kill him in the same day or force him to commit suicide. (Gentil 2007:225–26)

The connection between this published text and the autobiography is evident. There are, for instance, similarities in style and in some of its premises, especially that of female sexual agency. Maybe Doétiro wanted to barter his daughters for cultural goods, but Ëmësewii, the Heaven's House, is not a trading post. It is a power center where sexual pleasures and the girls' fondness for the sacred copula are the origin of life.

Moreover, Gentil offers a curious variant of the Yurupary story (2007:247). According to this version, in early times power was exerted by female shamans, who subjected men to a womanlike condition, making them perform female tasks and even "forcing them, with violence, to give birth to children." These shaman women were overthrown by the sun, which killed them all because they were turning all men into "homosexuals." The salient features in this version of the myth are the following: First of all, sacred flutes vanish (they appear perfunctorily in Gentil's other narrations). Then, an absolute character, the sun, external to men and women performs the gender revolution, and this intervention is intended mainly to reestablish in its entirety the gender binomial. I am inclined to believe that Gentil was rethinking the whole Tukano cosmology, building a new one that rearranged the traditional themes around a dual sex nucleus instead of the male one that was dominant in ancient times. Being a low-ranked fellow with poor chances to stand high in the Tukano ritual hierarchy (his father was of high enough status only "to light the cigars of the priests in the ceremonies"), he managed to become a prestigious shaman in Manaus, far from his village, where all the ancient ways were fading away. He did so by transforming the traditional wisdom that was not his legitimate inheritance.

Gabriel did not have much experience with the Tukano traditional order such as the ideal pattern of residing in a patrilineal *maloca*; rather he had memories of a solitary father wandering in search of a wife. In fact, his autobiography describes a new epoch that is different from the "traditional" order. Page 133 reads:

> *Changes between 1968 and 1972*
> Three changes happened in Pari-Cachoeira, in the Tukano tribe.
>
> First, the white men from the COMARA arrived, [people] who fucked willy-nilly in front of the fathers.
>
> Second, the traditional chief, Manuel Machado, was deposed, and the democratic Indian community was created; they elected a provisory leader. The Salesian fathers dropped out of the soutanes and turned the altar of the church halfway around.[4]
>
> Third, Benedito Machado, nineteen years old, from the Tukano tribe, declared freedom, modern year, saying in 1971: "It's a modern year. From now on, we Tukano can marry among Tukano people, with the Tukano women!"
>
> This was the starting of the NEW TIME.

This is a most ambiguous announcement of the signs of changing times. Taken together, changes such as the Catholic Church's adjournment, the beginning of a democratic Indian movement (which we know Gabriel did not at all regard favorably), the arrival of a trading company whose workers promoted Indian prostitution, and the supposedly final victory of the missionaries over the Tukano exolinguistic rule would be very hard for a supporter of Indian traditions like Gabriel to accept. Considering the whole of Gabriel's memories, however, we can suspect that his strong proclamation (in uppercase letters) was not entirely ironic: he could endorse, at least in some measure, these *new times*. Likely he was not alone in such unorthodox feelings. In a PhD dissertation written under my supervision, Jakeline de Souza has researched the practices of urbanized shamans of Tukano descent living in Manaus. These shamans seem to be very fond of native *culture* (albeit in some hybrid Afro-Amazonian forms); however, they are far less concerned with native *social structure*, especially agnatic ideology (they indulge in cognatic calculus when speaking about their descent) and with exolinguistic marriage rule ("how could we marry someone we can't speak with?") than Tukano people of the past or current relatives who live in indigenous communities.

Brazilian Indians have seldom written life stories. When they do, they center them around two mainstream topics of Brazilian ethnology: ethnic friction (Indian-white relations) and traditional culture asserted as a diacritic or marker of identity. The life story of Gabriel Gentil is somewhat different. It is scarcely sensitive to the political trends of multiculturalism; it is theocratic and (if considered next to his other writings) culturally dense and innovative.

To some extent Gentil can be compared to the Rio Negro Indian messianic leaders who in the two past centuries led strong resistance movements against Western rule, but who also brought about deep changes in native social structures (Wright and Hill 1992) impelled to some extent by Western ideas. A prophet such as Venancio Kamiko was inspired by Christianity, and much later Gentil was inspired by a blend of Indian nativism and very Western, new age ideas about sexuality.

Gentil was well aware of the disturbing strength of sex in both Tukano and white cultures. Thus, the somewhat shocking quality of his autobiography is not innocent. His life story is in some way a disruptive tale that consciously confronts both Tukano and Christian order. It seeks to portray Gentil not as an accomplished Indian or Christian person but as a somewhat idiosyncratic individual. However, his extreme sexual longing is not a sign of Western individualism, since it conflates the powers that created *pajés* in older times, prior to the decadence and oblivion of indigenous wisdom. Gentil does not stress his own shamanic learning process, which did not occur or at least not in conventional ways. Yet when exposing his own sexual life, he is in some measure rehearsing the ritual that consecrated ancient shamans, after his own rendering of old times: he is making his own consecration public, in the best way possible with respect to the literate public in urban Manaus.

When describing current historical changes in indigenous societies in Brazil, anthropologists are eager to point to Indian agency and to its faithfulness to traditional identity or structures. The Indians do not surrender to Western order or cosmology; they do not convert to Christianity or to capitalism. They *pacify the whites* (Albert and Ramos 2002); they domesticate or transform for their own traditional uses, Christian rites, Western goods, money, technology, or literacy, as the Rio Negro ethnographers and historians have widely described (Wright 1999; Andrello 2006). It is, no doubt, a healthy view after so many years of romantic defeatism. Twenty years ago we know Indian societies were portrayed as vanishing worlds: an Indian wearing sunglasses or a T-shirt, not to mention a Christian or an urban Indian, was no longer considered an Indian. However, this new historical optimism should not lead us to believe that these indigenous social structures, which were once considered soft, fluid, precarious, or merely nonexistent, would now be better described as unspeakably solid and permanent. This permanence is, indeed, a paradoxical permanence, a transforming one; that is, the continuity of changes is indeed the sole continuity to remain untouched by changes. The "inconstancy of the savage soul" is so because it acts not only against foreign faiths but also against its own faith or its own culture (Viveiros de Castro 2002). The continuity of distinctive Indian ways has been postulated on legitimate versions of Indian culture, endorsed by established communities, leaders, and shamans. However, it becomes most interesting when seen in relation to the works and standpoint of a heretic. The autobiography of Gabriel Gentil is relevant because it emerges as an unusual case in a landscape where autobiographical expressions of Indian subjects are rare, but also because Gentil wrote it contrary to some of the strongest foundations of Tukano social order. Only a true Tukano would be so conspicuously deviant from Tukano rules.

Appendix

Original texts quoted in this chapter:

Comunidades indígenas democráticas, fazendo mais eleições, eleições, eleições, só se preocupam com as eleições. É assim o nosso mundo atual. Não estamos mais gerando os novos pajés, não existem as mulheres indígenas parteiras. (Gentil 2007:251)

Quando o Tukano Doétiro chegou na casa do Céu Ëmësewii, fez o ritual para abrir a porta. Ficou em pé na frente da porta, abaixou a cabeça, com a lança ritual fez os gestos de círculos. E disse estas palavras cerimoniais: "Oh! . . . Deus de Pedra Quartzo Branco. Estou aqui em pé, eu vim aqui para te pedir ajuda. No meu Mundo na Terra, nós povo Tukano estamos passando fome. Preciso fogo, comida, cerimônias sabedorias, semente de ipadú, mandioca e todo tipo de bens e valores. Em troca eu trouxe minhas duas filhas virgens bonitas, para você engravidar elas, fazer filhos com elas. Aqui estão elas! . . .

Deus Pedra, respondeu: "Hummmmmmmm, há, há, há, aaaaaaaa!.." Pegou nas moças e disse sorrindo: "Vocês são minhas agora. Fiquem à vontade, estamos na minha Casa do Céu. Onde é Casa de gostos, os gostos e gozos é que são origens de vidas. Aqui é centro de poder. Eu sou Deus de Pedra Quartzo Branco. Mantenham os olhos de vocês fechados, vamos nos gozar fazer amor, eu vou assoprar estando de longe. Vocês têm belas coxas, têm seus belos corpos."

As moças sorrindo responderam: "Ah!!! . . . nosso Deus de Pedra Quartzo Branco, você nos deixa loucas, estamos sentindo gostos." Dizendo assim deitaram no chão, abrindo as coxas. E disseram todas juntas ao mesmo tempo: "Vem em cima de nós. Nos assopra, nos goza, queremos mais."

Depois ficaram em pé, Deus de Pedra alisava os seios, acariciava, tocou nos órgãos genitais. As moças eram virgens, foram arrebentadas através de posições sagradas assopradas de longe. Riam de sentir as cócegas dos gostos.

Depois de sexos sagrados o Deus Pedra deu em troca os bens culturais, os objetos de valores para o Tukano Doétiro. Se alguém risse dele o Deus Pedra matava no mesmo dia ou obrigava se suicidar. (Gentil 2007:225–26)

Mudanças entre 1968 a 1972

Aconteceram três Mudanças em Pari-Cachoeira na tribo Tukano.

Primeiro, chegada dos brancos da COMARA, que fodiam de marra na frente dos pais.

Segundo, o Chefe tradicional, o Manuel Machado, foi afastado, e criaram a Comunidade Indígena democrática, elegeram dirigente provisório. Os Padres Salesianos tiraram as batinas, e viraram a mesa do altar da Igreja.

Terceiro, o Benedito Machado, de 19 anos, da tribo Tukano, gritou a liberdade, ano moderno, dizendo em 1971.

É ano moderno. Agora em diante nós Tukanos podemos já casar entre Tukanos, com as mulheres Tukanas!

Era o início do NOVO TEMPO. (Gentil n.d.:133)

Notes

1. I acquired a copy of this autobiography through Jakeline de Souza, a PhD student at the Universidade Federal de Santa Caterina. Jakeline has worked with Gabriel Gentil in Manaus during her previous MA research and was very close to him. My knowledge about Gabriel Gentil's life comes to a large extent from her personal communications. Interpretations or misinterpretations, however, are undoubtedly mine.

2. I am referring here to the main Indian characters from *The Last of the Mohicans*, by James Fenimore Cooper (1826), and *O Guarani*, by José de Alencar (1856). Both are in love with white women. In the Brazilian novel, however, chastity is somewhat abandoned in the final episode, which points to the eve of a mixed-blood nation.

3. Of course this is not an exclusively Tukano trait. Perhaps it is, on the contrary, a horizon to every dream of autochthony, as expressed by Lévi-Strauss in his experimental essay on the myth of Oedipus (1958). I myself found a similar panorama in my analysis of myths and rituals of northern Spanish peasants (Sáez 2002).

4. "Soutanes" refers to the Catholic priests' cassocks, abandoned by much of the clergy—mainly from its left wing—after Vatican II.

Bibliography

Albert, Bruce, and Alcida Rita Ramos
    2002 Pacificando o branco: Cosmologias do contato no Norte-Amazônico. São Paulo: Editora da UNESP.
Andrello, Geraldo
    2006 Cidade do Índio: Transformações e cotidiano em Iauaretê. São Paulo: Editora da UNESP.
Bidou, Patrice
    1979 A propos de l'inceste et de la mort: Un mythe des Indiens Tatuyo du Nord-Ouest de l'Amazonie. *In* La fonction symbolique. Michel Izard and Pierre Smith, eds. Pp. 107–38. Paris: Gallimard.
    2001 Le mythe de tapir chamane: Essai d'anthropologie psychanalytique. Paris: Odile Jacob.
Brumble, David
    1981 Annotated Bibliography of American Indian and Eskimo Autobiographies. Lincoln: University of Nebraska Press.
Freyre, Gilberto
    1964 The Masters and the Slaves: A Study in the Development of Brazilian Civilization. New York: Alfred A. Knopf.
Gentil, Gabriel de Santos
    2000 Mito Tukano, quatro tempos de antigüidades: Histórias proibidas do começo do mundo e dos primeiros seres, vol. 1. Frauenfeld: Verlag im Waldgut.

2005 Pueblo Tukano—Cultura, historia y valores. Manaus: EDUA.
2007 Bahsariwii—A casa de danças. História, Ciência, Saúde—
Manguinhos, Rio de Janeiro 14 (suplemento):213–55.

Gregor, Thomas
1985 Anxious Pleasures: The Sexual Lives of an Amazonian People.
Chicago: University of Chicago Press.

Hugh-Jones, Stephen
1996 Shamans, Prophets, Priests and Pastors. In Shamanism, History,
and the State. Nicholas Thomas and Caroline Humphrey, eds. Pp.
32–75. Ann Arbor: University of Michigan Press.

Kopenawa, Davi
2000 Sonhos das origens. In Povos indígenas do Brasil 1996–2000.
Carlos Alberto Ricardo, ed. Pp. 19–23. São Paulo: Instituto Socioambiental.

Kumu, Umusin Panlon, and Tolaman Kenhiri
1980 Antes o mundo não existia: A mitologia heroica dos indios
Desana. Sao Paulo: Livraria Cultura Editora.

Lévi-Strauss, Claude
1958 Anthropologie structurale. Paris: Plon.

Lizot, Jacques
1976 Le Cercle des feux. Recherches anthropologiques. Paris: Editions du Seuil.

McCallum, Cecilia
1997 Comendo com Txai, comendo como Txai: A sexualização de
relações étnicas na Amazônia contemporânea. Revista de Antropologia USP 40(1):104–47.
2001 Gender and Sociality in Amazonia: How Real People Are Made.
Oxford: Berg.

Pereira, Manuel Nunes
1967 Moronguetá: Un Decameron indígena. Coleção Retratos do
Brasil 50. Río de Janeiro: Civilización Brasileira.

Raoni, and Jean-Pierre Dutilleux
2010 Raoni: Les memoires d'un chef indien. Paris: Editions du
Rocher.

Reichel-Dolmatoff, Gerardo
1973 Desana: Le symbolisme universel des indiens Tukano du Vaupés. Bibliothèque des Sciences Humaines. Paris: Gallimard.

Sáez, Oscar Calavia
2002 Las formas locales de la vida religiosa: Antropología e historia
de los santuarios de La Rioja. Madrid: Consejo Superior de Investiga-
ciones Científicas.
2006 Autobiografia e sujeito histórico indígena. Novos Estudos 76
CEBRAP:179–95.

Soares de Sousa, Gabriel

    1851 Tratado descritivo do Brasil en 1587. Edición de Adolfo de Varnhagen. http://www.brasiliana.usp.br/bbd/handle/1918 /01720400#page/1/mode/1up, accessed June 10, 2013.

Souza, Jakeline de

    2003 Aprender com os saberes de diferentes culturas: Um diálogo entre a maloca Tukano e a educação por Edgar Morin. Master's thesis, Department of Education, Universidade Federal do Amazonas (UFAM), Brazil.

Viveiros de Castro, Eduardo B.

    2002 A inconstância da alma selvagem. São Paulo: Cosac and Naify.

Wright, Robin, ed.

    1999 Transformando os deuses: Os múltiplos sentidos da conversão entre os povos indígenas no Brasil. Campinas: Editora da Unicamp.

    2004 Transformando os deuses: Igrejas evangélicas, pentecostais e neopentecostais entre os povos indígenas no Brasil, vol. 2. Campinas: Editora da Unicamp.

Wright, Robin, and Jonathan Hill

    1992 Venancio Kamiko: Wakuénai Shaman and Messiah. *In* Portals of Power: Shamanism in South America. Jean Langdon, ed. Pp. 257–87. Albuquerque: University of New Mexico.

Part Four

Hybridity, Dissonance, and Reflection

8

An Indigenous Capitão's Reflections on a Mid-Twentieth-Century Brazilian "Middle Ground"

Suzanne Oakdale

Because life histories and other genres of autobiographical narratives often describe a person's movement into a variety of social fields and his or her ability to understand and function within more than a single cultural logic, they can potentially offer a glimpse of the historically dynamic and synthetic nature of lowland South American indigenous people's lives. Many of the dominant modes of ethnographic analysis in the lowlands have tended to stress, on the one hand, shared cultural patterns, often associated with a language group, for example, the "Tupi-Guarani centrifugal dynamic" (Viveiros de Castro 1992) or the "Arawakan ethos" (Hill and Santos-Granero 2002), or, on the other hand, the common values orienting an interethnic system such as the Upper Xinguan value of peacefulness or language exogamy in the Vaupés. While previous modes of analysis such as acculturation studies have emphasized to a greater extent how people can simultaneously be oriented to more than one set of values, they tended to emphasize how the "traditional" values are replaced or at least how there is a movement in the direction of a complete reorientation toward the values and culture of the national society. The content of autobiographical genres as well as their form often highlight the simultaneous involvement in a variety of social fields, what could be called the "assembled" nature of social life. The "assemblage," as defined by Stephen Collier and Aihwa Ong, is "the product of multiple determinations that are not reducible to a single logic" (2005:12).[1]

Thinking in terms of "assemblages" means that those institutions and cosmologies that have led anthropologists to see, for example, Tupians as having a "centrifugal dynamic" do not completely fade from view but take a place alongside other institutions with other logics and in which other cosmologies are in play, such as that of government-sponsored "pacification" projects or Christian missions. Government policies or elements of Christian doctrine are not then viewed as meaningful for the people in question only in their own particular, culturally specific terms. Rather, from the perspective of "the assemblage," these social forms carry their own persuasive logics and habitus, socializing participants partially into them.

This "assembled" nature of social life is also more salient in certain periods and places and more salient for some individuals in comparison to others. Places and periods that fit what Richard White has termed the "middle ground" are contexts in which people would seemingly be most actively involved in navigating an assemblage of logics and social forms. According to White, the "middle ground" is the "place in between cultures, peoples, empires, and the non-state world of villages" (1991:x). The "middle ground" according to White is, first, a concrete historical space and time (for him the Great Lakes region of North America between 1650 and 1815). It is a historical space in which both a balance of power exists and an infrastructure has developed to support a process of partnership between distinct peoples (White 2006:9). Second, White uses the term "middle ground" to refer to a particular sort of process taking place in this concrete historical context. This process involves actors producing a "creative cultural misunderstanding," in other words, seeking out cultural congruencies, either mistakenly perceived or actual, in order to work together (2006:9). With respect to this second sense, "middle ground" as a process, White stresses the tenuousness, accidental, incorrect, and often ludicrous nature of congruencies that nonetheless seem to be accepted by both sides and are put to work (2006:9). With respect to the Amazon, Beth Conklin and Laura Graham (1995) have described beautifully the incongruities of the middle ground of the Amazonian indigenous/environmentalist alliance. As their discussion of this particular contemporary middle ground indicates, some indigenous Amazonians, such as leaders who interface with the environmental movement, are clearly involved in this process more than others.

This chapter focuses on portions of the autobiographical narrative of one Kawaiwete (formerly known as Kayabi) leader, Sabino, and describes an earlier "middle ground" in the lowlands, one that took shape around rubber extraction and government "pacification" of indigenous peoples. Sabino's life spanned the course of the twentieth century. He passed away as an elderly man in 1993 in the Xingu Indigenous Park, a location where he and the majority of the Tupi-speaking Kawaiwete people moved over the course of the 1950s and 1960s.[2] Before moving to the park in the mid-1950s, Sabino lived along eastern tributaries of the Tapajós River in the states of Mato Grosso and Pará.[3]

The Tapajós River and its tributaries during the rubber booms of the nineteenth (1860–1910) and twentieth centuries (1940s) was a middle ground in which a partnership was established between very different sorts of peoples.[4] Because rubber trees would not grow on plantations, the only way to increase rubber production in this area was to increase the number of tappers (Nugent 1993:189). During times when rubber prices were high, the value of indigenous labor combined with its mobility seemed, at least at moments, to balance the relations of power somewhat between indigenous tappers, traders, and rubber firms (for a similar dynamic in other areas, see Cooms and Barham 1994; Veber this volume; Weinstein 1986).

Here I focus on a few sections, excerpted from a much longer autobiographical narrative, in which Sabino recounts his memories of being a *capitão*. The *capitão*, or indigenous captain, was a hybrid sort of leader derived in part from indigenous leadership forms and in part created by rubber companies and the Brazilian government. The *capitão* was a position in which the different social arenas or fields, key to the middle ground, came together. It was itself a point of assemblage where the logics of SPI, missionaries, "contacted" and "uncontacted" indigenous groups, and the extended family household came together. As such those who held this position were automatically in place to be encouraged to think about how these various fields and their respective logics fit with one another.

For Steven Collier and Aihwa Ong, the presence of "multiple determinations" making up an "assemblage," as it is articulated in specific situations, encourages self-reflection and a calling into question of some of these constitutive logics or forms.[5] While they are more specific with respect to formulating why "global assemblages" lead to critical technological, political, and ethical reflection, I see the simple juxtaposition of these logics as potentially encouraging a consciousness and an evaluative stance. As Sabino describes his own experiences as a *capitão* in the 1940s and 1950s, he gives a glimpse of how he experienced the contrasting cultural logics of the "middle ground" of the Mato Grosso/Pará interior, at least as he remembered and reflected upon them in 1992. While there are some "misinterpretations" (as White would lead us to see) of colonial structures, his account is more notable for how it indicates that Sabino was aware of the way radically different logics and social relations from different social fields came together in tenuous, ill-fitting ways, for how he understood a variety of different perspectives.

After first describing the genres that Sabino drew upon when he told me about his life and then presenting an overview of some of his experiences (based on my reading of other sources as well as his account), I turn to what his narrative can tell us about two general features of the *capitão* position, the control of labor and the redistribution of goods. These two features were comprehensible to a range of players but not in exactly the same way by all of them. Sabino's account of his own experiences with controlling labor and the redistribution of goods shows how the *capitão* position brought different social fields to a point of convergence, but also how from the perspective of one individual, perhaps unusually familiar with many sides, this convergence was ultimately experienced as dissonant. The result was not so much a "creative misunderstanding" in which each side brought *only* its own particular culturally informed perspective and somehow still managed to work together as White (1991, 2006) describes, but rather a situation in which one individual had a kind of limited fluency in several cultural perspectives experienced and even actually embodied their clash and lack of fit. Excerpts from his narrative show how the dissonant cultural logics brought together in the *capitão* position impacted his sense of the developmental time of his life course and gave him a sense for the unviability of the resources upon which his position as a *capitão* was based.

Sabino's Account as a Mixed Genre

Sabino's son approached me in 1992 in the village where Sabino lived, located in the northern, "lower" or "downriver" section of the Xingu Indigenous Park. I was at that time conducting research on ritual performances and autobiographical narratives. He asked me if I would like to record his father "telling about his life and where he had traveled" (*contando sua vida e onde ele andou*). The narrative that resulted, when I did sit down to record Sabino's story, with his family sitting around him, was clearly a hybrid genre, a feature itself reflecting the fact that he had participated with some finesse in a wide variety of disparate social fields. Telling about one's travels is something that Kawaiwete leaders (at all levels) are expected to do, and while Sabino in 1992 was no longer even the head of his own household, having recently suffered a crippling stroke, for most of his life he had been a well-respected *capitão* as well as a much-loved leader (*wyriat*) of his extended family household. His account, at least with respect to its theme, was very much a type of "leader's talk," or *wyriara porongyta*, describing where he had traveled and with whom he had interacted.

His other son, however, said that Sabino "told about his life" because he did not know any myths or "stories of the ancestors" (*eyja porongyta*), like other elders did, and that he told his "own story" in place of these. While I do not include these sections here, Sabino began his account of his own travels by presenting the stories of the previous generation's encounters with "whites," that is, nonindigenous people, particularly his uncle's encounter. These stories recount the prowess of particular Kawaiwete individuals in warfare against particular named enemies. Ultimately, however, as a whole series they also describe the gradual "pacification" of the Kawaiwete. In this way Sabino prefaced his autobiographical account with stories of events that he himself did not witness, a feature of his account in keeping with the *eyja ̓porongyta*. Unlike most narrators when telling "stories of the ancestors," he did not use tense/evidential markers indicating that these events were not actually experienced by him.

With respect to the thematic content, these accounts were more like Kawaiwete Jawosi songs. Jawosi songs describe encounters with enemies, most recounting how an individual enemy was vanquished by a Kawaiwete warrior. These songs are also handed down from one generation of male relatives to the next much like Sabino's stories about pacification inherited from his uncle. Furthermore, the majority of Jawosi songs also do not employ tense/evidential markers. These songs are, however, much briefer, metaphorical, and more stylized, as well as sung with the accompaniment of a chorus.

Clearly a form of oratory and also influenced by myth tell-ing and perhaps Jawosi songs, Sabino's account also drew on a genre of talking about personal experiences developed over the course of living and working with researchers such as anthropologists—something Sabino had done periodically since the 1960s in the Xingu Park. A few years before my visit, in 1990, Sabino had participated in an education program headed by Mariana Kawall Leal Ferreira at a post (Diauarum) within the Xingu Park. Between 1980 and 1990, Kawaiwete individuals as well as others living in the Xingu narrated sto-ries about their past.[6] In this context Sabino narrated his "life story," and his son wrote it down in Portuguese. Even before this, however, Sabino had been telling "about his life" for other researchers. At least a small part of the narrative Sabino recorded for me in 1992 and for Ferreira in 1990 was also told to the German anthropologist Georg Grünberg in 1966 (Grünberg 2004:66).

While large parts of the Portuguese narrative found in Ferreira (1994) and the Kawaiwete narrative I recorded in 1992 describe similar events, they are also complementary, each including many events that the other does not. Sabino remarked that he wanted to give me stories that were dif-ferent from those he had recorded for Ferreira, a comment that suggests he had a sense for how his recording fit into the "research economy" of the Xingu Park, one of the most heavily researched areas in Brazil. The amount of overlap in terms of the content of the recordings done for Ferreira and myself does very likely mean, however, that Sabino had crafted his narra-tive into a relatively standardized account, one that attempted to discuss his "whole life," from childhood to the present. It was, in part, then, also a narrative that was created over the course of many years of interacting with different anthropol-ogists who had been requesting "life histories" for decades and one that was appropriately called forth by the presence of yet one more researcher such as myself. His "life history" in and of itself was a product of his entering into and learning the social dynamics of and discourse styles appropriate to anthropological research. His account therefore was "double voiced" in the sense that it called to mind both the narrative styles of the victorious warrior as well as that of the contemporary "research subject."

Sabino told his account, largely uninterrupted in the Kawaiwete language, and I later transcribed and translated his recording with the untiring help of two of the village's schoolteachers, who had been assigned by the village chief to work with me on language, Mairata and Aturi. Boys and young men also often requested that I play Sabino's tape recording in the months afterward. They would usually sit in silence, paying very close attention. It was, therefore, an account that others, beyond the researcher, found deeply meaningful.

Sabino's Life

As Sabino tells his story, he did not set out to be involved in so many social arenas. Rather, circumstances led him to this position. As a small boy his family took him to José Bezerra Post, a post set up along the Teles Pires River, where the Kawaiwete established their first sustained peaceable contact with the SPI in 1929 after destroying two other previous SPI posts in 1924 and 1927.[7] While at José Bezerra, Sabino's parents died during a measles epidemic, and he was taken to live with his older brother in a more remote Kawaiwete village. Later after his brother also died of measles, he was returned to José Bezerra and adopted and raised as a son by the white post chief. Sabino spent his adolescence working for this man and then worked at farms and ranches in the area. Fluent in both Kawaiwete and Portuguese as a young adult, Sabino began tapping rubber and organizing the labor of other young men living near posts. For a period after the Second World War, when the Brazilian government controlled and steadied rubber prices (Dean 1987:108–15), rubber companies tried to win Sabino's favor by giving him and his workers more manufactured goods than posts (Ferreira 1994:100). Post records indicate that he, like other men in his position, encouraged groups of workers to switch from tapping rubber for the SPI post to tapping for one of the local rubber-tapping companies (such as that of Renato Spinelli) (Dorilio 1954). In 1953 he was selected by Father Dornstauder, an Austrian Anchieta missionary, to translate Catholic doctrine for other Kawaiwete speakers. He was chosen, likely because he was already designated as a *capitão* and fully bilingual, but also because Sabino was in fact quite interested in Catholic spirituality and had developed a friendship with Father Dornstauder. After contacting remote groups living along the Peixes River for SPI in 1953, Sabino took Father Dornstauder to visit these groups in 1954 and 1955 (Dornstauder 1954:2; Meliá 1993:501). Sabino's early life and young adulthood was marked by a shuttling back and forth between remote villages uninterested in "contact" and villages that had relocated near posts and were involved in the debt-merchandise system of rubber tapping. It was also marked on the nonindigenous side by a movement between the SPI, rubber companies, and missions.

The Position of *Capitão*

Sabino said he was given the position of *capitão* by the SPI when his older brother who had had this position died. Prior to his brother, his uncle had also held this position (Ferreira 1994: 86, 89). The SPI established particular individuals as leaders in indigenous communities near posts so that they had an intermediary figure with whom they could conduct business. Prior to the existence of SPI, rubber traders had established certain indigenous men as *capitões* in the greater Tapajós area, and they functioned as intermediaries between groups of indigenous tappers and rubber companies (Murphy and Steward 1956). The French explorer Henri Coudreau, for example, describes meeting *capitões* among the Kawaiwete's neighbors, the Tupi-speaking Apiacá in 1895 (1941[1897]:101). Anthropologist Robert Murphy (Murphy and Steward 1956) comments that in the 1950s the nearby Tupian Munduruku had rubber-trader-appointed *capitões* at least as early as ninety years prior to his visit. He writes that they were at first distinguished from hereditary chiefs but by the 1950s had entirely replaced these chiefs all together.[8]

Prior to the active rubber trade in the Tapajós, the *capitão* position seems to have been established by the Brazilian government, though in this earlier period, *capitões* were nonindigenous men. English naturalist Henry Walker Bates describes meeting what he called "Captains of Trabalhadores" in 1852 on the Tapajós. These were men appointed by the Brazilian government to "embody the scattered Indian laborers and canoe-men of their respective districts" (Bates 1880:702). He continues, "A semi-military organization is given to the bodies, some of the steadiest among the Indians themselves being nominated as sergeants, and all the members mustered at the principal village of their district twice a year" (1880:702). By the time the SPI began to appoint Kawaiwete leaders in the 1930s, they were thus building on patterns set up by rubber companies and the earlier nineteenth-century Brazilian government.[9]

While *capitão* to whites in the 1940s and 1950s, Sabino reported that Kawaiwete often referred to him also as *wyriat*, a term that translates, "the owner or caretaker of a place."[10] In the early twentieth century a Kawaiwete *wyriat* was a very senior man who managed to keep his extended family, children, grandchildren, and great grandchildren living with him by virtue of his ability to provide for them. Some *wyriat*, reported in 1915 along the Teles Pires River, had several hundred people living in their large collective houses (Pyrineus de Sousa 1916).

Both the *capitão* and the *wyriat* positions rested on the control of labor and the redistribution of goods. A man could become a *wyriat* only once he had several children and his daughters began to be married. The institution of bride-service meant that a newly married son-in-law owed his wife's parents years of labor to pay for his wife, in the form of house building, hunting, fishing, and agricultural work. This labor was understood as paying the parents for the labor it took both to form the girl as a baby and to raise her as a child. The fish and game produced by these in-marrying young men were then redistributed in the form of cooked food by the *wyriat* and his wife. Ideally a *wyriat* would keep several generations of sons-in-laws in his household and perhaps even attract his own sons back with their wives and families after they had fulfilled their own bride-service (Oakdale 2005:36). To keep a number of generations working together required skill and charisma. *Wyriat* of the past were remembered in the 1990s as having the ability to talk all day, explaining to people how they should live. They were also supposed to be model workers, providing examples for others. In addition to these skills, they were to make life enjoyable, to have a good sense of humor, and to know how to encourage collective rituals.

Capitões appointed by rubber companies were also men who controlled the labor of young men and redistributed goods, though in this case the labor was largely the gathering of rubber and the goods were industrially produced items such as metal tools or clothing provided by rubber firms or the SPI. Murphy describes the Munduruku *capitão*'s authority and prestige as resting on his access to commercial goods. He writes that these men had more purchased goods than others and that "to increase the prestige of the trader-appointed chief, the trader often took his protégé on his annual trip to buy supplies in Belém, where the chief's position was confirmed by the governor or some other official" (Murphy and Steward 1956:342). In return, the *capitão* had "the onerous task of goading the people on to harder work in the rubber avenues" (1956:342). The SPI pursued this rubber company pattern with respect to the Kawaiwete as well. Sabino described going on a shopping trip in Cuiabá with SPI officials, much as Murphy described Munduruku *capitões* accompanying rubber traders in Belém (see Ferreira 1994:89).

The SPI, at least in the Kawaiwete case, also made the indigenous *capitão* a key figure in the pacification of remote, so-called hostile groups, those who had not settled at posts. "Pacification" was a SPI process that involved luring these groups to settle at posts by offering them gifts of industrially produced goods, particularly metal tools. Sabino describes how in 1953 he was told to go out and visit the still "unpacified" Peixes River Kawaiwete and give them gifts of knives and axes. Ultimately, through these goods, these groups were to be peaceably lured to posts and made into national workers. As Antônio Carlos de Souza Lima has pointed out, by becoming national workers, indigenous people were understood to be both joining contemporary history and the Brazilian nation (Lima 1992a:163, 1992b:254).

Despite the overlap between the *capitão* and the *wyriat* position with respect to the control of labor and the distribution of resources, these positions did not fit together seamlessly. Firstly, the position of *wyriat* was one attained only by senior men who had acquired a series of verbal skills in addition to having spent a significant amount of time as a parent and grandparent, maturing a family. Men in the *capitão* position, in contrast, were usually much younger, as these were the men who could speak Portuguese.[11]

The control of young men's labor and the redistribution of resources were also understood differently in these distinct social fields. In the context of the Kawaiwete household, both were understood to index a type of personally achieved social maturity, that a man had matured enough to understand how to lead people. In the social fields of the SPI and the rubber companies, they were interpreted as pointing to a collective type of social maturity, that the ethnic group as a whole was in

OAKDALE

the process of being brought into the national society, a process that unnaturally accelerated development, bringing them from "the stone age" or "historical stagnation" into "modernity" in one generation. During the 1930s the posts of "attraction" as well as posts of "vigilance and pacification" (for those people who had already been "attracted") were described, for example, by a Brazilian official as "awakening . . . peaceful, unarmed groups in their social infancy, the desire to participate with us in the progress that we have reached" (from Oliveira 1947:159, as quoted in Lima 1992a:166).

The control of young men's labor and the redistribution of resources were also understood in Kawaiwete local groups to be linked to self-sufficiency, that these men's households could function as a relatively self-contained unit on their own. In fact, Kawaiwete households often lived separate from one another, each as "its own village," as people in the Xingu explained to me. This self-sufficiency was also related to the leader being able to renew these resources through his hard work and charisma. In the social fields of the SPI and the rubber companies, the control of labor and especially the redistribution of resources was understood as part of becoming dependent on a huge political-economic structure, either that of the Brazilian nation or of the international rubber trade or both and, in the eyes of members of the national society, as leading to a much-needed end to local group autonomy. The resources on which this system was based were clearly not reproducible by leaders and were very much beyond their control, a situation of which Sabino at least in 1992 was well aware.

Sabino's Account of Being a *Capitão*

Sabino's recollections of being a *capitão* bring to the foreground the clash and dissonance of these logics in a very personal way. Sabino recalled the following about being appointed a *capitão* as a very young man.

Then at that time our chief died. He was my older brother. The chief in your white city [Cuiabá] called me and I went.

"Your chief has died," he said to me. "Your chief has died. Now you have to take his place," he said to me.

"No, no," I said to him. "I don't know how to work as a chief. I don't know how to speak like a chief," I said to him.

"No, you are definitely going to take over your brother's place," he said to me.

"No, no, no."

Then he got a little mad at me. "[If you do not take this position,] I will order you to go far away," he said to me, "from your children," he said to me.

The sense throughout this section of his narrative is that the developmental time of his life course was sped up, that he was forced to assume a position beyond his level of maturity and skill. He says, for example, to the SPI chief in Cuiabá, "I do not know how to work as a chief. I do not know how to speak like a chief," meaning that he had not learned these skills yet. Other Kawaiwete men have described growing up or "causing themselves to mature" as having been done by intentionally watching senior relatives in order to learn how to speak to people as a household leader. Here Sabino describes being rushed into the position of knowing how to speak and act like a chief before he was ready. At an earlier point in this story, after describing how the white chief of the post engaged him in all sorts of manual labor, he commented to me, "You whites who raise children don't let them grow up." This subjective sense of being rushed through the stages of the life course is consistent with the larger national project of encouraging indigenous people to enter into the process of human development, "helping" them to make up for centuries of lost time. In the initial portion of Sabino's autobiographical narrative (not included here), he recounts the "pacification" of the Kawaiwete over a long period of time as a process according to which Kawaiwete people are taught to eat increasingly more types of food much in the way that children slowly move from infancy into adulthood (see Oakdale 2008).

The second point of dissonance with respect to the *capitão* position for Sabino involves the erratic way goods and resources were controlled by SPI and rubber companies as well as their ultimate scarcity in contrast to the renewable nature of the resources on which a *wyriat* bases his authority. About his pacification trip to the Peixes River, Sabino recounted how he had been sent with too few industrially manufactured goods and so little food that he and his family starved along the way.

To return to Sabino's narrative (picking up where the last excerpt ended), he said the following:

> I returned to my village again. Then the [white] chief there said to me, "When you become chief do not stay still in one place. A chief should travel around a lot, guy. When you arrive [some-place] count two and two [four days]. Then you can go visit your [other] group. 'This is my group,' you think to yourself. You should go visiting with people. 'I am coming as a chief to see you,' you say to your people."
>
> I said to him, "That is good."
>
> "I hope you always do this," he said to me.
>
> [You know,] we like any sort of manufactured goods. Knives, we like any sort.
>
> Then I said to him, "Would you give me some [knives]? Would you give me some?" "These I will take directly up there [to his new group]," I said to him, to the chief.
>
> "That's good," he said to me.
>
> But the knives would not satisfy my whole group. The group was really large.
>
> "If this number of knives is not enough for everybody, I will come back to you," I said to him. "You will always give me help."
>
> "That's right," he said to me, lying to me.

Then I went home and I said to my wife, "Let's go visit our people." That is what I said to her.

Then I got ready to go. *Pooo* [the sound of getting ready] I was ready. I went walking without a trail. There wasn't one for me. I didn't take much food, only a little. Just like that without a trail I went. I went until I got to water. I got to the arm of the Teles Pires River. After that I went along next to the river. I was hungry. The manioc flour was all used up. The salt was used up. My shot was all used up. There was nothing I could do. I was stuck with just an ax.

[He continues here with a long account of how he and his family starved while on their way to the Peixes River.]

Sabino describes himself in this section as being duped into trusting that the SPI would provide the resources for him to be a successful leader (a *wyriat*) and provide and care for his Peixes River followers. As Sabino says, "The knives would not satisfy my whole group. The group was really large." In response to the scarcity of industrially manufactured goods, Sabino and his Peixes River relatives turned instead to Kawaiwete resources in order for Sabino to lay claim to *wyriat* status. This is initiated by the Peixes River people when they ask him to organize a festival of Jawosi singing for them.

Then the Kayabi took me, took me in the house. Then we slept. We slept [another night.] We slept and we slept. In the morning [of the fourth day] we went to visit other villages again. The next day I went to yet another village. There they called me *wyriat*."

"Is it true that you are a *wyriat*?"

"Yes, it is."

"Organize a Jawosi festival for us," they said to me.

Then I organized a Jawosi. I got a lot of people to come to it. Then I went visiting all those villages of the past. I went there and then I went over there. I was visiting all those people of the past.

Then I said, "I am going now, but I will come back again."

After a lot of time in the villages, I think about four months, I returned again to the Teles Pires. I went on the arm of the river, Jatwar'y [a small river that flows into the Teles Pires River]. Then I arrived at the mouth of the river again. I arrived where the people used to live on the Teles Pires again. I came to where people lived on the mouth of the river. From there I went upriver to see all those who used to live there. I arrived at other villages. I came to one and I came to another. Then I left that one. I went to the city following the river. *Woòoa.* [It took a long time.]

Jawosi requires a high level of commitment on the part of the local group, especially the women. This sort of singing can be done only if the women are consulted by the organizer of the ritual and a significant number of them agree to participate as a chorus. This chorus then asks each adult man to sing for it and accompanies the lead singers for several hours each night over the course of several weeks. While not described, the chain of requests involved in Jawosi singing would be called to mind by most listeners and is a sharp contrast with the very limited support Sabino received from SPI. Kawaiwete tradition, such as Jawosi, is portrayed here as a stable, dependable resource in contrast to commercial goods, which are in short supply and easily exhausted. Leadership based only on these goods supplied by SPI is portrayed as ultimately untenable.

Sabino's reliance on the distinctively Kawaiwete resource of Jawosi also meant that one of the first SPI "pacification" missions to the Peixes River Kawaiwete was done, ironically, through a celebration of warfare, for Jawosi songs feature stylized accounts of Kawaiwete warriors encountering enemies whom they ultimately vanquish. Sabino's 1953 visit based on this celebration of Kawaiwete warrior exploits also later paved the way for Father Dornstauder's visits in 1954 and 1955 to these same villages.

Making this same point concerning the fragility of access to non-Kawaiwete resources, the next exploit Sabino described is a failed expedition to tap rubber. Sabino organized workers to tap for rubber companies as well as SPI. Here the mention of the shortwave radio suggests he was working for the SPI in this instance. Picking up the narrative where the last excerpt ended, I quote,

> Then I went back to my village. [There, I stayed.] I selected workers there. I got a group of young, unmarried men together. "Let's go see the chief," I said. "I'm going to bring you," I said to my workers, to my relatives, followers, employees. I said to my employees, my many employees, "Let's go."
>
> Then after a while a boat filled with other whites came. I embarked on that one. My wife came with me too. The wife that is with me now. Then my son came in the middle of the big river. He was born in the middle of the trip. That one who is living here. My son was born to me. Then I took that baby, I took that baby far. *Wooo.* I took him until I came to my village.
>
> Then I took his mother with me, far away to the whites' lands. It did not work out very well. I arrived at the 'Ypytang [Red River]. There I stayed with my group of workers. I spoke by radio with the chief. Then the chief responded back to me by radio.
>
> He responded, "You are bringing your workers. Do not bring them. Do not bring them. There is not enough supplies or money," he said to me.
>
> "You are bringing them only to suffer hunger," he said to me, he emphasized to me.
>
> Then I responded, "Why did you let me go? Is there really nothing?"
>
> "Your workers will suffer hunger," [he said.]
>
> Then to another one of the whites I said, "I am going to go back."
>
> I really got mad at them [because of this]. "Because of this I am going to leave the chieftainship. I do not want to stay being a chief. The position doesn't allow me to visit the city [to buy supplies]," I said.

Then I said to some of them, to my workers, "I am going to leave the chieftainship."

"No, no don't leave. Keep on visiting our people, your people and your wife's people."

Then I said to myself, "Things are okay."

Here again, the supplies and support at least tacitly promised to Sabino are revoked and his boss warns him that he will be hungry. Either fluctuations in the demand for rubber or in SPI funding during this period might have explained the cancelation of this trip (see Hemming 2003:217 on the SPI during this period). Whatever the case, the erratic nature of SPI and the larger national economy contrasts with the renewability of Kawaiwete resources, this time, the goodwill and support of relatives and followers.

Conclusion

The indigenous *capitão* was a position that fit with indigenous patterns of leadership in that a *capitão* controlled the labor of young men and redistributed goods like the *wyriat*, a household or residential group leader, though the resources the *capitão* distributed were typically commodities, rather than cooked game, mature counsel, and the orchestration of rituals. Sabino's autobiographical narrative provides some purchase on the experience of inhabiting this position that was a part of so many social fields. While he was not completely fluent in all the different ways that the *capitão* position was perceived by different social sectors, he understood enough to sense that the way in which this position brought social fields and logics together did not result in a seamless fit. While "creative misunderstanding" may have been "put to work" in this Amazonian context as White (2006) concludes happened in the seventeen and eighteenth centuries around the North American Great Lakes, they did not function or "work" without personal cost. Sabino felt the stress of becoming a leader too soon and of having his resources dependent on the erratic funding of the SPI and the fluctuating price of rubber. These "misunderstandings" created a dissonance at the level of individual experience, a dissonance that when recounting his experiences in 1992 he was able to consciously evaluate.

Sabino's stories about these experiences as well as those of other people in similar positions may have been important forces in shaping these peoples' move to the Xingu Park in the following decades. Stories about the fickle nature of the larger political economy may also have played a role in encouraging Kawaiwete people to revive and invest in ritual life in the park, which they continue to do with great enthusiasm. The Xingu Park administration also emphasized the cultivation of indigenous tradition from its inception and was in a sense a space set up as a critique of the state policies of rapid, forced acculturation of indigenous peoples. My point with these suggestions about the possible impact of Sabino's recollections is that if cultural production is to be set within "the frame of encounter" of ethnic groups or social fields, a perspective Philip Deloria (2006) has seen as being opened up by White's concept of the "middle ground," then personal memories concerning the lack of fit and dissonance between cultural perspectives in this encounter are as important as the way these misunderstandings "work." These memories of dissonance, recounted by people like Sabino, may drive the choices of later generations with respect to how they will participate in new sorts of "middle grounds."

Acknowledgments

An earlier version of this essay, titled "The Formation of a Kaiabi Leader in the Mid-Twentieth-Century Brazilian Frontier," has been published in the Proceedings of the Tenth International Congress of the Brazilian Studies Association, Brasília, July 22–24, 2010. I would like to thank Jane Landers and Judy Bieber for their comments on this essay and their invitation to participate in their session at this meeting. I would also like to thank Centro Burnier Fé e Justiça, Cuiabá MT for allowing me access to Father Dornstauder's letters and reports and the Museu do Índio in Rio de Janeiro for access to its archive. The Latin American and Iberian Institute at the University of New Mexico provided the funding for these research trips in 2004 and 2007. In the 1990s my field research was supported by grants from the Fulbright Institute of International Education and the Wenner-Gren Foundation. I am very grateful to Aturi and Mairata for their work teaching me how to transcribe and translate Sabino's recorded narrative. Finally, I thank Sabino and his family for sharing part of their lives with me as well as their unending hospitality during my stay in their village.

Notes

1. They use the term "assemblage" in the phrase "global assemblage" to discuss how "global" phenomena (such as international standards or scientific knowledge) are articulated in specific situations with other, more local logics.

2. While individuals have changed their surnames from "Kayabi" to "Kaiabi" and the ethnic group as a whole has recently changed its name to "Kawaiwete," throughout the twentieth century they were known largely as "Kayabi" or "Caiabi."

3. As well as tributaries of the Arinos River, which flows into the Jure-ena, which then flows into the Tapajós.

4. Because of World War II the demand for rubber increased in the Teles Pires area after 1942, after having tapered off prior to 1920 at the conclusion of the first rubber boom (Grünberg 2004). After the war the price of rubber was artificially inflated by the Brazilian government, and it was used in the production of tires for the expanding Brazilian auto industry (see Dean 1987).

5. For them the copresence of multiple logics or forms allows actors to call into question the global forms.

6. Many of the stories narrated over the course of this program were circulated in the form of a mimeographed newsletter (Ferreira 1994:8). Ferreira subsequently published in 1994 Sabino's "life history," or "A História de Minha Vida" in Portuguese within *Histórias do Xingu*, a book that includes stories from many indigenous individuals residing in the Xingu.

7. These posts were built in 1922 on the Verde River and in 1925 on the Teles Pires (Grünberg 2004:57).

8. In the 1950s, as Munduruku people pursued their own exchanges with traders, Munduruku *capitões* were beginning to be selected by SPI agents and missionaries to function as intermediaries for them rather than having any role in the rubber trade (Murphy and Steward 1956:343).

9. The Kawaiwete, entered rubber tapping in 1927 (Grünberg 2004) and may have had *capitões* appointed by rubber companies at that point as well.

10. Father Dornstauder refers to Sabino in the 1950s as "Capitão Sabino" as do many of the post records (Dornstauder 1954, 1955). In the Kawaiwete's own language, *capitão* was often substituted with *wyriat* when people referred to Sabino.

11. Murphy suggests that indigenous *capitões* among the Munduruku were usually younger men as well (Murphy and Steward 1956:342).

Bibliography

Bates, Henry Walter
  1880 The Naturalist on the River Amazons. New York: J. Fitzgerald.
Collier, Steven, and Aihwa Ong
  2005 Global Assemblages, Anthropological Problems. *In* Global Assemblages: Technology, Politics, and Ethics as Anthropological Problems. Steven Collier and Aihwa Ong, eds. Pp. 3–21. Malden MA: Blackwell.
Conklin, Beth, and Laura Graham
  1995 The Shifting Middle Ground: Amazonian Indians and Eco-Politics. American Anthropologist 97(4):695–710.
Cooms, Oliver T., and Bradford L. Barham
  1994 The Amazon Rubber Boom: Labor Control, Resistance, and Failed Plantation Development Revisited. Hispanic American Historical Review 74(2):231–57.
Coudreau, Henri
  1941[1897] Viagem ao Tapajos, 28 julho de 1895–7 de janeiro de 1896. A. Miranda Bastos, trans. São Paulo: Companhia Editoria Nacional.
Dean, Warren
  1987 Brazil and the Struggle for Rubber. Cambridge: Cambridge University Press.
Deloria, Philip
  2006 What Is the Middle Ground, Anyway? William and Mary Quarterly, 3rd ser., 63(4):15–22.
Dorilio, Jair
  1954 Letter dated April 12, 1954. Microfilm 0025, 205. Archives of the Museu do Índio, Rio de Janeiro, Brazil.
Dornstauder, Father João
  1954 Resumo 1954. Fasísculo 14. Centro Burnier Fé e Justiça, Cuiabá, Brazil.

1955 Viagem ao TATUI. Fasísculo 16. Centro Burnier Fé e Justiça, Cuiabá, Brazil.

Ferreira, Marianna Kawall Leal
1994 Histórias do Xingu. São Paulo: Fundação de Amparo á Pesquisa do Estado de São Paulo.

Grünberg, Georg
2004 Os Kayabi do Brasil central. São Paulo: Instituto Socioambietal.

Hemming, John
2003 Die if You Must. London: Macmillan.

Hill, Jonathan, and Fernando Santos-Granero, eds.
2002 Comparative Arawakan Histories. Urbana: University of Illinois Press.

Lima, Antonio Carlos de Souza
1992a O Governo dos Índios sob a Gestão do SPI. In História dos Índios no Brasil. Manuela Carneiro da Cunha, ed. Pp. 155–72. São Paulo: Editora Schwarcz.
1992b On Indigenism and Nationality in Brazil. In Nation-States and Indians in Latin America. Greg Urban and Joel Sherzer, eds. Pp. 236–58. Austin: University of Texas Press.

Meliá, Father Bartolomé
1993 Os Caiabis Não-xinguanos. In Karl von den Steinen: Um Século de Antropologis no Xingu. Vera Penteado, ed. Pp. 485–510. São Paulo: Editora da Universidade de São Paulo.

Murphy, Robert F., and Julian Steward
1956 Tappers and Trappers: Parallel Processes in Acculturation. Economic Development and Cultural Change 4(4):335–55.

Nugent, Stephen
1993 Amazonian Caboclo Society: An Essay on Invisibility and Peasant Economy. Oxford: Berg.

Oakdale, Suzanne
2005 I Foresee My Life: The Ritual Performance of Autobiography in an Amazonian Community. Lincoln: University of Nebraska Press.
2008 The Commensality of "Contact," "Pacification" and Inter-Ethnic Relations in the Amazon: Kayabi Autobiographical Perspectives. Journal of the Royal Anthropological Institute 14(4):791–807.

Oliveira, Humberto de
1947 Coletânea de leis, atos e memorias referentes ao indígena brasileiro. Conselho Nacional de Proteção aos Índios 94. Rio de Janeiro: Imprensa Nacional.

Pyrineus de Sousa, Antonio
1916 Exploração do Rio Paranatinga. Publicação 34, Anexo 2. Rio de Janeiro: Comimissão de Linhas Telegraphicas Estrategicas de Matto-Grosso ao Amazonas.

Viveiros de Castro, Eduardo
  1992 From the Enemy's Point of View. Chicago: University of Chicago
  Press.
Weinstein, Barbara
  1986 Persistence of Precapitalist Relations of Production in a Tropical Export Economy: The Amazon Rubber Trade, 1850–1920. *In*
  Proletarians and Protest: The Roots of Class Formation in an Indus-
  trializing World. Michael Hanagan and Charles Stephenson, eds. Pp.
  64–69. New York: Greenwood Press.
White, Richard
  1991 The Middle Ground: Indians, Empires, and Republics in the
  Great Lakes Region, 1650–1815. Cambridge: Cambridge University
  Press.
  2006 Creative Misunderstandings and New Understandings. William
  and Mary Quarterly, 3rd ser., 63(1):9–14.

Fluid Subjectivity

*Reflections on Self and Alternative Futures in the
Autobiographical Narrative of Hiparidi Top'tiro,
a Xavante Transcultural Leader*

LAURA R. GRAHAM

Walking back from the river with a group of women and
children one July afternoon in 1984 in the central Brazilian
Xavante community of Eténhiritipa Pimentel Barbosa, I heard
the mournful sound of a woman's ceremonial keening. "E tiha?"
I asked my companions, "What is it?" "Da-wawa, watsini hã
te ti-nho're ti'ra dzo." (It's keening. Our in-law is keening for
her son.) I walked across the central plaza to the house from
which the lament emanated, and a small group of children
who had assembled to witness the excitement motioned me
to go inside. There, sounded by her sisters and other children
on her sleeping mat sat Zefa, tears streaming down her face as
she lovingly stroked the head, arms, and legs of a small boy,
also crying. He was Canambre, the six-year-old son that Zefa
had told me about with pride a year earlier and who, despite
residing in the community for nearly six months, I had never
met. Canambre was one of a small group of boys chosen by
the elder men to study in Riberão Preto, a city in the interior
of São Paulo State over a thousand kilometers away.[1] Zefa's
emotion was palpable in her tuneful lament. I could feel her
release the pent-up grief that had accumulated during the six
months since she had seen her last-born child.

Beginning in the late 1970s, sending boys to live among the
waradzu (non-Indians)—to learn to speak, read, and write Portuguese and to manage numbers—has been a fundamental pil-

lar in strategies some Xavante communities have developed for coping with the dramatic changes that accompany their decisions to enter into peaceful relationships with and live within Brazilian society.[2] During each major school holiday for the next eleven years, until Canambre made the transition back to living full time in Eténhiritipa Pimentel Barbosa, his "adopted *waradzu* family" returned him to his natal community, and the emotional reunion I witnessed in July 1984 was repeated. Like other Xavante boys who have gone to live in Brazilian cities "to learn the ways of the whites,"[3] Canambre was initiated into the *hö* (bachelors' hut) and became part of an age set; he participated in the major ceremonials and activities that, over time, molded him into a Xavante man. Yet he was different. He lived in, across, and between lifeworlds (George 2010), and transitioning between them was difficult for him, for his Xavante family, and no doubt for his "adopted" *waradzu* family.[4]

While the situation of each is unique, transcultural Xavante boys such as Canambre who were (and are) sent to study in Brazilian cities experience exceptional social and psychological pressures as they live and move within, across, and between two distinct social worlds. In both places they are different, unlike their peers. In the city they are both exotic and strange, sometimes celebrated as icons of romanticized Indians and also subject to discrimination and prejudice, the teasing and taunting of other children. And in Xavante communities, although they retain strong ties with their families and participate in many of the ceremonials that socialize them into cohorts, these boys are nevertheless unhinged from the routine mentoring, social formations, and activities that cement male bonds and provide structure and support for adolescents as they transition into adulthood (see Maybury-Lewis 1974; Graham 1995; Welch 2010). These boys are *chosen* to be different; then they are groomed to become go-betweens, to mediate relations and transactions between Xavante and the Brazilian society that increasingly threatens to engulf them.[5]

These boys also live with the stress of tremendous expectations. Their elders expect them, sooner or later, to step into prominent leadership roles in which they will negotiate the increasingly complex challenges that contemporary Xavante face as they seek to sustain their identity and culture within an uncertain and rapidly changing world; the region they inhabit has, over the last twenty years, rapidly transformed to become Brazil's largest soy-producing and exporting area. Elders' expectations put enormous pressure on these youth. This is exacerbated by the fact that these boys have had few, if any, role models who provide positive examples of becoming and being transcultural, living in and across the physical and social divide between "the city" and community life.

Autobiographical narratives recounted by Xavante men who, as boys, were sent to Brazilian cities to live and study among the *waradzu* provide glimpses into the experience of indigenous youth and leaders who move between worlds (Karttunen 1994). These narratives offer windows into the subjective experiences associated with being dislocated from the local community, its ceremonial life, and social formations; facing the challenges of life in the city; and moving between social worlds. In 2000 and 2001 I recorded autobiographical narratives recounted by Hiparidi Top'tiro, a visionary Xavante leader and activist from the Sangradouro Indigenous Territory. Hiparidi's narratives reveal the stress associated with his attempts to cope with the terrific expectations of self, family, and community that young indigenous leaders confront along the way.

I solicited Hiparidi's narratives in the context of research I was conducting to understand Xavante efforts to project their culture into national and international arenas, something to which several communities increasingly devoted themselves beginning in the mid-1990s (see, for example, Serebu'rã et al. 1997; Núcleo de Cultura Indígena 1994; Graham 2005, 2014). At the time I recorded his narratives, Hiparidi had received his undergraduate degree from the University of São Paulo (USP), with a major in anthropology, and was a graduate student at the Catholic University in São Paulo (PUC). Hiparidi is among the first group of Xavante to graduate from high school and the first Xavante to graduate with a bachelor's degree from a major Brazilian university.[6] Given my interests in cultural outreach and performance, Hiparidi came to my attention because he was then active in coordinating cultural events at PUC and USP, as well as in other public spaces, to bring support and attention to projects he and others were implementing in his community.

In 1996 Hiparidi along with members of his family had taken the bold step of severing from the Salesian mission community in Sangradouro and founding a new community, which they called Idzö'uhu (Abelinha in Portuguese or Little Bee in English). Although fissioning to establish new communities is a well-documented pattern among Xavante groups (see Maybury-Lewis 1974; Graham 1987, 1995:50–55) at the time of this move, no other group had left the mission community at Sangradouro since Xavante had taken refuge there in the late 1950s, a subject to which I return later. This group's establishment of Idzö'uhu was a deliberate and powerful rejection of the Salesians, the Catholic Church, and also choices made by Xavante who lived in the mission community.

Simultaneously with the founding of Idzö'uhu, Hiparidi established, and became president of, the Xavante Warã Association (Associação Xavante Warã, henceforth Warã).[7] The purpose of this nongovernmental organization (NGO) was to sponsor, receive, and channel funds to support community projects such as beekeeping (Associação Xavante Warã n.d.), building and maintaining a school, and the development of pedagogical materials.[8] It also sponsored cultural events in Brazilian cities.[9] At the time Warã located its administrative headquarters in São Paulo, and Hiparidi moved and worked between the metropolis and Idzö'uhu. In the years since

Hiparidi founded Warã, he has become increasingly active as an indigenous-rights advocate. He has also extended his work beyond Idzö'uhu; he now works to unite Xavante and mobilize other indigenous groups in efforts to protect their traditions and lands from the devastation of massive agribusiness in the central Brazilian *cerrado* (savanna). Hiparidi is visible as an indigenous and environmental activist on the national scene.

The autobiographical narratives he recounted emphasize the psychological struggles he experienced during childhood and adolescence and his reflexive critiques. His story illuminates the difficulties he had moving between Xavante society, which emphasizes collective identity and solidarity during youth and adolescence, and life in Brazilian cities, where he stood out for his uniqueness and difference and, as a result, experienced both prejudice and admiration. In both narratives, as his story progresses, it merges into discussion of the work he was doing at the time of his narrative and his plans for future projects. It reveals that his involvement in collaborative projects on behalf of his community have helped him resolve this tension. Even now, years later, Hiparidi continues to experience the tremendous stress that accompanies his role as a transcultural community leader. He lives with the unceasing pressure of high expectations, both from himself, family members, and other Xavante, as well as a multiplicity of non-Xavante expectations.

Crises of Subjectivity: Paths to Alternative Perspectives

Hiparidi was born in 1970 in the Xavante community of Sangradouro. He is the last of five children born to Top'tiro and Batika Dzutsi'wa. Hiparidi's autobiographical accounts of his childhood and youth revolve around a central trope that I call "crises of subjectivity." He emphasizes moments of extreme stress and confusion, then resolution that develops from his recognition and eventual acceptance of leadership and advocacy roles, informed by his understanding that

Xavante leadership ultimately involves collaboration and shared responsibility. I suggest that Hiparidi's moments of confusion and stress are effects of the dislocations, discrimination as well as exoticization and its allure, or "seduction" as Hiparidi terms it, and the liminal status that he experienced—indeed still experiences—while living "between worlds." I propose that these "crisis moments" provided critical opportunities, for they are contexts in which Hiparidi developed critiques of the social conditions that existed in his community and of *waradzu* (non-Xavante) institutions, especially the Salesian mission that dominated life in Sangradouro. These critiques have guided and informed Hiparidi's subsequent work. Moreover, these crises and the critiques that emerged from them enabled Hiparidi to imagine alternative possibilities for Xavante futures and to develop ideas and paths for potential change. Indeed Hiparidi has acted upon these imaginings, and they continue to inform his life's work.

Eduardo Viveiros de Castro (1998) and others (see, for example, Vilaça 2000) suggest that the ability to adopt different perspectives is a fundamental existential paradigm of native Amazonian social experience. The disposition to view the world they inhabit from different vantage points is an integral part of native Amazonians' social experience. Inspired by this idea, I suggest that the subjective crises that Hiparidi experienced during his youth enabled him to rotate his perspective; through them he began to view conditions in his community, especially the role of the Salesian mission at Sangradouro, in new ways. The turbulent moments that Hiparidi lived while moving between social worlds provoked him to critically reflect on the conditions in the Sangradouro community, as well as on the Xavante's circumstances within broader social, economic, and political arenas. I suggest that during his adolescence, when he was relatively detached from the firm social grounding that roots Xavante males' experience within their communities, Hiparidi experienced crises that afforded him new vantage points and opportunities for looking in fresh ways at life in his community and at Xavante circumstances in general. Hiparidi emerged from these crises with critiques of the missionaries who influenced much of Xavante life within Sangradouro during his childhood, of state institutions and policies that oppress Xavante, and of the social and economic situation in which Xavante live.

Xavante and the Sangradouro Context

Xavante are a central Brazilian Ge-speaking people who today number approximately 15,315 people (Instituto Socioambiental 2013). They now live in more than two hundred autonomous communities dispersed across separate indigenous territories in eastern Mato Grosso State. Before contact Hiparidi's parents and grandparents lived in a region known as Parabubure that lies along the margins of the Couto Magalhães River, a tributary to the Xingu River.[10] For two decades beginning in the late 1940s, when the Brazilian state targeted the area Xavante inhabit for colonization and capitalist expansion, Xavante groups experienced violent clashes with settlers who were moving into their lands. Hiparidi's mother, Batika Dzusti'wa, still has a bullet in her thigh from a gunshot wound she received as a girl during a settler's attack in the mid-1950s.

In the midst of these hostilities, Batika Dzusti'wa's father had a dream in which he saw a tall tree in a peaceful locale. Guided by this dream, he led his family to the place of his vision. According to Hiparidi, when the group found the tall tree, his grandfather announced, "This is the place I saw in my dream. Here we can live in peace."[11] The tree was located next to the Salesian mission at Sangradouro, and despite their rivalry with the Bororo Indians, whom the Sangradouro mission originally served, the beleaguered Xavante settled adjacent to the mission along with other Xavante refugees who came seeking shelter.[12] Decimated by violence and measles epidemics and exhausted from their search for shelter, the beleaguered Xavante acquiesced to Salesian catechism in exchange for succor.

Salesians discouraged social practices and ceremonies that they deemed immoral and inappropriate for the Christian subjects they were forming. They opposed polygamy and the women's naming ceremonial, *pi'õ nhitsi*, which involves extra-conjugal sexual relations. The Salesians collected and sold artisanal work, and like the government agencies in charge of Xavante nonmission areas (the Indian Protection Service, SPI, and later the National Indian Foundation, FUNAI, which replaced the SPI in 1967), the Salesians actively endeavored to transform the traditionally seminomadic hunter-gatherer Xavante into Western-style farmers.[13] They forced them to work in gardens and in the late 1970s and 1980s introduced a massive project of mechanized rice cultivation (see Graham 1995; Garfield 2001). Mario Juruna, a famous Xavante leader from São Marcos, deplored the Salesians' treatment of mission Xavante and accused them of practicing slavery (Juruna et al. 1982).

One of the most effective strategies that Salesians employed to indoctrinate Xavante was taking control of the bachelors' hut, the *hö*. This is perhaps the most important institution for the education and social formation of Xavante boys (see Maybury-Lewis 1974). Depending on their physical size and maturity, Xavante boys between the ages of eight and eleven are initiated into the *hö*; these boys become part of an age set at this time and are known as *wapté*, or members of the pre-initiate age grade. They are also designated "residents of the bachelors' hut," or *hö'wa*. During this pre-initiate phase, boys live apart from the rest of the community for a period of approximately two to five years.

Separated from their natal families during the *wapté* phase, pre-initiate boys learn everything they need to know to become fully social adult men during this period of seclusion.[14] The *wapté* are assigned to a group of senior mentors who are responsible for teaching them skills for life in the *cerrado*, or *'ro* as Xavante call the physical and spiritual environment they inhabit. With their mentor-sponsors the *wapté* learn how to hunt, fish, make camp, and cook. The mentors also subject their young charges to various tests that build the strength, stamina, and cooperative skills that are necessary to physical and spiritual well-being. *Wapté* also participate in numerous collective activities with their mentors; they regularly perform *da-ño're*, a form of collective song and dance, which they often practice in the middle of the night, under the hot sun as well as during rainstorms. Through their participation in these activities, boys develop a strong corporate identity that gives each a firm sense of his place both within his age set as well as within society as a whole (see Graham 1994, 1995). *Wapté* also learn about Xavante spirituality and how to mediate relations with the ancestors and other spirits who are part of the Xavante lifeworld. Thus the period of boy's semi-isolation and bachelors' hut residency is extremely important in the social and spiritual formation of Xavante boys.

The Salesians at Sangradouro co-opted the institution of the *hö* by merging it with their educational and religious assignment. They implemented a boarding-school experience in mission communities and moved the *wapté* into the mission. Because *wapté* traditionally live in a separate house apart from the semicircular ring of houses that forms a traditional Xavante village, the bachelors' hut institution could be conveniently adapted to fit the Salesians' boarding school. When the *wapté's* mentors and senior men came to visit and orient their youth, their activities were subject to the Salesians' supervision, oversight, and control. By incorporating the bachelors' hut into the boarding school, Salesians spatially and experientially dominated the creation of male social subjects and undermined senior Xavante men's control over the physical, social, and spiritual formation of younger generations. Even after Vatican II in 1964, which mandated greater respect for indigenous cultures and practices, the Sangradouro boarding school continued to function as the *hö* until 1978. All boys in Sangradouro were secluded in the mission school during their *wapté* phase.

Hiparidi attended the Salesians' school. As a child he did not have a developed critique of the institution, but the dislocation that he experienced from his natal community that came when he was sent to study among *waradzu* afforded him the opportunity to reflect on the Salesians' control over Xavante socialization. The critique he developed of the Salesians has informed much of his life's work, as we shall see in Hiparidi's autobiographical narrative. In narrating his life story, Hiparidi points to significant disjunctures between Xavante ways of being, thinking, and self-expression, and the waradzu values he was encountering during the unusual (from a Xavante point of view) life experiences he had at specific life phases and historical moments. Hiparidi points to a series of confused moments during his early life, then again during his adolescence when he moved between the city and his natal community. Eventually, as we shall see, Hiparidi succeeded in establishing a balance between his urban and community identities as he assumed a role as an organizer and architect of political events and, more recently, Xavante and interethnic social movements. According to his narrative he proposed the formation of a new community that would be completely autonomous and separate from Salesian presence or influence; members of his family followed through and made this into a reality by establishing Idzö'uhu. As this idea was fulfilled through others' actions, he became increasingly integrated, both within himself and into his community. As he worked to advance projects in the new community he helped to found, he has achieved a balance between competing pressures and become more comfortable in his role as a transcultural go-between.[15]

Fig. 3. Hiparidi Top'tiro at a 2006 protest in Nova Xavantina, Mato Grosso. (Courtesy of David Hernández Palmar)

Hiparidi's Autobiographical Narrative

In what follows I present excerpts of the autobiographical narratives that Hiparidi recounted to me in 2000 and 2001 along with analytic commentary.[16] To highlight his voice and to separate it from my own, I have chosen to put Hiparidi's words into block quotations. I draw primarily from the 2000 narrative, using excerpts from the other in only a few places to clarify points that he elaborated more fully in the second narrative.[17] I have not included my own comments, which primarily seek clarification of points and do not alter the narrative flow.

Hiparidi frames his biographical narrative within the tumultuous postcontact period. It is notable that the theme of disruption and confusion recurs throughout the narrative of his childhood and adolescence. This is resolved as Hiparidi assumes a leadership role and begins to take action that, informed by the critiques he develops through adopting alternative critical perspectives, seeks to improve Xavante's contemporary conditions. Toward the end of his narrative, he deemphasizes his individual responsibility, as well as accountability, and recognizes actions as cooperative achievements, even through the use of pronominal forms. Hiparidi's narrative thus illustrates a distancing from his focus on individuality, which he emphasizes in the account of his "seduction" by the city and its values, and movement into a Xavante frame of mind with an increasing emphasis on a collaborative leadership style (see Graham 1993).

Hiparidi begins his narrative by underscoring the confusion he experienced as a boy living in the context of what he increasingly came to understand as an oppressive Salesian regime. He speaks of his childhood as a period of general "disorganization," a turbulent time when "our parents were really disgusted." At the time, however, he had not yet developed the critical framework in which to understand or express his feelings as critique. In the following excerpt, the opening of his autobiographical narrative, we can feel Hiparidi's resentment of the Salesians; his cynicism is pointed, especially in statements such as, "[The Salesians] think it is nice when everyone [all the innocent children] goes to church."

Childhood and Early Adolescence:
Developing Critiques of the Salesians

I was born in Sangradouro. When I was born in Sangradouro it was a very difficult moment because the Salesians controlled everything. Our parents were really disgusted because the Salesians wanted to change our lives.

I heard this a lot: our mothers are still revolted, our parents, because the Salesians raped them. This is true. So I was born in a difficult time.

I was born in the decade of the 1970s, when everything was really disorganized, with the religion and with the Salesians. I was, in fact, educated by the Salesians.

I studied in a Salesian school. My brother taught my class.[18]

I didn't actually have class with the Salesians, but I went to a Salesian school in the mission at Sangradouro. I completed fifth grade. When I was there, the school went to fifth grade.

I went to church like all the innocent children. We had to go. [The Salesians] think it is nice when everyone goes to church.

I began to notice some things when I became a *ritai'wa* [novitiate]. I began to resist more. Then they [the Salesians] started to exclude me. I started to have problems with other people. They [the Salesians] pitted us one against the other. We couldn't speak about this because we were *'ritai'wa* adolescents.[19]

As Hiparidi entered adolescence, the novitiate phase that Xavante call *'ritai'wa*, he began to perceive the disjuncture between Xavante ways of teaching and raising children and the Salesian educational regime. He was beginning to develop a critique of the Salesians and their work, and he began to resist. His commentary suggests that he saw the coexistence with the Salesians as one that "created problems among Xavante." He states that the Salesians pitted Xavante against each other. His comment, "We couldn't speak about this because we were *'ritai'wa* adolescents," expresses the frustration he felt because of his obligation to follow Xavante rules: as a *'ritai'wa*, a member of the novitiate age grade, he was not allowed to speak in public. *'Ritai'wa* must be humble and do not have a public voice. Hiparidi occupied a life-cycle phase for which Xavante etiquette prescribes silence just as he was beginning to develop a critique of the Salesian regime. Hiparidi could not express his ideas or comment on the oppression he was beginning to notice. Instead he internalized the critique. His growing resentment of the Salesians and his inability to speak is one reason why he considers his childhood "traumatic."

I began to reflect on all of these things. My childhood was traumatic. It was traumatic [because of this conflict over the Salesians].

Today I don't like the church. I don't even want to hear about it because I was traumatized in one major way: We were forced to go to church. And if you didn't go, you were expelled from school.

This still happens even today in the Salesian schools. If you don't pray you are expelled from school. You are discriminated against.

They [the fathers] screened films [of Xavante celebrations]. [They said,] "If you don't go to church, you can't watch this film!" So this was a difficult moment for me.

In the preceding excerpt Hiparidi recounts some of the ways he perceived the Salesians as coercive; he speaks of their "forcing" Xavante to follow their rules. Children who did not go to church were threatened with expulsion from school. Salesians also bribed Xavante to go to church by showing films that Salesians had made of Xavante ceremonials in Sangradouro and in São Marcos, the other mission community.[20] If a child didn't go to church, she or he could not see the films, which of course all Xavante wanted to see. Hiparidi objected to these forms of seduction and coercion and was increasingly troubled by the Salesians control over life in Sangradouro. His distaste for the Salesians and the ways he saw them manipulating Xavante is unmistakable in his speech.

Adolescence: Study in the City and the Stress of Not Fitting

Since the Salesian school in Sangradouro went only to fifth grade, elders sent some young boys to the nearby Brazilian city of Barra do Garças to continue their studies. This frontier town's economy centers around agro-industry and promoting frontier expansion and development. It was not a welcoming place for Xavante.

The leaders, the elders, wanted the boys to continue their studies. They sent us to Barra [do Garças]. We were sent to Barra, Barra do Garças for one year. There were just a few of us. There was no structure. And so we came back. No one wanted to stay there because there weren't any other indigenous people. It wasn't a place for Indians anyway.

In Barra do Garças and also the town of Primavera do Leste that he had to pass through en route, Hiparidi first experienced discrimination. Unmoored from his family and community and the firm grounding of Xavante social relationships, he found these experiences particularly disorienting. They were exacerbated because he was severed from the ceremonial activities that give support to and structure adolescent *'ritai'wa* life within Xavante communities. There were no mentors, no one from his sponsor group, to counsel or guide him.

> I was insecure. I confronted preconceived notions from our neighbors in the city, in Primavera [do Leste] and in Barra do Garças. There is a tremendous prejudice against us. It is really strong. I was very young.
>
> So, when I entered into the middle of that [*waradzu*] society, I cut my hair just like the *waradzu*. I was really young. And young people don't know what to do. Do you understand? Even though I was a *'ritai'wa* [when Xavante admire physical beauty and long hair], I cut my hair to fit [into *waradzu* society].

Hiparidi speaks of being "insecure" and succumbing to pressure "to fit in" to the *waradzu* lifeworld. His decision to cut his hair Western style demonstrates how much pressure he felt to conform, "to fit in." He took a deliberate decision not to show signs of his Xavante identity, for coiffure has particular social significance in Xavante society, indeed in Ge societies in general. One's haircut signals one's identity as Xavante, and manipulations of hair mark significant social transitions (see Maybury-Lewis 1974). Hiparidi's decision to abandon his Xavante haircut underscores his desire to look like a *waradzu* instead of a Xavante.

Despite his Western haircut, Hiparidi experienced discrimination. He says his mind "exploded" from all the stress. In retrospect, speaking from the present vantage point, Hiparidi conveys the impression that this explosion, while a painful crisis moment, provided him with the ability to see Xavante conditions in Sangradouro in new ways. He began to look at things in his community from a different vantage point. And at this point, as Hiparidi adopted a new perspective, he began to develop a critique of the Salesians and conditions in Sangradouro. The stress he experienced, this "explosion," enabled him to eventually develop significant critiques that have, in fact, informed his adult leadership work.

> I studied there. I stayed one whole year in Barra do Garças, When I was an adolescent ['ritai'wa]. That was when my head exploded. I think it was too much, not participating in the rituals. It was so complicated for me when I was a novitiate ['ritai'wa]. In this phase it was difficult to be in the middle of the *waradzu.*
>
> I began to be very critical. But I really didn't know what I was talking about. I didn't have any emotional structure because I was an adolescent ['ritai'wa].
>
> Also I didn't have an argument ready to critique the Salesians. I wasn't against them. But I thought things needed to be thought through. Everything needed to be rethought.

After Hiparidi had studied for a year in Barra do Garças, an opportunity presented itself for him and another boy to study at Palas Atena, a boarding school in São Paulo State.[21] This was an alternative middle school where most teachers and students, many who were awaiting adoption, were more open minded than peers in Barra do Garças. In this environment, away from the discrimination of eastern Mato Grosso, Hiparidi succeeded academically. This was a relatively tranquil year. He completed seventh and eighth grades and high school at Palas Atena.

> Some people came from a school called Palas Atena Association. Palas Atena is a school for children who don't have fathers, who

GRAHAM

don't have mothers. I think children went there to be adopted. It was in Monteiro Lobato [a city in the interior of São Paulo State], near Campos do Jordão.

I lived with them. It was an excellent school with land around it. It was good for me to be there after that bomb fell on me. This was in 1989. It was good because I came here [I got away from Mato Grosso]. I got away from the city and lived on the land. I stayed there and studied with the other young people. I was about seventeen or eighteen years old then.

Hiparidi's peers at Palas Atena were not privileged, nor were they judgmental. They were, as Hiparidi notes, waiting to be adopted. At Palas Atena Hiparidi did not feel that his difference was stigmatized, as it had been in Barra do Garças. In fact at Palas Atena, he felt supported. This school offered a positive environment and provided a safe place in which Hiparidi was able to reflect on the situation at Sangradouro. He comments that around this time he was inspired by Mario Juruna, a Xavante leader who took the Xavante's fight for land into the center of national conscious (see Juruna, Hohlfeldt, and Hoffman 1982; Garfield 2004; Graham 2011). For a boy who had few role models, Juruna was a likely figure, for he had lived among the *waradzu* and developed a critique of the Salesians. He had dedicated his life to fighting for Xavante and indigenous rights, but Hiparidi was not thinking of himself in terms of leadership at this point.

I paid attention to everything. Many people inspired me, especially Mario Juruna, whom I saw a lot [in the media]. In his last speeches Juruna spoke a lot about how tired he was. He urged the Xavante, especially the younger generations, to take action too. This made me think a lot.

I saw him in the papers, in magazines, and I became inspired by him. I was really inspired by Juruna.

Inspired by Juruna, Hiparidi began to think that he too could make a difference in the Xavante's future. Given the state's emphasis on incorporating Xavante into Mato Grosso's agricultural economy, Hiparidi thought that studying agronomy would best prepare him to assist his community. So he took the entrance exam for agricultural technical school. He was devastated when he did not pass. Hiparidi couples his failure to enter agronomy school with a remark from a teacher that he remembers as offensive, and these two negative experiences combined to unhinge him again. He lost sight of his desire to help his people. Away from his home, family, guidance, and institutions that structure youth's experiences, Hiparidi felt lost and alienated.

> When I didn't pass [the entrance exam], I was in bad shape. Another thing happened at the same time. A history teacher accused me. He said that I was ashamed to be an Indian. I said, "How could I be ashamed of being Indian?"
>
> "What do you mean?" That was complicated.
>
> For me, this built up inside. It made me think about these critiques. It really made me think. And I began to react. I began to challenge the police. I really did.

Hiparidi's comments suggest that he became angry, to the point where he even "challenged the police." This is another moment of crisis. Among the *waradzu,* Hiparidi felt himself to be in a hostile environment. Then, as his next remark suggests, he returned to his community where he experienced pressure from another side: from his family. His father "came down hard on [him]." Both in the city and also when he returned home, life was difficult and challenging. Experiencing pressure from both sides, he was vulnerable to various forms of "seduction" that he next experienced when he moved from Monteiro Lobato to São Paulo, where he got jobs as a model.

Then, my father came down on me. He really gave it to me. It was around then, between 1995 and 1996, that I started to make appearances in the media.[22] But I didn't really know what it meant to appear in the media. They featured me as a "handsome face," with my long hair. And then a lot of people started chasing me. A lot of women came after me. This really messed with my head.

Hiparidi's comment, "This really messed with my head," underscores the disjuncture he felt between the pressures of the city and those of his natal family and community. He began to be "seduced" by the desire to have "fame," to have an individual voice and attention. These desires conflict with values that Xavante emphasize for young men during this life-cycle phase. Xavante practices promote attention to collective activities, such as *da-ño're* collective singing, that deemphasize individuality and minimize attention to individual personae and values young men acting collaboratively in groups (see Graham 1994, 1995). His city life and values were out of sync with Xavante values and practices. Hiparidi felt a tension and disjuncture. This then was a source of internal conflict and subjective crisis.[23]

After several years of city life, of "seduction" by media attention and desire for fame, Hiparidi indicates that he began to perceive that he was paying a high price for his city life. His narrative expresses that he felt torn, that he was "losing control," "losing himself." His awareness that he was becoming distant from his community and estranged from Xavante morals and values caused him immense internal conflict. Again it prompted him to reflect.

Then I began to realize that I wouldn't be able to accomplish anything alone.

Then my head began to mature. I saw that things were really complicated. I recognized that I might lose myself, for I was, in truth, losing control. Really I was subject to a lot of seduction.

I let my hair grow long for mourning when one of my relatives passed away. I mourned by letting my hair grow really long. And this was something that [city] people saw. They started to see me as a "beautiful Indian," a symbol, really, of indigenous sexuality. All kinds of women came after me. And this messed with me.

This seemed important to them, indigenous sexuality.

And I paid a price for this. I began to realize that each day I was getting farther and farther from my people. By appearing [in the media] with my long hair and handsome face and a lot of people chasing after. Many women coming on. And this also moved me.

In this moment of recognition, when Hiparidi was "moved," he again shifted his perspective. He speaks of his realization that his life in the city—the media, money, women—was distancing him from Xavante. The "movement" he felt prompted him to see things in a different way. He recognized that the glamour of media attention made scant contributions to improving life in his community. His comments also point to an acknowledgment of the ethos of Xavante leadership and the idea that work is accomplished, not by focusing on the individual, but through collaboration.

Shifting Perspective and Action: Establishing Idzö'uhu and Community Projects

The crises that Hiparidi describes as "moving" caused him to reflect, to reconsider Xavante circumstances, and to rotate his perspective. They jolted him into awareness of how distanced from and out of touch with life in Sangradouro he had become. They moved him to think about things in new ways and from different perspectives. As he reflects on this period of his life, he recalls conversations, especially with his brothers, and indicates that these also motivated him to reflect on others' perspectives on *him*. This was something new and different; he stepped out of his field of vision and looked at himself, as others would look at him.

I was a symbol for them [people in the community], a symbol of hope. I was a model for them. They didn't understand the craziness that I had inside me. This internal crisis within me. They saw me as a person with resolve, who was well prepared. So I was a model for them, a person they had to follow. This is how they thought of me.

I began to feel even more isolated. Everyone in the community was coming after me, everyone in the community. This was really difficult.

As Hiparidi rotated his perspective to consider how others' saw him, he began to feel new forms of pressure, specifically a pressure to try to improve things in his community. In this section of his narrative we glimpse his realization that members of his community thought of him as some sort of savior. He states that people thought of him as the "hope of the community." This expectation carried a heavy burden. His desire to have distinction as an individual, was cultivated by the attention he received in São Paulo, conflicted with Xavante norms and values that favor the "depersonalization" of individual achievements (Graham 1993) and collaboration. At the same time that he was a model for others, he recognized that he was wracked by internal conflict; this amplified his stress. On the one hand, he felt drawn to the attention he received as a "symbol of indigenous sexuality, of sensuality, as exotic," but he was beginning to experience dissatisfaction with this fame and even saw it as a form of "prostitution." He began to turn toward thinking of his community and how he would relate to it.

I began to think about things, to put my head in order in about 1995. I spoke a lot with my brothers. They provided me with a strong reference point. This provoked me, and I began to forget my dreams, personal dreams of stardom.

Every time I came [to the community], they spoke with me. They had high hopes for me. Really, they expected me to become someone, to become someone who would represent Xavante culture, not someone who was lost.

Hiparidi describes conversations he had with his brothers. They elaborated their critique of the church, and Hiparidi internalized their expectations.

> [My brother] Lucas began to lay his expectations on me. We began to talk about the issue of the church. He had dreams for me. My parents did too. And this was a shock to me when I returned [to the community]. This helped me, knowing that others held hopes for me.

With time Hiparidi states that he began to integrate his critique of the Salesians with a plan to liberate his family from the missionaries' control. He began to develop the idea of establishing a new community that would be entirely separate from the Salesians and the mission. It would be, he says, a place that the "Salesians would not enter." In 1996 Hiparidi and his family founded a new community named Idzö'uhu, Abelinha, or Little Bee in English. The new community was conceptualized as a reaction to and an escape from the Salesians at Sangradouro. Hiparidi was in many ways following the model of Mario Juruna, who had in 1974 established the community of Namukura to get away from the Salesians and the mission at São Marcos. Idzö'uhu took this a step farther; not only would its inhabitants be distancing themselves and asserting their independence from the Salesians; they were also reasserting their traditional economy and lifestyle. The political impetus for the new community was therefore complex; it would be wholly independent from the Salesians, and it would seek to revive practices that had been abandoned as a result of the Salesians' influence.

> So, it was like this, I had the idea to form a new community. I came up with the plan, as a result of having lived away. I thought about how it would be organized. I had it all in my head. It wasn't written down.

I thought of everything, really. The village needs to work like this: The church will not enter. It will have bathrooms. Everything will be nice and neat.

But in practice, all of this is really difficult. The project itself was simple, the new village. The idea was simply to raise bees and to be self-sustaining. Everything would be collectively managed. It would have a community garden where everyone would work. Whoever worked less, would get less as well. So there wouldn't be any inequality, like there is here [among the *waradzu*].

After a while we started to raise bees. They started to give honey a little while ago. This is an alternative project.[24] It doesn't depend on FUNAI. We are dependent on ourselves.[25]

The project was like this: Xavante recapture their psychological force as well as political force and the economy and culture. This was clear for us from the outset.

While according to Hiparidi the initial idea to form the new village was his, it was his brothers, Lucas Ruri'õ in particular, who implemented the plan. Hiparidi remained divided, however, seduced by the attention he received in the city. Again his father spoke frankly and caused him to think critically about the attention he received.

At this time I was appearing a lot in the media. My father said, "Wait a minute! This seduction is normal. This is what the whites do. They make you into a star and then soon you are not from here. If you don't take care of yourself, and take care of your connection with your community, the people who support you, you won't have anything."

This was a big shock for me. This made me think about many, many things. It really did. It hit me hard. My father said I was not what he and my mother had imagined. And I thought about this every time I went home.

Hiparidi's inner turmoil was exacerbated by the disjuncture between how he was understanding himself and the ways that others, both in the city and in Sangradouro, thought of and treated him.

> I had many followers [in Sangradouro]. A lot of people wanted to follow me. Young people were idealizing me. This left me in crisis. My father's words troubled me. He spoke frankly, with hard words. I needed to find peace inside me; otherwise I would lose myself. Totally lose myself. And then I wouldn't accomplish anything. Without the connection to the community, when you cut your hair [like a *waradzu*], you can lose everything. It is very complicated.

Hiparidi characterizes this period, when he appeared in the media, when he was "a star," as "very complicated." "Seduced" by the city but not wanting to lose his connection with his community was stressful and confusing. Again his brother pressed him to think about his situation, to see himself from a different angle. Again in the midst of crisis, and prompted to reflect on his situation by his brother's and father's words, Hiparidi rotated his view.

> I succeeded in feeling like a star. This was worrisome, really. This was a bad phase. I thought that I was everything. It was very complicated. This phase lasted about a year and a half. Everyone was worried about me.
>
> My brother kept at me but in a subtle way. He talked with me, showed me that I was important in the community. And I decided that I wanted to be important there.
>
> I began to cut off my contact with the press. I stopped calling attention to myself. I didn't want to appear in the press, even when I was involved in projects for the community.
>
> This made me think a lot about things in the community, about all the projects that need to be done there. And now I am more secure.
>
> We are doing work. Everyone is eating. For me, this is good. I don't need to appear in the media anymore. Before my objec-

tive was to appear in the media. Now, if the media wants to do stories on my work, that is fine. But the media itself is not the objective.

This was a critical turning point for Hiparidi. His crises, together with the counsel he received from family members, especially his father and brother, caused him to reflect on what he had done with his life. He questioned his values, particularly his fascination with stardom. This prompted him to realize that he risked losing his connection with his community and "those who support[ed] him." He acknowledged that without this support, he would be lost.

As Hiparidi recounts this critical turning point in his life, a point at which he moved from a primarily ego-focused stance to one in which he positioned himself, as well as his ideas and actions, as part of larger collective efforts, his narrative begins to shift, fitting into a pattern that is recognizable for Xavante leadership. He no longer focuses so exclusively on himself. He shifts his narrative to focus on collective actions and decisions and to credit others' contributions. A good example of this is his description of his family's move to establish Idzö'uhu, the new community that is separate from the Salesian mission and the missionaries' control. Although Hiparidi relates that the initial idea was his, he emphasizes that it was his brothers, and especially Lucas, who implemented it. His comments about being the one who took the brunt of the heat of the Salesians' backlash can also be seen in this way. Hiparidi absorbed the conflict, deflecting it away from others.

They [my brothers] began to make [my idea] more sophisticated.

[My brother] Lucas, the director of the school, took on some of the greatest responsibility. He is the one who is most responsible. He took the idea and transformed it [into action]. He stopped teaching classes there, with the Salesians. That is how it began.

He [Lucas] started a war with the Salesians. Then they [Salesians] began to blame me.

But my brother is the one who really took control of the plan. I made the suggestion. I made the suggestion to everyone. He is the one who really took it on. He took it on. And he did it.

From this point on in his narrative, Hiparidi focuses attention on projects that he *and* others are involved in to support the community. He removes himself from the spotlight and in so doing, his behavior conforms to Xavante ideals of leadership: he deflects attention away from himself and emphasizes the collectivity and collective effort. The rest of his narrative is not so much an autobiography as it is a description of projects and activities. Hiparidi moves away from a focus on himself; he effaces his ego as he becomes absorbed in descriptions of community projects.

Conclusion

Hiparidi's narrative provides one window into the experiences of Xavante boys, like Canambre and others, who left their communities to study in Brazilian schools.[26] He and his family, like others, experienced difficult times but also in many cases great rewards. In each of the cases that I know of, when Xavante boys have moved between community and city to study, the experience as well as their transitions, have been taxing.[27]

Hiparidi's autobiography also offers a window into the stresses and struggles of emergent leadership and of challenges that indigenous leaders experience when they live and move across porous social boundaries. Few accounts exist that help us to understand the experiences of native Amazonian leaders from Brazil who act as go-betweens, transcultural individuals who move fluidly, but not without stress, between worlds (but see Dutilleux 2010; Kopenawa and Albert 2013; Oakdale 2004). My hope is that this chapter will help stimulate more attention to the subjective experience of these individuals. Hiparidi's autobiography reveals the difficulties he experienced as a result of his movement between his community and the city, the challenges of being different in multiple places and being fragmentarily, as opposed to consistently, integrated into the forms of social organization that help structure and guide Xavante youth through adolescence. His narrative also emphasizes his struggle to develop a critique of the Catholic Church.

I have argued that Hiparidi lived through several periods of subjective crisis and that he emerged from these with new perspectives and ability to see Xavante conditions in new ways. He developed critiques of the Catholic Church, of the state, of city life, and eventually a vision for improving conditions in his community.

As he reintegrated himself into Xavante society and accepted his leadership role, Hiparidi began to assume qualities of Xavante leadership that deemphasize individuality and ego. I have noted how, toward the end of his narrative, he emphasizes others' participation in projects he was involved in implementing.

I recorded versions of Hiparidi's autobiography in 2000 and 2001, when he was still relatively young and inexperienced as a leader. Since then he has continued to develop projects to improve conditions in Idzö'uhu, to bring attention to the destruction that rampant and massive unregulated soy agribusiness is causing to the *cerrado* environment in which Xavante and many other indigenous peoples in live. Recently he has begun to develop a project to link Xavante territories, which are tiny islands in a vast sea of intensive soy cultivation and formed a coalition of distinct *cerrado* groups that are confronting devastating consequences resulting from the massive agribusiness in the region.[28]

I conclude with an excerpt from a narrative that I recorded in 2006 in which Hiparidi speaks about projects that the Xavante Warã Association, which he founded to administer projects in Idzö'uhu, developed to protect the environment in which the Xavante live. This excerpt shows the evolution of

Hiparidi's discourse, the way he emphasizes the importance of collective effort and incorporating different sectors of the population, including women. He also speaks of cultivating future leaders. In his discourse he immerses himself into the positions of others. He states that in order to succeed, projects cannot be solely associated with him; others must be committed, involved and invested.

In making these statements, Hiparidi speaks in the first-person plural. Instead of speaking as "I" as he did through much of the narratives I recorded in 2000 and 2001, Hiparidi speaks of "we" and "our." By shifting to "we," Hiparidi underscores his integration into the community and the submersion of his own ego into it.[29] This is a marked departure from the "I" and focus on his personal ego of his earlier narrative. This discourse shows that he has embedded his own self into the broader collectivity; in his discourse he has reintegrated himself into the Xavante and the collective subjectivity that successful leaders express.

> We are seeing,
> We are learning,
> We are getting results.
> We are always working on ambitious projects.
> Through *our* work we are always discovering new leaders.
> *Our* ambition is for each project that Warã undertakes
> *We* will discover new leaders.
> A project shouldn't be only "Hiparidi's" or "Hiparidi's work"
> It can't be this way.
> Everyone needs to be involved, saying the same things.
> This is a question of experience.
> Juruna said this.
> Other leaders also said it.
> I tried this, my own experience shows it.
> And we are seeing with increasing clarity that the youth and
>   the women [want to participate].

Men and women. . . .

This is a long-term project [to get all Xavante communities to work together].

It is a project that will involve a lot of people.

Do you understand?

Postscript

Hiparidi currently resides full time in Idzö'uhu. He is now married in the community, and rather than making trips from his city residence to Idzö'uhu, he travels from the community to the city and back. He devotes a great deal of time to recording his father's memories and the oral histories of other elders. In addition to continuing his activist work, he is thus fulfilling a dream he possessed when he entered the graduate program in anthropology at USP.

Acknowledgments

I would like to thank Suzanne Oakdale and Magnus Course for inviting me to contribute to this collection. I thank Suzanne especially for her encouragement and productive editorial suggestions, as well as comments from anonymous reviewers. Support for research was provided by a Global Scholar Award from the University of Iowa and a Fellowship from the National Endowment for the Humanities. I am grateful to the Associação Xavante Warã and its associates, the community of Idzö'uhu, members of Hiparidi's family, Xanda de Biase, Daniela Lima, and above all, Hiparidi Top'tiro for sharing his life and work.

Notes

1. Several elder men had developed contacts in Riberão Preto, and for this reason boys went to this location.

2. The Xavante contact spanned over twenty years beginning in the late 1940s. The group that resides in Pimentel Barbosa was the first to agree to peaceful relations with government representatives, and they

have been able to remain in the general area since contact (for an excellent overview of the history of Xavante contact, see Lopes da Silva 1992). In the late 1970s six boys were sent to study in Riberão Preto; Canambre and Caimi Waiassé followed in their footsteps in the early 1980s. Individuals from the first group and members of their adopted city families reflect on their experiences in documentary film *Estratégia Xavante* (Xavante Strategy) (Franca 2007).

3. Xavante refer to all nonindigenous peoples as "brancos" or "whites." I use the label *waradzu* here, conforming to local usage.

There is no standard orthography for writing Xavante, and for historical and political reasons, communities use slightly different characters to represent the sounds of their language. For example, communities in Pimentel Barbosa represent the alveolar affricate *dz* and *ts* as *z* and *s*. The name for non-Indian is thus differentially rendered as either *warazu* or *waradzu*. Because this chapter focuses on an individual from the Sangradouro Indigenous Territory, I employ its orthography here.

4. In general Xavante have been fortunate to place their boys with middle-class and professional families, although their experiences have been quite diverse: One boy lived for a time in an orphanage and also worked in a shoe factory; another lived with a family of well-to-do ranchers, while two others lived for a time among a group of delinquents in an adolescent community "modeled after" a Xavante village. Many indigenous children are less fortunate; they are often taken in as domestics and frequently suffer abuse.

5. In her analysis of seventeenth-century cultural mediators who brokered relationships between Portuguese and indigenous societies, Metcalf (2005) identifies three types of cultural go-betweens: physical, cultural, and transactional. Of these Canambré was expected to be a transactional go-between, mediating social and economic transactions.

6. There are now several universities with special programs for indigenous peoples and some that grant MA degrees for indigenous educators so that they can teach in secondary schools in indigenous communities. Hiparidi became increasingly involved in community leadership and activism and has not yet completed his graduate degree.

7. *Warã* is the name of the central plaza in Xavante communities where meetings are held. For further discussion of Xavante political meetings, or *warã*, see Maybury-Lewis 1974 and Graham 1993.

8. Beekeeping was the first project implemented in Idzö'uhu, conceptualized to generate income from sales as well as honey for local consumption. This was followed by projects to raise chickens and later others that focused on greater participation of women, including "Flowers and Fauna" conceptualized to document, validate, and revitalize women's knowledge of traditional *cerrado* foods (developed in collaboration with anthropolo-

gist Mariana Ferreira 2004), and another focusing on midwifery developed in collaboration with Daniela Lima and Maria Lucia Gomide (Gomide and Lima n.d.). In addition Warã sponsored numerous cultural projects designed to raise money and also awareness of Xavante and the *cerrado* environment in which they live (see Graham 2014); for further discussion of Idzö'uhu, see Vianna 2011; Gomide 2008; Ferreira 2004, 2013. Ruri'õ, Stilene de Biase, and Ôwa'u (2000) is a children's book that tells the story of Idzö'uhu.

9. Xavante began founding NGOs in the late 1980s soon after Brazil's 1988 constitution enabled indigenous peoples to directly receive funds from outside sources without the National Indian Foundation acting as intermediary. The first Xavante association was established by members of the Eténhiritipa community in the Pimentel Barbosa Indigenous Territory (see Graham 2000). Now almost every Xavante community has its own association, or NGO.

10. There are currently twelve distinct Xavante Indigenous Territories (see Instituto Socioambiental 2013). The area Xavante know as Parabubure is now demarcated into three distinct indigenous territories: Parabubure, Ubawawẽ, and Chão Preto.

11. The basic point of this account of the Xavante's arrival at Sangradouro is corroborated in the elder Alexandre Tsereptsé's recollection in the film *Tsõ'rehipãri, Sangradouro* (Tserewahú Tsereptsé 2009).

12. The Xavante contact spanned more than two decades. The first group to establish peaceful contact with representatives of the national society in 1946 was the easternmost group, led by Apõwe that lived along the margins of the Rio das Mortes.

13. For a good account of Salesians' treatment of Xavante in mission communities, see Menezes's description of São Marcos (1984). Mario Juruna (Juruna, Hohlfeldt, and Hoffman 1982) also describes the situation of mission Xavante at São Marcos as one of slavery. For more information about Mario Juruna, see Juruna, Hohlfeldt, and Hoffman 1982; also Garfield 2004. Graham 2011 shows how mainstream media manipulated images of Juruna to advance elite political agendas.

14. *Wapte* may make brief visits to their natal homes and their mothers after dark. Their fathers, like all adult men, may visit the *hö* bachelors' hut at any time. Women neither approach nor enter the *hö*; they prepare food for their sons and send meals via the conveyance of young girls.

15. Hiparidi conforms to all three types of go-betweens in Metcalf's scheme. He has two children with a Brazilian woman, Xanda de Biase, who was a significant partner in Warã activities during the late 1990s and the first decade of the twenty-first century, making him a "physical go-between." As an organizer of cultural events, he is a "cultural go-between." He also mediates political and economic transactions and could thus be

considered a "transactional go-between." His example shows that, while Metcalf's heuristic is useful for thinking through the different types of (inter)actions in which native intermediaries are involved as transcultural individuals, in practice it is not always easy to separate these roles and activities.

16. Excerpts in this chapter are taken primarily from Hiparidi's 2001 narrative. In a very few instances, where Hiparidi makes the relevant point more clearly, I have used excerpts from the 2000 narrative. The two narratives present much of the same material but differ in their elaboration of certain points. Differences between the two narratives may be the result of clarifications I asked for and also because my understanding of Hiparidi and his work was more extensive at the time of the second interview. In another work it would be interesting to analyze these differences.

17. I do not formally distinguish between excerpts of the two narratives.

18. Hiparidi's older brother, Lucas, was his first teacher. After completing the first grades at the Salesian mission when the school was taught by missionaries, Lucas was sent to Kuluene where FUNAI had a school that went through sixth grade (Mariana Ferreria, personal communication). He then returned to Sangradouro, where he taught the primary grades in the mission school.

19. At the end of the *wapté* phase, boys undergo initiation and become members of the *'ritai'wa* novitiate age grade, which Xavante gloss as "adolescence" in Portuguese. During this period boys must show respect for women and their elders, and this is made explicit in a number of behaviors such as speech taboos. Except during song/dance performances, *'ritai'wa* do not appear or speak in public, and they must keep their heads bowed and eyes downcast.

20. Salesians practiced the same form of bribery when they visited other nonmission Xavante communities. In another work (Graham 1995), I describe a scene where Padre Giaccaria from the mission at São Marcos bribed members of the Pimentel Barbosa community to attend mass before seeing a film of a ceremonial from São Marcos.

21. http://www.colegiopalasatena.com.br/, accessed September 1, 2010.

22. In the 2000 interview Hiparidi recalled that he did commercials for Guaraná (a soft drink) and the television network, A Globo. He also appeared in propaganda for banks.

23. Around this time Hiparidi entered USP as a graduate student in anthropology. He developed a fascinating critique of anthropologists, which unfortunately I do not have time to explore here. I leave this topic for future exploration.

24. Hiparidi's use of the word "alternative" (*alternativo* in Portuguese) to describe this project illustrates that he is immersed in the discourse of NGOs and is fluent in the current terms of discourse circulating in the NGO

community at the time (for discussion of indigenous leaders' use of the language of global arenas, see Graham 2002).

25. Independence is a critical component of this project, for the National Indian Foundation, FUNAI, had implemented economic projects in Xavante areas beginning in the late 1970s that created intense dependency throughout Xavante areas (see Graham 1995; also Coimbra et al 2002; Garfield 2001).

26. Paulo Supretaprã briefly describes how difficult life among the *waradzu* was for him in the *Millennium* film series (Meech and Grant 1992).

27. In nearly thirty years of working with Xavante, I am very familiar with ten cases.

28. In 2006 Hiparidi founded the Mobilization of Indigenous Peoples of the Cerrado (MOPIC).

29. In another work I have shown how Xavante leaders submerge ego into larger collectivities through use of pronoun shifting (Graham 1995). This pattern is found among other Ge groups (see, for example, Urban 1989) and may be part of a broader areal pattern.

Bibliography

Associação Xavante Warã
  N.d. Flier.
Coimbra, Carlos E. A. Jr., with Nancy M. Flowers, Francisco M. Salzano, and Ricardo V. Santos
  2002 Xavante in Transition: Health, Ecology, and Bioanthropology in Central Brazil. Ann Arbor: University of Michigan Press.
Dutilleux, Jean-Pierre
  2010 Raoni: Mémoires d'un chef indien. Paris: Edicions du Rocher.
Ferreira, Mariana Kawall Leal
  2004 The Color Red: Fighting with Flowers and Fruits in Xavante Territory, Central Brazil. Indiana 21:47–62.
  2013 Acting for Indigenous Rights: Theatre to Change the World. Minneapolis: University of Minnesota Human Rights Center.
Franca, Belisário, dir.
  2007 Estrategia Xavante (Xavante Strategy). 86 min. GIROS and IDET. Rio de Janeiro, Brazil.
Garfield, Seth
  2001 Indigenous Struggle at the Heart of Brazil: State Policy, Frontier Expansion, and the Xavante Indians, 1937–1988. Durham NC: Duke University Press.
  2004 Mario Juruna: Brazil's First Indigenous Congressman. In The Human Tradition in Modern Brazil. Peter M. Beattie, ed. Pp. 287–304. Wilmington DE: SR Books.

George, Kenneth

2010 Picturing Islam: Art and Ethics in a Muslim Lifeworld. Chichester, West Sussex, UK: Wiley-Blackwell.

Gomide, Maria Lúcia

2008 Marãna Bödödi: A territorialidade Xavante nos caminhos do Ró. PhD dissertation, Faculdade de Filosofía, Letras e Ciências Humanas, Universidade de São Paulo.

Gomide, Maria Lúcia, and Daniela Lima

N.d. Livro das Parteiras. Unpublished MS, Associação Xavante Warã.

Graham, Laura R.

1987 Uma aldeia por um "projeto." *In* Povos Indígenas no Brasil-85/86. Aconteceu Especial 17. Carlos A. Recardo, ed. Pp. 348–50. São Paulo: Centro Ecumênico de Documentação e Informação.

1993 A Public Sphere in Amazonia? The Depersonalized Collaborative Construction of Discourse in Xavante. American Ethnologist 20(4):717–41.

1994 Dialogic Dreams: "Creative Selves Coming into Life in the Flow of Time." American Ethnologist 21(4):723–45.

1995 Performing Dreams: Discourses of Immortality among the Xavante of Central Brazil. Austin: University of Texas Press.

2000 Xavante Wildlife Management: Lessons in Collaboration. *In* Indigenous Peoples and Conservation Organizations: Experiences in Collaboration. Ron Weber, John Butler, and Patty Larson, eds. Pp. 47–72. Washington DC: World Wildlife Fund.

2002 How Should an Indian Speak? Brazilian Indians and the Symbolic Politics of Language Choice in the International Public Sphere. *In* Indigenous Movements, Self-Representation, and the State in Latin America. Jean Jackson and Kay Warren, eds. Pp. 181–228. Austin: University of Texas Press.

2005 Image and Instrumentality in a Xavante Politics of Existential Recognition: The Public Outreach Work of Eténhiritipa Pimentel Barbosa. American Ethnologist 32(4):622–41.

2011 Quoting Mario Juruna: Linguistic Imagery and the Transformation of Indigenous Voice in the Brazilian Print Press. American Ethnologist 38(1):164–82.

2014 Genders of Xavante Ethnographic Spectacle: Cultural Politics of Inclusion and Exclusion in Brazil. *In* Performing Indigeneity: Global Histories and Contemporary Experiences. Laura R. Graham and H. Glenn Penny, eds. Lincoln: University of Nebraska Press.

Instituto Socioambiental (ISA)

2013 Xavante Povos Indigenas no Brasil. http://pib.socioambiental .org/pt/povo/xavante, accessed April 15, 2013.

Juruna, Mario, with Antonio Hohlfeldt and Assis Hoffman

1982 O Gravador do Juruna. Porto Alegre, Brazil: Mercado Aberto.

Karttunen, Francis

1994 Between Worlds: Interpreters, Guides, and Survivors. New Brunswick NJ: Rutgers University Press.

Kopenawa, Davi, and Bruce Albert

2013 The Falling Sky: Words of a Yanomami Shaman. Cambridge MA: Belknap Press of Harvard University Press.

Lopes da Silva, Aracy

1992 Dois séculos e meio de história xavante. *In* História dos índios no Brasil. Manuela Carneiro da Cunha, ed. Pp. 357–78. São Paulo: Companhia das Letras, Fundação de Amparo á Pesquisa no Estado de São Paulo, Secretaria Municipal de Cultura.

Maybury-Lewis, David

1974 Akwe-Shavante Society. 2nd ed. New York: Oxford University Press.

Meech, Richard, and Michael Grant, dirs.

1992 Millennium: Tribal Wisdom and the Modern World. 10-part series, 60 min. segments. Meech Grant Productions Ltd. Toronto.

Menezes, Claudia

1984 Missionários e índios em Mato Grosso (Os Xavante da reserve de São Marcos). DSc dissertation, Faculdade de Filosofía, Letras e Ciências Humanas, Universidade de São Paulo.

Metcalf, Alida

2005 Go-Betweens and the Colonization of Brazil, 1500–1600. Austin: University of Texas Press.

Núcleo de Cultura Indígena

1994 Etenhiritipá: Cantos da tradição Xavante. Quilombo Music/ Warner Music Brasil Ltda. Brazil.

Oakdale, Suzanne

2004 The Culture-Conscious Brazilian Indian: Representing and Re-working Indianness in Kayabi Political Discourse. American Ethnologist 31(1):60–75.

Ruri'õ, Lucas, with Helena Stilene de Biase and João Lucas Õwa'u

2000 Daró Idzô'uhu Watsu'u: A historia da Aldeia Abelhinha. São Paulo: Pancast/Master Book Editora Comércio e Representaçãoes Ltda.

Serebu'rã, Hipru, with Rupawê, Serezabdi, and Serennimirãmi

1997 Wamrêmé za'ra/Nossa palavra: Mito e história do povo Xavante. São Paulo: Editora Serviço Nacional de Aprendizagem Comercial.

Tserewahú Tsereptsé, Devino

2009 Tsõ'rehipãri, Sangradouro. 29 min. Video in the Villages. Recife.

Urban, Greg

1989 The "I" of Discourse in Shokleng. *In* Semiotics, Self, and Society. Benjamin Lee and Greg Urban, eds. Pp. 27–51. Berlin: Mouton de Gruyter.

Vianna, Fernando de Luiz Brito
    2008 Boleiros do Cerrado: Indios Xavantes e o futebol. São Paulo: Annablume.
Vilaça, Aparecida
    2000 O que significa tornar-se outro? Xamanismo e contato interétnico na Amazônia. Revista Brasileira de Ciências Sociais 15(44):56–72.
Viveiros de Castro, Eduardo
    1998 Cosmological Deixis and Amerindian Perspectivism. Journal of the Royal Anthropological Institute 4:469–88.
Welch, James
    2010 Hierarchy, Symmetry, and the Xavante Spiritual Life Cycle. Horizontes Antropológicos 16(34):235–59.

Autobiographies of a Memorable Man and Other Memorable Persons (Southern Amazonia, Brazil)

BRUNA FRANCHETTO

Nahu (Nahum), who later changed his name to Utu Hususu (Old Fish Trap) when his first grandson was born, died in 2005 at over eighty years of age at Ipatse, the main Kuikuro village.[1] I wanted to realize one of Nahu's biggest wishes, implicitly expressed in his narrated autobiography, by writing his obituary for the *kagaiha* (whites) to read and know about him (Franchetto 2006:679, translation by David Rogers):[2]

> Among the great Kuikuro elders, Nahu was an admired *akinha oto*, "master of narratives," *eginhoto*, "master of songs" (a ritual specialist), a living memory of the Kuikuro history of the twentieth century and their ancestors in the previous century. Nahu played a leading role in the history of the last sixty years: he had been a guide and interpreter for the Villas-Boas brothers, responsible along with others—as he always emphasized—for the elaboration of the project for the Xingu Indigenous Park. But while the names of the whites (Rondon, Villas-Boas, Darcy Ribeiro, ministers and presidents of the republic, researchers) were enshrined as part of written history, Nahu's name would have disappeared had it not been for his own insistence on remembering and being remembered, and his desire to record his life history and glory for his grandchildren and all those who in the future might want to rewrite the park's history. A Kwaryp was held for Nahu in August 2005, the like of which had never been seen before, given the

extraordinary number of white and indigenous visitors. In 2009 another homage was a Hagaka (Javarí), a ritual intended to send away for good the deceased, who, homesick, still wanders the village, accompanying living kin, and to celebrate the memory of Nahu as a great ritual specialist (like the great *kindoto* [wrestlers] and *anetü* [chiefs] of the past and the present).[3]

Writing these lines I was wrought with emotion and felt that, in a way, I was performing a catharsis, paying homage to a man I had once hated deeply and with whom I had only become reconciled during the final years of his life, after dealing with what were ambiguous feelings, to say the least. This text is also a polyphonic narrative or an intersection of distinct as well as interdependent trajectories, revolving around the central figure of Nahu and providing complementary perspectives of him.

First, Nahu's life is told by himself, as well as in fragments by myself and Ellen Basso—both of us researchers, anthropologists, and linguists—and by his grandson Mutua.[4] Second, in describing my encounter with Nahu, I am describing my own trajectory from 1976 to the present among the Kuikuro. And finally Mutua describes his own trajectory as an inevitable legacy from Nahu. His narrative is almost a hagiography: he *is* Nahu, or part of him, exemplifying the "reproduction" of the person (or aspects of the latter) from grandparent to grandchild. In the narratives of Nahu and Mutua, as we shall see, having linguistic knowledge, having skill as a translator as well as mastering the whites' language, are central questions.

From a dangerous "owner of witchcraft" to an outstanding and supralocal "owner of a great name," Nahu led an intense life. He was feared, hated as well as admired. His memory survives not only in his descendants. Nahu needed the white people at the same time that he hated them. As time went by our relationship gradually improved, until, toward the end of his life, it turned into an ambiguous friendship, steeped in diplomacy but nonetheless sincere. I learned to admire Nahu's political abilities, his capacity of building around himself an extensive family group that protected him from repeated accusations of witchcraft, and helped him to construct and increase his fame as a great ritual specialist and as one of the last men with knowledge of traditional songs and music. Nahu grew as a *tuhutinhü* and *tikaginhü* (well known, famous) person.

Kagaiga oto, tisakisü oto: Nahu by Himself

In two recordings made in 2001 and 2003, Nahu, lying in his hammock, by now almost deaf and blind, told his life story (in Kuikuro).[5] These "texts" are very different.

In the first one Nahu told his life to his son, Jakalu, and to me, as hearers and what-sayers of a true *akinha*, a traditional oral genre involving all the markers of narrative structure. Two years later, when he was asked once more to tell the story of his life, Nahu was much weaker and more confused. This time his listeners—his grandson Mutua and the anthropologist Carlos Fausto—were much more like interviewers than what-sayers. While in the first recording the voices of the addressees merely punctuated the oral performance, guided by the flow of recollections structured by the narrative framework, in the second recording the addressees were full-fledged interviewers, incisively provoking responses in large part based on their hearing-reading of the first recording. The outcome was a pseudo-narrative broken up by numerous interventions. In fact the stimulus given by Nahu's interlocutors resulted in little more than the addition of a few more details, some of which were undoubtedly relevant, but neither enriching the narrative itself nor changing the mnemonic anchors and the communicative aims of the narrator-interviewee.

Here, therefore, I present the first narrative (Nahu1), inserting where necessary comments derived from the second (Nahu2).

The start of Nahu1 is significant: the narrator had asked

his son to summon me to record his life history, aware that he was soon to die.

Nahu: engü kaha egei uametati kaha eheke egei Bruna
You're willing to record me, aren't you, Bruna?
atütüha ekugu uakiti
I . . . I like the idea a lot.
ukanne uka.. ukametüe tiha
You can rec . . . you can really record me!

Nahu1, with its historical references, is constructed as a traditional narrative genre. Any linguistic analysis must focus on the linking of events, the discourse strategies used to highlight or obscure elements in the foreground or background (through the construction of focus and deictics), the inflections of aspect and mood, and the expressions of tense values. Given the limits of this chapter, I only mention the use of epistemic markers, which appear in bold in the extracts of both narratives, because they characterize the specific autobiographical or life's story subgenre and the contextual difference between the two "texts."[6]

Two of the Kuikuro epistemic markers (EM) occur in the introductory utterances of Nahu1: *kaha* and *tiha*. *Kaha* means strong doubt awaiting a positive answer.[7] The EM *tiha* is far more frequent in Nahu's story and indicates strong visual and firsthand evidence. *Tiha* is followed in frequency by *wãke*, also an EM with a tense value indicating distant past and marking the statement uttered by an authoritative voice. Another important EM is *ngapaha* (maybe, perhaps), marking doubt in relation to the speaker's own weak memories or another's reported speech or memories. There is only one occurrence of *tsüha* and no occurrences at all of *tsügü*, *tüha*, and *kilü*, EMs founded in Nahu2. *Tüha* and *tsüha* have similar values: with *tüha* the speaker expresses lack of direct evidence; *tsüha* indicates the speaker's uncertainty concerning facts related by others. *Kilü* is basically a tense marker: the utterance within its scope describes events in a very distant past and already pertaining to the collective memory. *Tsügü* means that the information comes to the speaker through transmission from preceding generations, a chain still present in the speaker's memory.

Table 1 summarizes the frequency and the linguistic nature of these markers in the two narratives.

In Nahu1, Nahu starts from the beginning:

listen![8]
I was born in Kuhikugu (village), when Kuhikugu still existed
I was born from my mother's belly
inside the *tajühe*, the "chief's house" of my grandfather
    Kahalati

This is an opening formula where Nahu already mentions his connection to a chiefly status (*tajühe* is the big adorned house collectively built for a chief). This opening formula is also founded in Nahu2 but only after several lines of "adjustments," combined with a verbal etiquette and strategy intended to situate the interaction with a literate young man and a still poorly known *kagaiha* at the right level from the outset. To the opening question addressed to him by his grandson: "Where were you born, in Kuhikugu, is that right?" Nahu answers: "I don't remember . . . I was just a little child . . . you are literate, you know . . . we [Nahu lists all the Upper Xingu groups] are all *ngikogo* ("wild Indians," a word usually employed to refer to non-Xinguano people, to non-true-people), we don't know how to read and write."

A few months after his birth, Nahu moved with his parents to Alahatua, a new village built "on the other side" of Kuhikugu, where some years later his father, Jakalu, died.[9] He was raised by his widowed mother and five maternal siblings, who played a fundamental role in his early upbring-

Table 1. Kuikuro epistemic markers

EM	Nahu1	Nahu2	Morphosyntax	Position	Meaning
tiha	48	37	Clitic	2nd position	First evidence (visual)
wãke	15	64	Free form	Free	Past tense, authority
kilü	0	6	Free form	Immediately post-verbal	Past tense, collective memory
tsügü	0	2	Clitic	2nd position	Transmission from one generation to the next, still controlled by the speaker's memory
tiŋ(ha)	0	2	Clitic	2nd position	No firsthand evidence, speaker's distance from narrated events
tsü(ha)	5	7	Clitic	2nd position	No firsthand evidence, speaker's distance from narrated events

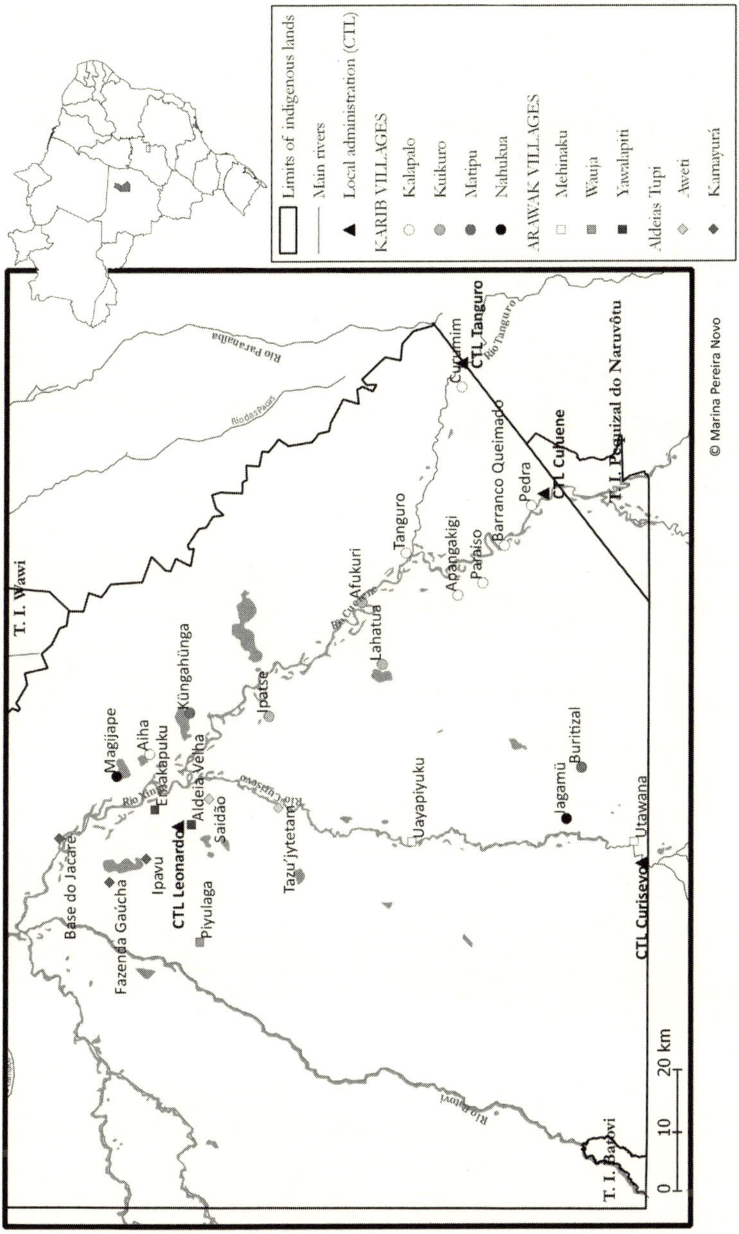

Map 2. Map of the Upper Xingu within the southern portion of Xingu Indigenous Land. Inset shows the entire Xingu Park and its location in Brazil. (Courtesy of Marina Pereira Novo)

ing. When he was, presumably, seven years old, the event that would mark the turning point in his life took place. We know that it was 1931:

> so . . . when perhaps I was seven
> the airplane landed
> it landed on the water, over there, downriver
> there at the place where the Matipu bathe
> over there, at the mouth of the Curisevo

The person arriving by flying boat in the upper Xingu was the Italian American military officer, adventurer, and explorer Vincent Petrullo, who would publish an account of his visit to the area in 1932. Many from the Agahütü (Yawalapiti), Kamayura, Mehinaku, and Kuikuro villages ran to see the novelty. They saw many Bakairi from Pakuera village, the SPI (Serviço de Proteção ao Índio, the Indian Protection Service in Brazil) Post located on the upper Batovi River. The Bakairi knew that the flying boat had set off from there.

> I didn't understand *kagaiha* (Portuguese)

However, there was a Bakairi man (Pügitsa) who knew the Jagamü language (a variant of Upper Xingu Carib), and he explained:

> this white man has come in search of his brother
> a long time ago a white man came here and became lost
> I've no idea where he went, but these men have come to look
>   for him

Petrullo led the first expedition in search of the English colonel Percy Fawcett, who had disappeared at the end of the 1920s after setting out from a Kalapalo village.[10] Petrullo was not the first *kagaiha* to visit the Upper Xingu, but he was the first *kagaiha* to appear in flesh and blood in front of Nahu (and the other Upper Xinguanos who gathered around the flying boat).[11] Two days later the flying boat took off and returned to Pakuera, along with the Bakairi by canoe.

> my uncle Jahila said
> let's go there with them, he said, let's go there with them
> let's get knives from there instead of the Bakairi
> my mother said, let's go there
> many people. . . . Kamayura, Aweti, Wauja, those who went, the people of Jagamü
> Kuikuro, five peoples
> of those who went, everyone came back
> along with my mother, we both stayed there
> maybe a year, maybe two
> I learned the Bakairi language
> so my uncle Atahu left here and went there [to Pakuera] again
> he went by canoe, it took twenty days [paddling]
> we returned, we arrived in Alahatua
> I had grown a bit

Nahu, like many Upper Xinguanos, would return to the Bakairi several times, part of an almost continuous to and fro between the Kuikuro village and the SPI posts in the Bakairi area (Batovi and Paranatinga), traveling via the upper Curisevo or upper Batovi Rivers. The basic motive for these trips was always to acquire tools. Nahu accompanied his uncles on these journeys. Mutua, Nahu's grandson, remembers that the Culiseu or Curisevo River served as the primary route for entering and leaving for those people who wanted to acquire tools from the whites: "Many are said to have died on the journey because the enemies used sorcery. The elders fought a lot because of the whites" (Mutua Mehinaku, personal communication, 2009).[12]

The journeys between the Upper Xingu villages and the SPI posts in the Bakairi area, "where there were whites," as Nahu says, travelling up and down the Curisevo and Batovi

Rivers, took place at the turn of the nineteenth and twentieth centuries.

> Nahu2:
> the elder Kamayura were always going to get (things)
> [they say that] they always journey up the Curisevo river, to
>   there
> [they say that] they returned from there with knives, hoes,
>   scythes
> they didn't [buy], [they say that] the head of the post gave us
>   them as presents
> that's what attracted them
> there was no money at the time, money didn't exist
> the Jagamü people were the first to obtain knives
> afterward it was the turn of the Mehinaku people, they
>   acquired knives
> the Aweti obtained [them]

From then on, Western goods and diseases arrived hand in
hand, confirming the equation *kagaiha engikogu=notoho=kugihe*
(white goods=disease=sorcery). Desire and envy were always
the main source material for sorcery attacks and accusations
(Figueiredo 2010).

The history of the Bakairi has interwoven with that of the
Upper Xinguanos for some centuries: participants in the Upper
Xingu system until the end of the nineteenth century, the Eastern Bakairi abandoned their villages on the Batovi and Curisevo to join the "tame" Paranatinga Bakairi, living close to the
SPI posts on the upper Batovi, and finally on the Paranatinga
River itself, the center of successive and partially successful "civi-
lizing" projects (school, plantation labor, clothing, forced learning of Portuguese, and so on) (Collet 2006). The Bakairi posts
became the launch point for "contact" with the Xinguanos with
the initial aim of attracting them to the aforementioned posts
and thus freeing up their rich lands for colonization:

Nahu2:

the Bakairi knew how to wrestle, they were always wrestling
    fighting
they painted themselves with annatto, the women used the
    uluri [belt]
the Bakairi were like that, though not any longer
it was the SPI who put an end to all that
"forget your language, forget your language"
the Bakairi's whites told the Indians
"talk in our language!" No, this was wrong
they celebrated the Kwaryp festival
Other Bakairi people came from Aünoho
the SPI brought them
Marechal Rondon ordered them to be united
so they could relocate there
they gave a rifle to my father, to Jakalu
my father understood Portuguese, I became just like him
my father spoke the Bakairi language, my mother spoke the
    Bakairi language
I speak the Bakairi language too

From the 1940s onward a new chapter was opened in the history of the Xinguano peoples, merging with the history of the creation of the Xingu National Park. In 1943 the Roncador-Xingu Expedition (ERX) was set up as the vanguard of the Central Brazil Foundation with the aim of occupying Brazil's central regions. A member of the ERX, Nilo Veloso, arrived in the Upper Xingu with the task of preparing the territory and the Indians for the definitive installation of the state/SPI. Nilo Veloso was the second *kagaiha* to mark Nahu's life.

Nilo Veloso appeared when I was already an adult
I was the only one who spoke the whites' language
my uncle Jahila said, let's go there to see
you can be the master of our words (translator)

(Nilo Veloso) went to the Kamayura village, so we went to visit
   him
we all greeted him
we came here to meet you, in search of knives
but I have some there
I'll give you some, he said, Nilo Veloso said
he took photos there
so, afterward we returned
our food ran out, we traveled upriver again
and afterward I returned from there, from Alahatuá village
my uncles said, let's go there with them, let's get ourselves
   some knives
we arrived in Pakuera
so
in the Bakairi village
on the way, I met Nilo in the Mehinaku port
Hi Nahu, he said, where are you going? he asked
let's go there, there I've got beads, I've got knives
I've got axes, hooks, I've got them there
Nahu, he said, I'm going away now to Rio
I'm not going to take you with me, he said
okay, I'll stay here then
next year I'll come back
so you can take me to your Kuikuro village
okay
we stayed working at the Pakuera village, at the SPI post still
FUNAI [Fundação Nacional do Índio, the National Indian
   Foundation of Brazil] replaced [the SPI]
from there we came to Matuhi
the truck full of whites arrived
along with Nilo Veloso
he was coming to the Kuikuro village
he brought a lot of things
clothing, shirts, lots of knives, hooks, and fishing line
he [Nilo] embraced me

Nahu, he said, have you been here since that day?
I was waiting for you here
this time you're going to take me to your village
we slept and slept and slept
we docked at the Jagamü village port
from there we arrived [at the Mehinaku]
Nilo approached me to speak: Nahu, tell them to bring our
    food!
João fired a shot, toooooo . . . tooooo
everyone came running to see us
it's been so long, Nahu, they said, have you just arrived?
yes, I've just arrived
the whites are here
have many of them come?
of course, I said
do you think he's got knives or hooks?
of course he has
wow, a lot of Mehinaku
with flour, they put it in the bag
their chief, Katupula
the Mehinaku chief was Katupula, he's dead now
so
we slept three days, then we arrived at the Kuikuro
I wasn't yet married, I was still single
so the whites slept in my village
they took lots of photos
they stayed for ten days
where's the payment? they asked
calm down, I'm going to pay, he [Nilo] said
his things, shirts, axes, hoes, knives and scissors
mirrors, mirrors
Bruna! that's what I did
that's why I understand a little bit of Portuguese
Nahu, I'm going now, he [Nilo] said
go with me!

if you accompany me, I'll pay you
but I stayed
my companion, the late Luis, he went
he went with Nilo

In 1946 the Villas-Boas brothers arrived in the region of the Xingu headwaters; Orlando Villas-Boas was the third pivotal personage in Nahu's life:

Orlando appeared there on the Sete de Setembro River
I grew up as an orphan
I hadn't had a father or mother for a long time
my father died first, afterward my mother died
someone came to summon me, a Kalapalo messenger arrived
[Orlando] arrived at the Kalapalo village
there was nobody who understood Portuguese
that's why they invited me
I went there, we went to visit Orlando
afternoon! afternoon! I said [in Portuguese]
Nilo was there too, he was the trail guide
this is Nahu, he said, Nahu
I greeted them all
the old wrestling champion lived there
Sagagi approached me
my friend, he said, you're here?
yes, it's me
I was the one who sent the messenger to summon you
for you to be the master of our words [translator]
when the whites spoke, I translated
everything they said, I translated
I translated for the Kalapalo elders
Orlando called on me to work with him
Nahu, you'll be the chief, you'll be the chief, he said
it was Nilo Veloso who chose me first
there in Pakuera
so I became Orlando's friend and worked with him

I translated for the other peoples
I translated for the Aweti, the Kamayura, the Wauja
especially for the Kuikuro, for the Kalapalo too
just me

Nahu even traveled as one of the Álvaro Villas-Boas's (the youngest and less famous of the Villas-Boas brothers) employees to the city of Cuiabá, the capital of Mato Grosso State, where he worked for a time as a builder's assistant. He returned to Alahatuá and married Sesuaka; soon afterward their children were born. At this point he clearly presented himself as a *kagaiha oto*, master of the whites, and, at the same time, a chief "made" by the whites.

the whites always came to my house
and there was always a lot of news arriving
when Orlando was there

Nahu describes himself as one of the main protagonists in the creation of the Xingu Park, a protagonist who was silenced by history, as officially told. He recalls the difficult negotiations, many of which he felt directly responsible for, that led various Upper Xingu groups, scared after the 1954 smallpox epidemics, into accepting their dislocation to areas near state assistance posts, thus abandoning their traditional territories. These were subsequently taken over by farms, nowadays the foci of environmental degradation affecting the upper course of the rivers running through the park. These ambiguous alliances between Nahu and white people had major consequences for the future.

Nahu, [Orlando Villas-Boas] said
you're in trouble, you're in trouble, he said
you've lost your lands, they're no longer yours
the governor of Cuiabá took them from you
the Matipu are outside [the park boundary]
yes, the Kalapalo are outside

and you're outside too

that's the situation you face

we returned with the Kalapalo, with the Kalapalo

to the mouth of the Tuatuari River and there we stayed

so, they were talking

a Kamayura man was with them

that's why the Kalapalo ended up staying at Aiha [Kamayura
territory]

their villages were at Kunugijahü, that was their place

further upriver from the Kuikuro

I didn't like it [the news] at all, I kept shaking my head

choose a place where you'd like to live [Orlando said]

the boundary was like that, at the mouth of the Curisevo

Nahu, how do you like it? Stay at the mouth of the Curisevo

relocate

which do you like, Nagija or another place?

there's Morená, which you're going to pass by

there's Auara'in, there's the place where the Pavuru folk live

I didn't like it

do you like it? I asked my people

they didn't like it

sometime later, listen to what I say [I said]

I'm going to stay in Ipatse, I'm not going there, I'm going to
Ipatse

you have to increase the park's area for me

you have to increase the area, I saw it expand three times

the governor of Cuiabá lost out

the Xingu made him lose heavily

and Nahu gained a lot

all the Indians here gained

and that's when the creation of the park began, Orlando created the park

only I helped him

there was only the demarcation left to do

the trail that needed to pass through your area

okay

we along with Orlando and Claúdio created the park

Orlando and I, me alone

only me at that time, I was still the only one who understood
Portuguese

I've told you everything, I'm done

Nahu's life told by Nahu himself ends at this point, when he was in his forties, in both versions: the apogee of his political trajectory began when the Villas-Boas brothers arrived to the Upper Xingu and when the Xingu Indigenous Park, the first and largest indigenous reservation in Brazil (22.000 km²), was founded. At the end of Nahu2, his son, Jakalu, promises that his father's story will be divulged. From that moment, other tellers are needed and with them other perspectives and stories arise.

Nahu by Alena, *akuku kagaihagü*

When I was back in Rio after my first field trip, two articles written by Ellen Basso on the Kalapalo (Basso 1975, 1984) drew my attention because there I found a careful account of some details of Nahu's life between 1966 and 1971.[13] At this point Nahu was searching for a husband for his daughter. Nahu was depicted as an enraged man, at the limits of the acceptable behavior, a *kugihe oto*, master of witchcraft. Basso analyzes strategies for the selection of spouses through the detailed description of two cases, and Nahu is mentioned in both.

Fall 1966: the first case described by Basso involves the search for a husband for Wambü, Nahu's daughter, as well as a search for a wife for Kaluene, the only son of Apihu, the chief of the Kalapalo village of Aiha.

> The fact that Wambü had not been committed to a man until her last puberty seclusion was quite unusual not for lack of suitors, but because Nahu had rejected all the proposals of his fellow villagers, the Kuikuro. . . . Nahu was one of those individuals so common in the Upper Xingu, who find themselves belonging,

either by reason of birthright or sentiment, to none of the village groups of the area. Allied by kinship to only one man (Luis, his cousin and companion), whose household he shared, he was accused of witchcraft by many of the Kuikuro. This in itself would not have been a problem, since most adult men are accused of this crime by at least some persons, but the fact that Nahu did not have the support of a large number of relatives, who would block his assassination in the event of a crisis, made him highly vulnerable in case of a sudden death. (Basso 1975:223)

Nahu's strategy was to marry his daughter to a man outside the Kuikuro village and thus find a way to move out, with his family, to the son-in-law's household. The marriage of Wambü with Kaluene was a good solution, but "Nahu's insistence upon living in Aiha, in the very house of his son-in-law, was inconsistent with his own position. Behaving as if he was a man of a great influence and prestige, he disrupted the household of a man who was actually more powerful then he and demanded continual obedience from his son-in-law, even though his daughter was still in seclusion. Such behavior was only acceptable for a man whose son-in-law had moved in with him, not vice versa" (Basso 1984:40).

For many months overt conflicts and gossips impelled successive "comings and goings" of Wambü (and Nahu) between the Kuikuro and the Kalapalo villages, apparently caused by the unsatisfied Nahu's growing demands, until the engagement was definitively broken.

In the fall of 1967, a second Kalapalo man asked to marry Wambü. Lamati was a young man whose sister was married to Luis, Nahu's single supporting kinsman among the Kuikuro. However, once more Nahu tried to impose his own desires on the determined Lamati.

When Basso left the Upper Xingu, Wambü was once more alone in the Kuikuro village with her angry father. Basso says that in 1971 "Nahu barely escaped being executed only managing to do so by fleeing to FUNAI's Post and seeking asylum with the Park personnel" (1975:224).

A few years later, I arrived to the Kuikuro village, and Nahu was there. Wambü and Lamati were a happy couple; his son, Jakalu, was peacefully married with a great chief, sister of the young Ahukaka, *hugogo oto*, master of the plaza. Ipi, the other daughter, had married a Mehinaku belonging to the powerful faction of a Mehinaku headman.[14] Nahu succeeded in building around him a large, strong household with his sons-in-law and daughter-in-law.

Nahu by Bruna, *kuhikugu kagaihagü*

Nahu forms part of an important chapter in my own life story, and even today I'm surprised by the intensity of my memories of him, feelings that are still ambiguous despite the "peace" we attained in the last years of his life and consolidated, in my spirit, by supervising the master's course of his grandson Mutua.[15]

A short while before I first set off on fieldwork, the new director of the Xingu Indigenous Park told me to speak directly with the "traditional chief," the young Ahukaka (who was about my age, around twenty-five years old), and avoid the "captain," *kagaiha oto*, master of the whites. This represented a "new policy" in the park's management, an island in FUNAI's administration that was still otherwise controlled by military personnel: dismantle the prestige of the "false" chiefs constructed during the course of "contact" over the last few decades and support the rise to power of the "true" chiefs. I followed the director's "advice" to the letter.

I arrived in Ipatse in 1976, and Nahu was waiting for me at a bend in the Culuene River some distance before the Kuikuro "port." The people who were taking me (members of Ahukaka's family) accelerated the pace of the canoe paddles to cross quickly to the other side of the river. Once in the village I was taken to Ahukaka's house, and there I stayed. I was inexorably incorporated into one of the two village factions, the one on the south side. Nahu arrived soon afterward and went to his house to the far north of the village. He would not forgive this affront for a long time.

I was called by Nahu to the middle of the village, a public place for welcoming visitors. I sat next to him with trepidation because of the many things I'd heard about him: mean, ugly, had failed to complete his reclusion properly, a dangerous *kugihe oto* (master of sorcery). Nahu directed the distribution of the few presents I had brought and immediately started to "tell," *akinha,* since "anthropologists want to know the names of kin and stories." Being a linguist was still a mysterious identity. Nahu was nervous, as was I. I was irrevocably involved in the disputes between factions and chiefs and in the accusations hurled from all sides of the village.

I have many memories from fieldwork associated with Nahu. In my thesis (Franchetto 1986) I wrote:

> The wanderer N. had traveled with the Bakairi, worked at the Simões Lopes Indigenous Post, and visited the big cities. He had been a guide and translator for the Villas-Boas brothers and assumed the role of official mediator with the whites. Until just a few years before my arrival he was the only speaker of Portuguese. He therefore thought of himself as the key informant, which allowed him to maintain the prestige of accessing the information brought from the white world and the goods that could be demanded or exchanged. This prestige was a strategic means of defense for a social position continually threatened by accusations, a tension he always tried to circumvent through careful political maneuvers. (Franchetto 1986, vol. 1:17)

From the outset the relationship with Nahu was difficult and tense, despite maintaining the appearance of Upper Xingu etiquette. His strong personality scared me. I avoided him, trying to defuse the risk of an open conflict, even though he was the most sophisticated interpreter-translator. He was a recognized

Fig. 4. Nahu leading the ear-piercing ritual (the initiation of young boys from chiefly lines), with jaguar skin on his head, a symbol of his status as headman and ritual specialist. (Photo by Bruna Franchetto)

ceremonial specialist, a skilled "storyteller," and a living memory of the history of contact. However, he didn't understand my linguistic work and expressed a mixture of impatience and intrigue, the staunchest propagator of the idea that researchers "steal" the indigenous culture, material production, and, in my case, language in order to sell them and become rich. The researcher's "presents" were, in his view, a malicious con. For me Nahu ended up becoming a figure of love and hate, respect and disdain, fascination and repulsion, since he touched on my feelings of guilt and the unequal game played with the Indians. Our relation only began to change in the final period of research when I was able to appreciate his narrative and rhetorical performances and his skill in providing exegeses during the translation of mythic texts and ceremonial discourses.

Nahu would not accept the changing times. Other Kuikuro emerged as protagonists of contact, competing with him. Ahukaka and his faction already understood that usurping or sharing the status of "master of the whites" was a prerequisite for a leader and that the political setting for them was favorable: they had the support of the new park administration.

I returned to Ipatse in 1977. In 1978 Nahu denounced me to the Brazilian military, claiming that I had failed to respect his authority and intermediation as *kagaiha oto*, "master of white people." I only regained my authorization to conduct field research in 1981, after a formal defense on my behalf by the Brazilian Anthropology Association. I returned to Ipatse full of anger and frustration.

From my field notes:

Sept. 27, 1981—Being a researcher in the field leaves me with a deep sense of unease, both psychological and physical. The Indians "know *caraíba*" now. More and more they have the feeling (one that partly corresponds to the truth) that they know what the whites are all about. As Nahu says, the diseases come from the whites: *kagaiha notoho*, as in the old discourses of the chiefs. They come from somewhere, nobody knows for sure, but they come from the whites. The flu viruses come one after the other. Each flu outbreak is treated by the shamans and by myself (and Tabata) through the distribution of metamizole, aspirin, erythromycin, or sulfametoxazol for the children. When I arrived I found the children vomiting and with diarrhea and fever. All of them have heavy coughs with a lot of catarrh. And the flu weakens them. Each shamanic session costs dearly. Whites and illness are almost synonymous: *Kagaiha=kugihe* (witchcraft)/*notoho* (illness)=*engikogu* (goods). . . .

And I find myself in this game. Without resources (real or potential); who is favored by me, accepts me (I also have my own bribery policy); some try to understand my work or evaluate me according to what I can teach about whites. I can teach them to read and write, something fairly highly valued. The image of researchers, especially anthropologists, constructed by FUNAI under military control has a big influence.

It seems clear to me now that the entire story with Nahu was the work of Colonel Zanoni. Jakalu told me that he overheard the following conversation between Nahu and Zanoni: "Tell me, Nahu, why do you like anthropologists? They don't do anything for you; it's FUNAI who pays travel costs, buys craftwork, sends medicine, takes Indians by plane for treatment and recreation. Anthropologists don't do anything. They steal your language, sell it and become rich. FUNAI needs to rest a bit and you need to ask for money from the anthropologists."

This was the content of the denunciation. The anthropologist eats the Indian's food, not FUNAI. In sum FUNAI is powerful, orders people around, guarantees land (or not, as the case may be). The most essential things on which the survival of the Indians depends. Anthropologists are useless or harmful.

The rumors circulate through the village. Nahu asked me for money again: "You need to save money to hand over to me when I go to Rio; I need to talk with your boss there at the Museum. . . ." The brothers-in-law/factions continue in a tense relationship.

Nahu is a friend of FUNAI. An old-style alliance: I corrupt you; you keep your mouth shut and say everything is okay. So the airplane trips as far as the highway, the good craftwork sales, the promise of a boat and outboard motor. Nahu feels strong and secure: "I'm the one who bosses the whites, that lad only bosses the people here, Orlando was the one who made me the chief, even today. . . ."The other faction is my friend. The gossip and accusations spread. . . .

Not to mention the entire issue of payments. I'm manipulated. . . . Nahu arrives on the scene. Politely a woman informs Nahu, in my presence, that I recorded *tolotepe* and promised to make a payment (1kg of beads). Nahu's ears twitch hearing the word "payment" and he remembers the payment for the recorded narratives. I try to persuade him with the argument that there's no payment for *akinhá* . . . no luck. I touch on the subject of gossip with FUNAI, no luck. Tension, I leave exhausted and depressed.

Oct. 23, 1981—Nahu requests me to teach, saying: let's see, I'll speak with the president of FUNAI to keep you here to teach our people. Nahu asks the meaning of words like society, social, community, attention, hope, program. . . . This constant asking tires me out, sad, annoying, irritating. On the other hand, who told me to "study them"? The equilibrium is reestablishing itself at a new level of exchange: me instructing, teaching the alphabet? Them studying us outside, in the city? They really do have a lucid sense of exchange, defend themselves and make us feel outsiders, intruders; neither side likes the other.

Nov. 6, 1981—Jakalu, Nahu, and his family returned from the swidden. Again the old man's control. I hate him, and yet he also fascinates me, his curiosity to know more about the world of the whites. He asks me for words in Portuguese; I explain their meanings. I write down speeches, phrases. Nahu is the one who brought the whites, who persuaded everyone to move village from Lahatua to Ipatse. It seems that "people held him responsible." A woman recounts that the transference from Lahatua was extremely painful. As well as the numerous deaths, Lahatua was situated in the territory historically used by the Kuikuro in their migrations. Large, beautiful village, two large lakes full of fish, many *pequi* trees, and many swiddens. Images of abundance: water snails, *asankgu* full of flour and swiddens full of ripe manioc were abandoned. In Ipatse people were hungry and thirsty. Children grew thin. Deaths from measles and the rapid change led to some traditions being forgotten.

Nahu is a hoarder of goods, a skilled centralizer, he created around himself a strong group with good alliances. He has an ideal son. He managed to place the whites-anthropologists on equal terms. Not with FUNAI, where the relationship involves his submission, servitude, and exploration; tokens, crumbs of power, and he manipulates the intermediation between the Kuikuro and the post. With researchers it's different; he orders people around, establishes equality. He is the anthropologist on the other side. A fine mirror. He appropriates any written paper, magazines, thumbing through them innumerable times, commenting on them as he flips the pages, on the houses, the men and women.

Nov. 21, 1981—N. has plotted my downfall. When he acts as the mediator between researcher and informant, it's all over: an aggressive closed shop swings into action, the defense of authorial rights, demands for respect and distance.

Nahu won: with his brilliant, even if costly, political strategies he succeeded in pacifying the conflicts around him, and at the end of the eighties he was definitely a respected old ritual specialist and singer.

My Grandfather and Languages: Nahu by Mutua

Mutua, born in 1982 at the Kuikuro village of Ipatse, is one of the grandchildren of Nahu. His life trajectory exemplifies

Fig. 5. Nahu painting a kinsman of a dead chief before the *egitsü* (*kwaryp*), the great ceremony held in honor of dead headmen. (Photo by Bruna Franchetto)

the success achievable by a young man keen to transform himself into a leader, a future chief, *kagaiha bama* (a specialist in "whites"): a teacher, president of the Kuikuro Association, and responsible for various cultural projects. He completed his indigenous teacher training course, followed by an undergraduate course at Mato Grosso State University, before enrolling in 2008 in an *ekugu*, "true," postgraduate course in anthropology at the Museu Nacional in Rio de Janeiro.

Hearing, transcribing, and translating Nahu's life history, which I recorded in 2001, left Mutua particularly moved. After this work the references to his grandfather open and close all the texts he has so far written since the teacher training course. His words contain Nahu's dense and contradictory legacy.

Mutua tells his life story in the introduction to his master's thesis (Mehinaku 2010). He spoke about himself to the whites for the first time in a text he wrote in Kuikuro and which he read in 2008 at an international event at the University of São Paulo (Semantics of Under-Represented Languages, SULA 4) and later at a lecture at the Museu Nacional, in the same year, when he wanted to introduce himself to staff and students. Significantly enough, the text was titled, "My Grandfather and Languages."

Mutua wrote:

> I remember I was two years old when I saw a television and the *kagaiha* for the first time; at the same time I got to know my grandfather Nahu, who knew how to speak Portuguese. During this period I heard my grandfather say that whites are dangerous, especially the farmers, who he described as very bad people: "farmers steal our people's land." And they gave poisoned food to the Indians so the *kagaiha* could take control of their lands after they died. These stories scared me a lot, and I cried when I heard about the *kagaiha*. This was the image that parents and other people instilled in children's heads. . . . I continued to grow up without hearing anything said about schooling. I only

heard what the older people, including my grandfather Nahu told us: school was an institution for assimilating indigenous peoples, which wasn't good since it killed off the traditional rituals of our people. My grandfather had witnessed the effects of the work of the priests, Catholic missionaries, as well as of the governmental officers (SPI), who arrived in the Bakairi village in the 1930s and the start of the 1940s, and who destroyed the culture of the Bakairi and denied their freedom. The Bakairi also speak a Carib language and live to the southwest of the Upper Xingu.

My grandfather used to tell many stories about the missionaries. Hearing these, everyone became afraid of the school. This is why he didn't want to have a school in the village and why there wasn't a school during my childhood.

Those who knew how to speak a little Portuguese included my grandfather and his cousin Luis, who learned the language of whites at the old Simões Lopes Post, in Bakairi territory, run by the Indian Protection Service, a Brazilian government institution that was later replaced by the National Indian Foundation, which still exists today. My grandfather and his cousin left the Xingu at the end of the 1930s; they traveled up the Xingu River, then journeyed on foot as far as the Bakairi. There they worked as manual laborers. At the time the SPI forced Indians to work in the fields and help build the post. . . .

At that time, we Xinguano people didn't know any Portuguese, so my grandfather stood out as the only person who could communicate with whites. He worked as a translator after the Roncador-Xingu expedition encountered the Upper Xingu peoples in 1946. The years following the expedition saw the arrival of numerous state functionaries, researchers, doctors, and above all the Villas-Boas brothers. My grandfather became a professional translator. Hence, when the team from the São Paulo Medical School arrived in the village to vaccinate us, my grandfather acted as the interpreter; he translated from Portuguese to Kuikuro or from Kuikuro to Portuguese. Seeing this I became curious, wishing to speak and understand what they were saying too. So I began to think a lot, asking my grandfather whether Portuguese was difficult to understand and how I could learn to speak it. So he told me it wasn't easy; it was difficult. I remained curious, therefore, really wanting to understand it, always staying by grandfather's side. . . .

When I reached the age of seven, I saw that some people knew how to speak Portuguese, as well as read and write. This had a big impact on me. I vividly recall when a lad who had learned at the FUNAI post school began to give lessons to any boys who were interested, perhaps as a joke. One day I went to watch his lesson. I sat there watching. Wow! It made me eager to have school material to study too. All of them were so proud to be students and intelligent in comparison to poor me. They seemed happy. After the lesson one of the students said to me: "If you want to study with us, since you haven't got a notebook, pencil, or eraser, you can write on your clothes and when you make a mistake, you can rub it out with your flip-flops." They laughed at me. I laughed *sininhüki,* "painfully." Afterward I went home thinking a lot, wanting the same. Meanwhile my parents wanted me to stay in reclusion so I could become a champion wrestler, *ikindoto.* The elders were worried about *katsagihakijü,* "turning white." The school and television were already getting in the way of young men's training to become *ikindoto.* Parents expected their sons to become *kuge hekugu,* "true people," strong, special.

Even so I continued to think a lot. I asked my grandfather whether Portuguese was difficult to understand and how I could learn to speak it. He told me it wasn't that easy; it was difficult. I remained curious, wanting to understand for real and I stayed constantly by his side. . . .

I'm fairly certain that in 1992 my cousin learned Portuguese from a boy who studied at the post. So I asked him to teach me, which he did. A month later I was able to connect words and managed to read and write in Portuguese. After I was able to study alone, there was also another lad who helped me a lot. He took an interest in my work, giving me the books he'd acquired from the FUNAI teachers working at the post. As a result I succeeded in expanding and improving my knowledge. I would also ask my grandfather about the meaning of words and phrases in Portuguese. Afterward I managed to learn in the village itself without needing to leave to study in the city.

My grandfather was the one who took bad news back to the village. He died in January 2005, and his life is testimony to the contact between Indians and whites. He was a teacher to me. Accompanying my grandfather inspired me to learn more and more. He told me lots of stories of missionaries and other *akinha* of our people. But hearing these stories, everyone became afraid of the school, which is why he didn't want one in the village. That's why there was no school during my childhood.

The spirit of my project is always linked to my grandfather. He taught me to respect others, to avoid fighting, and to know how to treat people who come to stay with you or those you go to visit. Afterward I discovered that when we learn many new things, we become better people. Better at understanding others and the world. My grandfather said that every person is important and has their place to be important. Without him as my reference point, I wouldn't be where I am today. (Mehinaku 2008, trans. David Rogers)

Mutua is now back in his village, a literate "native" anthropologist, with a good background in linguistics, just as his grandfather, almost illiterate, was and just as he wished his own grandson would be.

Final Remarks (by Nahu)

On the evening of October 23, 1981, Nahu made a chief's speech, *anetü itaginhu*; he spoke of the dams ("What, are we going to die? Are we all going to die?") and mentioned me as a friend for telling them about the dams.[16] It was a long and "good-right" (*atütü*) speech in front of the *kwakutu*, already dark, all the houses listening and commenting. *Anetü itaginhundagü*, "the chief is speaking," they remarked not without a degree of irony. Nahu told me: "I am the only one who speaks like a chief; the other one doesn't speak." The young chief said that he used to speak, but that he had given up, letting Nahu speak alone. The speech was a work of verbal and rhetorical art in which he foresaw a sad future for which he was, even if only partially, responsible. Nahu, the decaying "captain," criticized the whites for all the misfortunes they bring: illnesses and changes.

> dance, celebrate, all of us
> from somewhere the pain of whites' sickness will come
> before this, celebrate, all of us
> answer to your sisters
> this could be our last dance

He criticized the youngsters for not wanting to dance or paint themselves anymore, always wearing white people's clothes, and he called everyone to the festival, vehemently and dramatically.

> come here to celebrate
> don't wear the whites' clothes all the time
> remember our old way of being
> we used to paint ourselves with annatto
> we used to paint with annatto the women's foreheads
> like this we used to live
> don't try to wear the whites' clothes, children
> stay here, children
> don't go
> where are we going?
> now that we are in the hands of the whites

Finally, with great skill, he defended himself from the accusations spreading through the village, defining himself as an *eginhoto,* master of songs, "equal to a chief," and concluded with words that today sound like his own epitaph:

> the master of songs is like a chief, as old people used to say
> like a chief, look, like a chief, he stays together with the chief
> our old people used to say the same about the master of songs
> we need a chief
> in the same way we need the master of songs
> the sickness didn't grab me yet, but when it will grab me, you
>   all will speak well of me
> even if during my life I deceived you all a little bit
> listen to me, listen to what I always and modestly say to you all

Appendix

Nahu1:
tsakeha
uankgilü tiha Kuhikugute geleha Kuhikuguteha
uankgilüha amanhu tehualüpengine
apitsiha Kahalati üngümbüaha tajühe ata . . . .
aiha . . . igia tingapaha sete anos ngapaha uatai
ahijão üntegagüha
tunga kualü üntegagü egenaha tapitsiha egenaha
ekü Matipu nakagagü apakilüna
tigatiha ahijão kugitihu huta tugonkgu
ugetiha kagaiha tatela. . . .
engü akatsange kagaihai esei tühisuügü uhinhi
tsühügüi ina kagaiha enhügü inde leha atanhenügü
ikomundengapaha etelü hüle uhinhi hüle agoi. . . .
auaju kilüha Jahila kilü
kigekeha ikeni nügü iheke kigekeha ikeni
kutahogukoha ketsake Makaigi ituna
amanhu kilü kigeha

kaküngibeha tihu . . . Kamajulaha Aütüha Augaha Jagamü
   otomopeha
Kuikuguha a nhatüi ítagü
akagope tütenhükope tatüte isinünkgo leha
ama aketiha tisuge tsügütse tita geleha uinhügü
aetsi tungakuna takeko tungakunangapoha
aiha ugipanenügü Makaigi akitiha
aiha auajuha Atahu indongopeingine ütelü gehale
ehuaha ütelü tatute hügape
tisenhügü leha tisetimbelü leha Alahatuana
a kapehetsetse letiha uge leha. . . .

Nahu2:
itsi belaleha ingilango ige otomo kamaiula
ege engaha kugitihu engaha etelüko kilü an ilá
lepe leha titalüpengine leha isinünkgo kilü tahoha ande eue
   üha pose
inhalü egea gele posto anetügü heke kengikombalü kilü gele
üle tsaha inhuhekitako heke egei
inhalü hüle tinhegü inhalü benaha tinhegü ilá fundoi gele
Jagamü nago itagüha akagoi taho ihetinhi hotugui
tütemi leha sinünkgo meinaku nago ngipi taho
Aütü nago ngipi. . . .
tikindinhüpe Makaigi tutu tutu ikinduko kilüha
umüngiki pokü pokü itão ulu. . . .
langope tsaka Makaigi hoje não mais
tahaki leha spi heke
eitaginhukopeha opokinetüe eitaginhukopeha opokine
enenongokoha Makaigi kagaihagü kilüha ngikogo heke
tisakitiha não ta errado
festa kuarüpiha ailikoha
aünoho tongokopeha akagoi makaigi kuegüiha
üngeleha spi hekeha
Marechal Rondom nago ulegüiha itsuhutegatühükoha

itigatiha itsokomi
kagahina tunügü apa inha tsüha Jakalu inha
apajuha portugues uhute isagagetiha uatühügü gele
en apajuha makaigi uhute amanhuha uge ama Makaigi uhute
ugetiha makaigi itaginhu uhute la. . . .
Nilu Veloso apakilüha utükipügü atai letahüle leha utükipügü
  atai
ugetiha kagaiha akisü tate ajetsi
auaju kilü Jahila kilü ekü kunhita
engü tisakisü otoi
kamajulanaha ütelü isukugegüi hüle egei titselü
a itagimbakita tiheke a tatute
ande atsange tisetsagü ina einhaha taho hangamitigiha
e angi letaleha ungipiha
a tunümingo nügü iheke Nilu Veloso kilüha
fotogra fotografaiha ila
aileha ülepe engü ahütü tisenhügü leha
tisinhangope etsimbükilü leha tisugonkgulü gehale
Alahatuana tongopengine leha uenhügü
auajuko kilü kigeke gehale ihekeni kutahoguko uketsake
e engüha engüna Pakueranaha tisinhügü e Pakuerana
ai leha
ehe Makaigi ituna letsale

TRANSCRIPTION OF *ANETÜ ITAGINHU*

PERFORMED BY NAHU (OCTOBER 23, 1981)

kukangundüngi kukailundüngi
inkomunda isininhü kutaüpüaoko notoho etimbelüingo
üle igakaho kukailundüngi

ehisüko hoho engitütsüete
ületsügüi akangige kukailundagüha. . . .
ailundeketsüha
ahütü akatsange hoho tipaki kutaüpüaoko ingü ipoinjüla
  ehekeni

kuketingungingikügükotsüha

egikutsülükotsüha

atagihisutelüko muketsüha

ilatsüha enhügükotsüha küngamuke

ojo kutaüpüaoko ingü apepolü hoho ehekeni küngamuke

indemuke geletsüha kutengatüngitsüha küngamuke

ahütü hoho etelükola

unama kutenalüko

kutaüpüaoko inhakugulati igei kukanügüko atehetiha. . . .

kuge unkgugu ~egiki akatsangeha iginhoto ihatagüha wãke
  kukotomoko heke wãke

igia agageha kuge unkgugu inke apa kuge unkguguha
  ukihondelü iginhoto heke ukihondelü

ilakanga wãke kukotomoko heke eginhotomo ihatagü muke
  wãke

ukuge unkgugu ethijü

isagage gehale eginhoto tetuhisi gehale

utsugihütenu kugonda muketiha

utsugihütepügü atai muketiha

igiagage muketiha ande mukeletalüha ehekeni

uanügü ateheha igei taloki higei einkguginalüko muketiha
  uheke

igia agage taloki muketiha higei ukingalü ehekeni

Notes

1. The Kuikuro are a Carib-speaking people living in the headwater region of the Xingu River in the north of Mato Grosso State, Southern Amazonia.

2. The data in Kuikuro language are transcribed using the current orthography established by the Kuikuro teachers with the aid of the linguist. The correspondences between written symbols and the sound they represent (when not obvious) are as follows: *ü* (high central unrounded vowel), *j* (palatal voiced consonant), *g* (uvular flap), *ng* (velar nasal), *nh* (palatal nasal), *nkg* (prenasalized voiced velar plosive). It is an agglutinative, head final, and ergative language.

3. The 2009 Hagaka was the subject of an ethnography presented as an MA thesis by Penoni (2010).

4. Mutua obtained his master's in December 2010, at the Graduate Program in Social Anthropology at the Museu Nacional, Federal University of Rio de Janeiro.

5. *Kagaiha oto* means "master of whites"; *tisakisü oto* means "master of our (exclusive we) words/language."

6. I acknowledge the inspiring work of anthropologist Ellen Basso on epistemic markers in Kalapalo, the other "sister" variant of the Upper Xingu Carib language (Basso 1987, 1995).

7. Epistemic markers (EM) are present in most of the Kuikuro sentences that become utterances with communicative efficacy. Kuikuro seems to employ a rich repertoire of forms to make explicit the nature of force as a component of CP (the upper tier of the sentence structure, bridging syntax to discourse), synthesized by Haegeman: "[Force] guarantees anchoring to the speaker and is implicated in the licensing of, among other things, illocutionary force and epistemic modality. . . . (Epistemic modality) expresses the speaker's stance concerning the likelihood of the state of affairs/event, which is anchored to speech time" (2004:164). See Franchetto and Santos 2010 for an analysis of Kuikuro EM as elements of the cartography of expanded CP.

8. From this point onward the reader will find only the translation of the narratives told by Nahu; the transcription, using the current orthography for the Kuikuro language, is in the appendix to this article.

9. In Nahu2, Nahu recalls all the chiefs who led the faction that left Kuhikugu to found Alahatua. The references that allow the temporal localization of events are normally the names of the toponyms-villages with their chiefs and the genealogies of the latter (two generations above and below), as well as the performance of rituals such as *iponge* (male initiation) and *unduhe.*

10. In 1906 Colonel Percy Harrison Fawcett, as a member of the British Royal Geographic Society, was hired by the Bolivian government to delineate the country's borders with Peru in response to an intense dispute over the frontier. In 1908 the colonel decided at his own behest to chart Bolivia's borders with Brazil too, the only part of the map that remained blank. Nahu told us a very interesting version of the same facts, similar to the narrative collected by Basso among the Kalapalo and published in *The Last Cannibal* (1995).

11. The Kuikuro narratives recall the raids by *bandeirantes* (slave raiders and explorers) between the second half of the eighteenth century and the beginning of the nineteenth. After Karl von den Steinen's expeditions in 1884 and 1887 (Steinen 1940), other ethnographic or military expeditions entered the region: Hermann Meyer (1897; 1900, referring to the voyage made in 1896) and Max Schmidt (1905; 1942, referring to the voyage made in 1900–1901).

12. In fact in the first century after European conquest, the large Xinguano communities experienced catastrophic demographic losses, most probably the result of the first epidemics of contagious diseases. A drastic population decline between 1500 and 1884—when the written history of the Upper Xingu began—is clearly indicated by the significant reduction in the size and number of villages across the region from the later prehistoric phase until the twentieth century (Heckenberger 2001a, 2001b). From 1915 onward, exploration of the Xingu headwaters intensified with the participation of military personnel from the Rondon Commission: Ramiro Noronha (1952, referring to the 1920 voyage); Vicente de Vasconcelos (1945, referring to the 1924–25 voyage). The Carib groups remained in the same locations recorded by Steinen and Meyer. All the accounts register an incredibly rapid process of depopulation. Agostinho (1972) provides us with an estimate of the impact of this bacteriological and viral shock. Between the end of the nineteenth century and the mid-1950s, the region's population was reduced from 3,000 to 1,840 people in 1926 and a little more than 700 at the end of the 1940s.

13. Akuku was the denomination of one old village (and one old group) of the people known as Kalapalo; then Alena (Ellen) is or was referred as *Akuku kagaihagü*, "the white of Akuku people."

14. In his thesis Mutua, Nahu's grandson, analyzes the story of the marriage between his father and mother (Ipi), based on recordings where they tell their lives to their son. Nahu's performance as strategist for the accomplishment of this marriage too is outstanding.

15. *Kuhikugu kagaihagü*, "the white of Kuikuro people."

16. See Franchetto 1986 (vol. 3) for an analysis of this specific *anetü itaginhu*.

Bibliography

Agostinho, P.
    1972 Information Concerning the Territorial and Demographic Situation in the Alto Xingu. *In* The Situation of the Indian in South America. W. Postal, ed. Pp. 252–79. Geneva: World Council of Churches.
Basso, E.
    1973 The Use of Portuguese Relationship Terms in Kalapalo (Xingu Carib) Encounters: Changes in a Central Brazilian Communicative Network. Language & Society 2(1):1–21.
    1975 Kalapalo Affinity: Its Cultural and Social Contexts. American Ethnologist 2(2):207–28.
    1984 A Husband for His Daughter, a Wife for Her Son: Strategies for Selecting a Set of In-Laws among the Kalapalo. *In* Marriage Practices in Lowland South America. Ken M. Kennsinger, ed. Pp. 33–44. Urbana: University of Illinois Press.

1987 In Favor of Deceit. Tucson: University of Arizona Press.

1995 The Last Cannibal. Austin: University of Texas Press.

Collet, Célia Letícia Gouvêa

2006 Ritos de civilização e cultura: A escola Bakairi. PhD dissertation, Programa de Pós-Graduação em Antropologia Social, Museu Nacional, Universidade Federal do Rio de Janeiro.

Figueiredo, Marina Vanzolini

2010 A flecha do ciúme: O parentesco e seu avesso segundo os Aweti do Alto Xingu. PhD dissertation, Programa de Pós-Graduação em Antropologia Social, Museu Nacional, Universidade Federal do Rio de Janeiro.

Franchetto, Bruna

1986 Falar Kuikúro: Estudo etnolingüístico de um grupo caribe do Alto Xingu. 3 vols. PhD dissertation, Programa de Pós-Graduação em Antropologia Social, Museu Nacional, Universidade Federal do Rio de Janeiro.

2006 Kuikuro: Anos de muita agitação. In Povos Indígenas do Brasil: 2001–2005. Beto Ricardo and Fany Ricardo, eds. Pp. 69–80. São Paulo: Instituto Socioambiental.

Franchetto, Bruna, and Gélsama Mara Ferreira dos Santos

2010 Cartography of Expanded CP in Kuikuro (Southern Carib, Brazil). In Information Structure in Indigenous Languages of the Americas: Syntactic Approaches. José Camacho, Rodrigo Gutierrez-Bravo, and Liliana Sanchez, eds. Pp. 87–114. New York: De Gruyter Mouton.

Haegeman, Liliane

2004 Topicalization, CLLD and the Left Periphery: Proceedings of the Dislocated Elements Workshop, ZAS Berlin, November 2003. 2 vols. B. Shaer, F. Werner, and C. Maienborn, eds. ZAS Papers in Linguistics 35. Pp. 157–92.

Heckenberger, Michael J.

2001a Epidemias, Índios bravos e brancos: Contato cultural e etnogênese xinguana. In Povos Indígenas do Alto Xingu: História e culturas. Bruna Franchetto and Michael J. Heckenberger, eds. Pp. 77–110. Rio de Janeiro: Editora UFRJ.

2001b Estrutura, história e transformação: A cultura Xinguana na longue durée. In Povos Indígenas do Alto Xingu: História e culturas. Bruna Franchetto and Michael J. Heckenberger, eds. Pp. 21–62. Rio de Janeiro: Editora UFRJ.

Mehinaku, Mutua

2007 My Grandfather and Languages. Conference at SULA [Semantics of Under-Represented Languages] 4, May 24–26. São Paulo: Universidade de São Paulo.

2010 Tetsualü: Pluralismo de línguas e pessoas no Alto Xingu. MA thesis, Programa de Pós-Graduação em Antropologia Social, Museu Nacional, Universidade Federal do Rio de Janeiro.

Meyer, Hermann
1897 Über seine Expedition nach Central-Brasilien. Verhandlungen der Gesellschaft für Erdkunde zu Berlin 24:172–98.
1900 Berichte über seine Zweite Xingu-Expedition. MS.

Noronha, Ramiro
1952 Exploração e levantamento do rio Culuene, principal formador do rio Xingu. Publicação da Comissão Rondon 75. Rio de Janeiro: Departamento de Imprensa Nacional.

Penoni, Isabel Ribeiro
2010 Hagaka: Ritual, performance e ficção entre os Kuikuro do Alto Xingu (MT, Brasil). MA thesis, Programa de Pós-Graduação em Antropologia Social, Museu Nacional, Universidade Federal do Rio de Janeiro.

Schmidt, Max
1905 Indianer Studien in Zentral Brasilien 1900–1901. Berlin.
1942 Estudos de etnologia brasileira: Peripécias de uma viagem entre 1900 e 1901. Seus resultados etnológicos 2. São Paulo: Editora Nacional.

Steinen, Karl von den
1940 Entre os Aborígenes do Brasil Central. São Paulo: Revista do Arquivo Municipal. Offprint.

Vasconcelos, Vicente de Paula Teixeira da Fonseca
1945 Expedição ao Rio Ronuro. Conselho Nacional de Proteção aos Índio Publicação 90. Rio de Janeiro: Imprensa Nacional.

Contributors

Ellen B. Basso is professor emerita, School of Anthropology, University of Arizona, Tucson.

Pedro de Niemeyer Cesarino is a professor of anthropology at the Universidade de São Paulo.

Magnus Course is a senior lecturer in social anthropology at the University of Edinburgh.

Bruna Franchetto is a professor of linguistics and anthropology at Museu Nacional, Universidade Federal de Rio de Janeiro.

Peter Gow is a professor of social anthropology at the University of St Andrews.

Laura R. Graham is an associate professor of anthropology at the University of Iowa.

Casey High is a lecturer in social anthropology at the University of Edinburgh.

Suzanne Oakdale is an associate professor of anthropology at the University of New Mexico, Albuquerque.

Oscar Calavia Sáez is a professor of anthropology at the Universidade Federal de Santa Catarina.

Hanne Veber is a senior lecturer in social anthropology at the University of Copenhagen.

Index

Cesarino, Pedro de Niemeyer, 17, 149

Christianity, 38–39, 49, 54, 147, 195–96, 203. *See also* Catholic Church; missions and missionaries

Cobos, Enrique, 77

collective indigenous identities, 4, 113, 239

collective memory, 93–94, 113, 275

Collier, Stephen, 211–12, 214, 231n5

colonial situation, 94, 111, 113n1

colonization, 94, 95–96, 100, 112, 241, 280–81

communication, 165–84

Conklin, Beth, 213

contextualization, 13, 183

cosmological deixis, 14–15

Coudreau, Henri, 219–20

Course, Magnus, 18

crises of subjectivity, 239–40, 250, 252–54, 258–59, 261, 262

cultural mediators, 21–24, 51, 218–23, 235–37, 260, 264n6, 271, 284–87, 290–92, 295

Curisevo River, 279–80, 286

da-ño're, 243, 253

da Silva, Mandu, 7

Datura Stramonium, 157–58, 160n7

Dayuma, 35–36, 38–48, *43*, 49–50, 52–53

The Dayuma Story (Wallace), 35–36, 38, 39, 43–44, 49

death, 55, 122, 135, 139, 153–54, 159

de Biase, Xanda, 266n16

debt slavery, 101, 105–6, 108, 112

Deloria, Philip, 230

Descriptive Treatise of Brazil (Soares de Sousa), 192

de Souza, Jakeline, 202, 206n1

destiny, 144, 152, 154, 156–58

disease: Marubo and, 122, 125, 127, 131, 141; Xavante and, 241–42; Xinguanos and, 280, 285, 292–93, 295, 307n12. *See also* measles

dissonance, 22–24, 223, 225, 230

"dividual," 18, 153

Doétiro, 199–200

Dornstauder, Father, 219, 227, 232n10

doubles, 122, 123, 124–27, 129–30, 132, 134–37, 139

dreaming, 6–7, 25n3, 90, 125, 138–39

education for indigenous peoples, 238, 264n6

ego, effacement of, 259, 261, 262, 267n29

Elliott, Elizabeth, 49

End of the Spear, 39

environmental activism, 8, 213, 239

ERX (Roncador-Xingu Expedition), 281, 298

Estratégia Xavante, 264n2

Eténhiritipa community, 235–36, 265n9

ethnographic research, process of, 77–78, 217–18, 272–73, 289–96

Euro-American narrative conventions, 76, 78–79, 80–81

exchange relations, 19, 145, 153, 171–82

exemplary personal experiences: author's personal context and, 75–78; Dionisia Garcia's, 71–73; exclusion of emotionally extreme experiences from, 82–83; meaning of, 78–83; myths and, 86–90; overview of, 69–71; SIL missionary collection of, 83–86; as social experiences, 73–75; and teller's death, 82

fame, 273, 306n5

Farage, Nádia, 6

Fasabi, Artemio, 80–81

Fausto, Carlos, 273

Fawcett, Percy Harrison, 278, 306n10

Ferreira, Mariana Kawall Leal, 217, 231n6, 265n8

Fieta, Abel, 105, 114n7

Fiocruz Institute, 188

Fleck, David W., 168

Flores, Clara, 83–87

"Flowers and Fauna," 264n8

flutes, sacred, 198, 200

Fogelson, Raymond, 55

Franchetto, Bruna, 21, 23–24, 168

Freyre, Gilberto: *The Masters and the Slaves*, 193

Fŭcha Ñua, 158

FUNAI (National Indian Foundation), 242, 257, 265n9, 266n18, 267n25, 293–94, 295, 298

Garcia, Dionisia, 71–73

Gavino, Virgilio, 83

Gentil, Gabriel, 20, 188–90, 194–98, 199–204

global assemblages, 214, 231n1

Gomide, Maria Lucia, 265n8

Gow, Peter, 11, 13, 107; *An Amazonian Myth and Its History*, 87, 89

Graham, Laura, 23, 213

greetings, 148, 150, 154, 170, 178–79, 182

Gregor, Thomas, 191

Grünberg, Georg, 217

nongovernmental organizations (NGOs), 238, 265n9, 266n24

nshinikanchi, 80

Nuckolls, Janis, 7

nütramtun biography, 153

Oakdale, Suzanne, 23, 55

Ong, Aihwa, 212, 214, 231n5

ononki, 42–44, 55

ontology, 10–11, 14–16, 25n3, 122

"Our Late Mother Dionisia's Story about the Aeroplane," 71–73

Overing, Joanna, 14, 71

Pablo. *See* Rodriguez, Pablo

pacification, 212, 216, 222–25, 227

Painemilla, Teresa: "The Proud Horseman," 150–52, 160n5

Palas Atena, 250–51

Palm Beach killings, 38, 41, 43

Panã, 127, 130–31

Pañeta, 169, 170–81

Panĩpapa, 132–33

Parabubure, 241, 265n10

Paranatinga River, 280

Peixes River people, 222, 225–27. *See also* Kawaiwete

Pereira, Manuel Nunes: *Moronguetá*, 191

personal myths, 89–90

personhood: Mapuche, 148–49, 152–55, 159–60; overview of, 13–18; processes of, 17–18, 23, 146, 147–48, 149, 152, 153–54, 159; Waorani, 37, 50, 54

perspectives, paths to different, 240–41, 250, 254–55, 258–59, 261

perspectivism, 14–15, 16

Petrullo, Vincent, 278

pi'õ nhitsi, 242

Piro (Yine): discourse genres of, 70–73; and history, 80, 88–89; identity of, as civilized, 107; kinship of, 81–82, 88–89; multiplicity and, 11, 69, 79–80; personal myths of, 89–90; shamanism of, 82–83, 86; songs of, 74, 78

politics, Indian: activism and, 7, 8, 195, 196–97, 244; Asháninka and, 108–9; changing narratives and, 37, 51, 53, 56; Gentil and, 197, 244, 254–60

potential affinity, 145–46, 147–48, 149, 150–52, 159

Primavera do Leste, 249

prostitution, 197, 201

"The Proud Horseman" (Painemilla), 150–52, 160n5

Rabben, Linda, 7

Ramos, Alcida, 7

Raoni, 8, 195

Rappaport, Joanne, 7

Reeve, Mary-Elizabeth, 94

Reichel-Dolmatoff, Gerardo, 191, 198

relationships: Asháninka and Peruvian mestizo, 95–105; interethnic, 18–19, 20, 21, 50–51, 53–56; Kawaiwete and nonindigenous Brazilian, 218–30; Mapuche true persons and, 145, 147, 149, 150, 152–53, 159; of multiple persons, 134, 137, 139; between researchers and research subjects, 21, 289–95; ritual communication and, 166, 182

Riberão Preto, 235, 263nn1–2

Rio Negro region, 187–88, 198

rituals: Kawaiwete, 216–17, 226–27; Kuikuro, 272, *291*, 298, 301; little, 165–66, 167; Mapuche, 153; Marubo shaman, 122, 123–24, 139, 140; mortuary, 55, 153–54, 159; performance of, 122, 169, 180–81, 182, 184; Tukano, 196, 198, 199–200; Xavante, 248, 253

Rival, Laura, 46

Rivière, Peter, 81

Rodriguez, Pablo, 73–75, 77

romeya shamans, 122–23, 128, 133–34, 136, 142

Roncador-Xingu Expedition (ERX), 281, 298

rubber booms, 94, 98, 100–101, 107–8, 109, 112, 213, 231n4

rubber business: Asháninka and, 95, 97, 100–101, 106, 108; Kawaiwete and, 213–14, 218–23, 225, 228, 231n4, 232nn8–9; labor for, 101, 221

Rubenstein, Steve, 7

Ruri'õ, Lucas, 256, 257, 259–60, 266n18

Sabino: as *capitão*, 219, 220, 222, 223–30, 232n10; mixed genre of the story of, 215–18; overview of life of, 218–19; overview of narratives of, 23, 214–15

Sáez, Oscar Calavia, 4, 20–21

Saint, Nathan, 38, 41

Saint, Rachel, 38–39, 41, 44, 45, 49

Salesian missions: in Rio Negro region, 187–88, 201; at Sangradouro, 238, 240–44, 246–48, 250, 256, 259, 266n18, 266n20

Viveiros de Castro, Eduardo, 14–16, 79, 146, 147, 149, 240
voice, 16–17, 18, 19, 25n6, 149, 218

Walbiri, 88, 90
Wallace, Ethel Emily: *The Dayuma Story*, 35–36, 38, 39, 43–44, 49
Wambŭ, 287–89
Wamoñe, 40, 43, 57, 58
Waorani, 38, 39, 42–56; generational narratives of, 50–56; historical consciousness of, 50–51, 54; and history, 53–54, 55; and identity, 45, 50–52, 54; and outsiders, 42–50; and personhood, 37, 50, 54; rituals of, 55; sociality of, 44–46, 50, 56; and time of civilization, 45–50, 54, 56; urban interethnic relations of, 50–51, 55–56; victimhood of, 37, 39, 42–43, 44–45, 48–50, 51, 52–53, 54–55; and violence, 42–43, 44–45, 46–48, 55; and warriorhood, 50–52
Wapishana, 6
wapté, 242–44, 265n15, 266n19
warã, 264n7
Warã Association, 238–39, 261–62, 265n8, 266n16
warriorhood, 50–52, 103, 113n4
Wekorte, 135, *136*
White, Richard, 212–13, 229
Whitehead, Neil, 25n1

Williams, Raymond, 13
witnesses in narratives and myths, 87–89
Wright, Robin, 7

Xavante, 241, 253–54, 255, 260, 265n10, 265n12; adolescence, 242–43, 246–54, 266n19; cultural mediators of, 235–37, 260, 264nn3–4; discrimination against, 236, 249–50; and disease, 241–42; and identity, 239, 243, 249; Mario Juruna and, 251; NGOs and, 238–39, 265n9; rituals of, 248, 253; Salesians and, 241–44, 247–48, 265nn10–12, 266n20; and sociality, 236, 237, 240–44, 249; songs of, 243
Xavante Warã Association, 238–39, 261–62, 265n8, 266n16
Xinguanos, 279–81, 285, 292–93, 295, 298, 307n12
Xingu Indigenous Park, 213, 217, 230, 271, 277, 281, 285, 287, 289

Yakonero, 86–87
yine, 79
Yine (Piro): discourse genres of, 70–73; and history, 80, 88–89; identity of, as civilized, 107; kinship of, 81–82, 88–89; multiplicity and, 11, 69, 79–80; personal myths of, 89–90; shamanism of, 82–83, 86; songs of, 74, 78
yovevo, 122, 124–26, 129, 133–35, 140

OTHER WORKS BY SUZANNE OAKDALE

I Foresee My Life: The Ritual Performance of Autobiography in an Amazonian Community (University of Nebraska Press, 2005)

OTHER WORKS BY MAGNUS COURSE

Becoming Mapuche: Person and Ritual in Indigenous Chile (University of Illinois Press, 2011)